Improving
Assessment
of Schoolchildren

Jossey-Bass Publishers

San Francisco • Washington • London • 1981

IMPROVING ASSESSMENT OF SCHOOLCHILDREN
A Guide to Evaluating Cognitive, Emotional, and Physical Problems
by Carol Schneider Lidz

Copyright © 1981 by: Jossey-Bass Inc., Publishers
433 California Street
San Francisco, California 94104
&
Jossey-Bass Limited
28 Banner Street
London EC1Y 8QE

Library of Congress Cataloging in Publication Data

Lidz, Carol S
    Improving assessment of schoolchildren.

    Bibliography: p. 176
    Includes index.
    1. Educational tests and measurements.
2. Criterion-referenced tests.   3. Psychological
tests.   4. Ability—Testing.   I. Title.
LB3051.L468   1981   371.2'6   80-26130
ISBN 0-87589-488-7

Manufactured in the United States of America

JACKET DESIGN BY WILLI BAUM

FIRST EDITION

Code 8102

Preface

꙰꙰꙰꙰꙰꙰

This book examines the theory and practice of assessment in the school setting. It discusses specific assessment procedures and the multiple roles of the examiner, as well as each phase of the assessment process—referral, interviews, testing, interpretation of test results, and report writing. It strives to increase the professional's ability to derive information and recommendations that are appropriate to the educational situation, to utilize procedures that reflect the learning processes of the pupil, and to gain familiarity with procedures that are promising alternatives to those criticized as discriminatory. In the broadest sense, it aims to show psychologists and teachers how best to assess individual children, especially their deficiencies and potentials, to facilitate their education and progress in school. It places particular emphasis on the assessment of handicapped children, as well as on compliance with regulations pertaining to them as set out in Pub. L. 94–142; however, the content may be applied to all children from preschool to secondary school age who are referred for cognitive, emotional, and physical problems that interfere with classroom performance.

Recently, various IQ and standardized tests have come under the scrutiny of legislatures and public and other groups. Although this book does discuss many standardized tests as part of a broad assessment effort, it also includes many other useful procedures that together demonstrate the continuing validity of assessment as a professional activity.

The information contained herein will be of interest to school psychologists, clinical psychologists who assess schoolchildren, and other educational professionals who are responsible for assessment. The synthesis of the vast literature about assessment will also be useful to experienced and beginning professionals, as well as to advanced graduate students, who wish to review the current state of research and explore specialized areas in the field.

Chapter One outlines the background, issues, and problems related to the assessment of schoolchildren, all of which point to the need to consider alternatives to traditional assessment approaches.

Chapter Two defines assessment and describes a procedural model for conducting an optimal assessment. The model provides an array of alternatives rather than a single course of action and portrays assessment as an integral part of a consultation process.

Chapter Three begins the discussion of specific procedures and presents strategies that emphasize the student's ability to profit from instruction. These approaches include the most promising alternatives to those traditional measures that have been criticized as discriminating against ethnic minorities.

Chapter Four considers criterion-referenced procedures that assess the child's knowledge base in relation to specific school tasks. The chapter prepares the reader for evaluating the quality of these measures and describes criterion-referenced assessment as one type of procedure rather than as a panacea for all referral issues.

Chapter Five equips the assessor with tools for gathering information while observing the child in the classroom. This chapter also discusses measurement issues relating to observation as a technique and provides detailed examples of psychosituational assessment as an illustration of an educationally relevant observational strategy.

Chapter Six presents strategies for increasing the relevance of standardized traditional measures for the classroom situation. Such methods as testing the limits and task and error analysis are discussed in relation to specific measures familiar to most assessors. The chapter also reviews ways to increase the accessibility of children with a variety of more severe handicaps to the assessment process.

Chapter Seven describes a variety of procedures with clinical roots that show promise for application to the school setting. These include interview, play, and drawing techniques, as well as others that may be less familiar to the professional reader.

Chapter Eight is written by Robert E. Paul, a Philadelphia attorney. At the time of this writing, Paul works with an urban community mental health center and serves as its advocate for cases related to Pub. L. 94–142 issues as well as a consultant to the staff regarding this legislation. Paul analyzes Pub. L. 94–142 in relation to the assessment situation and draws inferences regarding the increased association between law and special education.

Chapter Nine concludes the book by considering how best to communicate assessment results. This chapter also looks toward the future of assessment in terms of current issues and trends.

This book grew out of ideas I have pursued in my work for several years. It represents information gathered from experience and research, which I have found professionally useful and which I wish to share with colleagues working in educational settings.

I would like to acknowledge and thank my husband, Howard Lidz, for his support and fortitude in weathering the course of preparation of the material for this book. I offer special thanks to Marilyn Paleologos, whose comments and criticism were particularly helpful. Janet Eisenstat offered her fine typing skills, intelligent criticism, and proofreading abilities. Finally, I feel that this book would not have been realized without my association with the Graduate School of Applied and Professional Psychology of Rutgers University, for which I particularly thank Donald Peterson, Jack Bardon (now at the University of North Carolina, Greensboro), Virginia Bennett, and Donald Clark.

Philadelphia, Pennsylvania   CAROL SCHNEIDER LIDZ
September 1980

Contents

Preface   vii

The Author   xiii

1. Major Approaches to Psychological Assessment   1

2. A New Model for Optimal Assessment   16

3. Methods for Estimating Children's Full Learning   33
   Potential

4. Testing for Knowledge of School Subjects   55

5. Observing Behavior in the Classroom   75

6. Modifying Traditional Methods of Administration   98

7. Interview, Play, and Drawing Techniques in Assessment 123

8. Legal Requirements for Assessing Handicapped   146
        Children
            Robert E. Paul

9. Communicating Assessment Results and Anticipating   160
        Future Trends

    References   176

    Index   215

The Author

✃✃✃✃✃✃✃

CAROL SCHNEIDER LIDZ is coordinator of the clinic team that provides assessment and consultation services to the Philadelphia Head Start programs (organized and administered by the United Cerebral Palsy Association of Philadelphia). She previously worked for several years as school psychologist for a community mental health center, as well as for a number of local districts in New Jersey and at the regional level in Pennsylvania. Her experience also includes college teaching, private practice, and a position on the staff of a rehabilitation hospital. She has had specialized experience in the assessment of learning disabled, gifted, physically handicapped, and preschool children, and has lectured and published on the topics of assessment and assessment of the preschool child.

Lidz received her B.A. degree in psychology from the University of Michigan (1962), her M.A. degree in school psychology from the University of Tennessee (1964), and her Psy.D. degree from Rutgers University Graduate School of Applied and Professional Psychology (1977). She was the first recipient of the Robert D. Weitz Award while at Rutgers.

To Howard Lidz

Improving Assessment of Schoolchildren

A Guide to Evaluating Cognitive, Emotional, and Physical Problems

Chapter 1

᚛᚛᚛᚛᚜᚜᚜

Major Approaches to Psychological Assessment

Psychological assessment is the process by which trained professionals collect information about an individual that enables them to identify problems that are interfering with the individual's functioning in his environment.* In this book, we are concerned with the assessment of school-age children

*The traditional use of the pronoun *he* has not yet been superseded by a convenient, generally accepted pronoun that means either *he* or *she*. Therefore, the author will continue to use *he* while acknowledging the inherent inequity of the traditional preference of the masculine pronoun.

who have problems—physical, emotional, or cognitive—that interfere with their performance in school. In the school system, the
assessment process is most often initiated by a teacher or parent
who notices that a child is having difficulty and shares this concern
with a counselor, school psychologist, or other professional trained
in assessment. The assessor then gathers various types of information about the problem—by testing, observing, and interviewing
the student, or by interviewing the student's teacher, parents, and
counselor—in order to identify the problem and make suggestions
for appropriate therapy, educational programming, or further
testing.

Assessment thus involves several individuals: the assessors,
the student, the student's classroom teacher, the student's parents,
and the school's administrators. The effective assessor must identify
the student's problems, make appropriate recommendations, and
share these findings with the other parties. In this chapter, we
explore some of the general practical and theoretical problems that
confront professionals who assess school-age children.

General Dissatisfaction with Assessment

The literature on psychological assessment suggests that parents, school administrators, and counselors have derived satisfaction from the results of traditional assessment procedures (Baker,
1965; Barclay and others, 1962; Gilmore and Chandy, 1973a; Tidwell
and Wetter, 1978; Waters, 1973). Administrators, and often counselors, tend to be primarily interested in the assessor's ability to
classify a child in order to place that child in an appropriate educational program. Traditional psychological assessment appears to
successfully meet this need (Fitts, 1972; Kaplan, Chrin, and Clancy,
1977).

Classroom teachers who are trying to devise a program for a
child who has problems have voiced the most complaints about the
usefulness of psychological assessment (Cason, 1945; "Do Specialists Help Teachers? . . . ," 1969; Szmuk, Docherty, and Ringness,
1979). Classroom teachers have complained that responses to their
referral requests are too slow and that reports are often incomprehensible or irrelevant (Baker, 1965; Brandt and Giebink, 1968; Gil-

more and Chandy, 1973b; Mussman, 1964; Rucker, 1967a, 1967b). They also suggest that the classroom teacher is not sufficiently involved in the assessment procedure and that the follow-up to assessment is inadequate (Baker, 1965; Grubb, Petty, and Flynn, 1976; Lucas and Jones, 1970; Roberts and Solomons, 1970; Waugh, 1970).

Teachers' dissatisfaction with assessment services reflects, in part, differences between the teachers' and the psychologists' academic training. The study of an academic discipline influences the professional's perception of behavior; it provides the professional with a method for observation and a structure for discourse. Thus, the assessment professional's language often sounds like meaningless jargon to the teacher (Moughamian, 1965). Morris and Arrant (1978) describe one example in which they found no correlation between the ratings of teachers and those of school psychologists on a questionnaire regarding the emotional disturbance of children referred for psychological assessment.

Teachers' dissatisfaction may also be related to their lack of awareness about the demands placed on the assessors who service their schools (Medway, 1977; Szmuk, Docherty, and Ringness, 1979). Teachers may base their expectations for service on unrealistic or incorrect assumptions, and their disappointment may reflect the system for delivery of services rather than the services themselves. For example, Gross and Farling (1969) surveyed Ohio school psychologists and found they handled between 100 and 300 cases each school year, while Dansinger (1968–1969) reports an average caseload of 220 students for Minnesota school psychologists.

The literature also testifies to the dissatisfaction of psychological assessors themselves. Engel (1966) summarizes five areas of dissatisfaction:

1. Disappointment with the lack of clear and direct relationships between test data and intrapsychic syndromes
2. Discomfort with the unavoidable factor of subjectivity in the interpretation of data
3. Uncertainty about selecting appropriate treatment
4. Anxiety regarding the presumed permanence of diagnostic labeling

5. Impotence resulting from the inability to always respond with an
   appropriate remedy

Another aspect of psychologists' dissatisfaction with assessment can be attributed to the historical antecedents of psychological practice. The early activities of the psychologist were defined
primarily as psychodiagnostic techniques subservient to the practice of physicians (Lewandowski and Saccuzzo, 1976). Although
psychologists have gained in status as mental health professionals,
assessment appears to continue to bear some of the negative associations of the discipline's early history. Other than reports of con-
sumers' satisfaction or dissatisfaction, however, we have few studies
that evaluate the validity of assessment as a professional activity.
Few researchers have explored to what extent the recommendations of the assessor are followed; how appropriate the assessor's
placement and programming decisions are; or which procedures
are most effective and efficient for which purposes. Some individual practitioners have studied the use and effectiveness of their own
recommendations (Fairchild, 1974; Pope and Haklay, 1974; Trione,
1958). Kaplan and Sprunger (1967) and Sternlicht, Deutsch, and
Alperin (1970) have conducted research on a larger, more generalizable scale, but more definitive work remains to be done. At this
time, we can only agree with Lewandowski and Saccuzzo (1976) that
"although the literature does not generally support psychological
tests, neither does it rule out their potential effectiveness" (p. 179).
Another source of difficulty for assessors relates to their
educational preparation. Levy and Fox (1975) report that more than
90 percent of psychologist positions in hospitals, community mental
health centers, traditional outpatient clinics, and school settings
require prospective candidates to be skilled in assessment. Yet
many student psychologists are in programs that do not prepare
them adequately in assessment skills. Inadequate training may be a
particular problem for professionals who work in school settings
(Holt, 1967; Rudnick and Berkowitz, 1968). While the number of
training programs in school psychology has increased (Brown and
Lindstrom, 1978), it is not clear that school psychologists feel satis-
fied with the quality of their training (Giebink and Ringness, 1970).
Although Chartoff and Bardon (1974) report a high general level of

school psychologists' satisfaction with their training programs, their respondents found the programs weakest in the areas most related to preparation for working in an educational setting.

A final dissatisfaction of assessors concerns the assessment measures themselves. While assessment is not restricted to testing, the administration of tests nevertheless plays a significant part in assessment. Considerable criticism of testing has come from both within and outside the profession. Critics raise such issues as invasion of privacy, negative effects of labeling, and the inappropriateness of existing measures for minority groups (Bowers, 1971; Cronbach, 1975). Psychologists criticize the technology of test development and the models of the assessment process (Anastasi, 1967; McClelland, 1973). This question of appropriate methodology for assessment leads us to a discussion of current competing methodologies.

Methodological Disputes

Assessors are sometimes unaware that any model underlies their approach to assessment and are thus unable to evaluate the usefulness of the model's applications. However, as McReynolds (1968) points out, "Whether aware of it or not, a psychologist does employ a model each time he develops or employs an assessment procedure" (p. 3). The model the assessor uses determines the variables that become the focus of the assessment, the measures that are selected for use, the interpretations of these measures, and the recommendations that result from these interpretations.

Perhaps the most frequently cited and discussed of the models for assessment is the medical, or etiological, model. Psychological assessment has traditionally functioned according to this approach, and has been condemned for doing so by many members of the newer establishment, who have offered alternatives. To a significant degree, psychological assessment is often equated with this model, and negative criticisms of this model have been used to challenge the assessment process itself.

Four assumptions describe and define the medical model: (1) An observed problem has a cause; (2) this cause lies primarily, if not exclusively, within the organism exhibiting this problem; (3) if found, the nature of the cause is suggestive of a particular treatment; (4) it is necessary to search for the cause in order to engage in treatment. Halpern (1960) applies the principles of this model to the assessment of school children: "For all children who cannot adjust to the classroom routine or benefit from what the class has to offer them, there is the need for special understanding on the part of those responsible for the child's development and education. Such understanding is only possible when the nature and causes of the child's difficulties are ascertained, when what he is trying to communicate through his aberrant behavior is understood" (p. 102). Halpern then summarizes the factors that underlie school maladjustment: "psychotic conditions, brain damage, limited mental endowment, special learning difficulties, exceptionally high mental endowment . . . [and] emotional problems" (p. 102). The assessor's task is to identify the causes of the individual child's problems by administering a battery of tests.

The most damning criticism of the medical model is that, even if the assumptions regarding the locus and existence of cause are correct, the identification of the causes of the child's problems does not result in recommendations that help the classroom teacher because there are, in most cases, no clear prescriptions for classroom activities associated with the presumed causes (Cohen, 1971).

An even more fundamental criticism of the medical model concerns the assumption that the cause of a child's problem lies within the child. There is little evidence that most emotional or personality dysfunctions have an organic source that is sufficient to account for the behavioral manifestations (Meyers, Sundstrom, and Yoshida, 1974).

Another frequent criticism challenges the assumption that it is necessary to locate the cause in order to proceed with treatment (Oakland, 1969). Furthermore, the medical model tends to justify the termination of assessment once the presumed cause has been found, as if this were a sufficient end in and of itself. Finally, the medical model tends to emphasize areas of weakness and failure rather than focusing on the child's positive coping strategies (Oakland, 1969).

Medical practitioners have attempted to revise and expand the traditional medical model, which Weiner (1978), a psychiatrist, equates with the "infectious disease model of the pathogenesis of disease" (p. 27). Weiner proposes a model for psychiatry that views disease "as a failure of adaptation" and considers "organisms in interaction with their natural, social, and cultural environments" (p. 32). This view appears compatible with many psychologists' criticisms of the traditional approach.

Defenders of the medical model point to instances in which organic factors have been demonstrated to relate to behavior, as in the cases of temporal lobe epilepsy and the affective disorders (Kaufman, 1967). Thomas and Chess (1977) suggest an organic predisposition to temperament; however, their work also supports the importance of the interaction between organism and environment, and shows that organic predisposition appears not to have equal importance for all individuals.

Kauffman and Hallahan (1974) object to what they call the confusion between a psychoanalytic and a medical model. They do not see the former as a fair or accurate representation of good medical practice; whereas the psychoanalytic model posits "unobservable variables [and] purely inferential techniques," medical science rests on "observation and empirical verification" (p. 98). These authors suggest that an optimal medical model is indeed appropriate for the psychological assessment of children, that the assessor should relate treatment to observed deficiencies in order to remediate these deficiencies. Their assessment procedure includes the search for cause of the problem and the delineation of deficits. While these authors acknowledge the contribution of contextual variables, they grant such factors little elaboration or focus.

Honigfeld (1971) argues that because "disturbed behavior may result from a variety of known, presumed, or unknown causes" (p. 289), the assessor must attempt to diagnose the cause so that the appropriate therapeutic technique can be prescribed. He cites the example of hallucinations, which "may be a final common path for alcohol or drug intoxication, lead poisoning, endocrinological disease, as well as supposed 'functional' or hysterical mechanisms" (p. 289). He suggests that in such cases one must search for the cause of the behavior since that cause has implications for treatment.

The term *diagnosis*, which is supposed to have implications for treatment and prognosis, is not always used in relation to etiology. Often a "diagnosis" merely labels a constellation of observed behaviors that are frequently perceived as reflecting a common etiology or are at least frequently associated with one. Thus, the assessor must distinguish between *diagnosis* and *etiology*. While the goal of diagnosis may be to identify etiology (Herron and Psaila, 1970), inferences regarding etiology have little to offer regarding treatment; etiology provides no basis for intervention.

Although diagnosis and etiology may not currently have clear implications for intervention, psychologists should not altogether dismiss the need to search for causes. As Bateman (1967), who is researching approaches to assessment that are educationally relevant, states, "the ultimate hope of the field [of learning disabilities] with respect to prevention and scientific treatment probably lies in more definitive knowledge of the causes of learning problems. Such knowledge of etiological factors may also eventually provide the best basis of grouping for educational planning" (p. 215).

We must also distinguish the issue of locating a cause from that of the locus of cause. The search for cause as a prelude to intervention may be a defensible assessment activity if we do not assume that the only place to seek the cause is within the organism. For example, a child's hyperactivity may result from an internal physical disorder or it may represent the child's reaction to a disturbing home environment. Indeed, the child's behavior may be an imitation of behaviors he sees in his family, behaviors he has learned from his parents that are reinforced by them.

In some cases, treatment cannot proceed effectively until the cause is established (for example, lead poisoning), while in other cases this identification is not necessary. Only further research can enable professionals to state which cases fall in the latter category. For example, although medical doctors do not know the organic causes of schizophrenia, doctors do prescribe treatment that provides symptomatic relief for patients who exhibit certain symptoms of the disease. In some cases, however, locating the cause appears either too time consuming or too costly, for example, in the case of repressed early traumatic experience. A psychologist or psychiatrist must then decide whether to proceed with a treatment that promises symptomatic control or to invest the necessary time or money to identify the cause. Further research is needed in this area to help professionals determine if the identification of the cause is critical to successful therapy.

Primarily because the medical model fails to generate recommendations relevant to the educational setting (Bateman, 1967), some professionals have proposed an alternative model that resembles the medical model in some of its assumptions yet differs considerably in others: the diagnostic remedial model.

This approach, like the medical model, posits that there exist causes of observed dysfunctions and that these causes are within the individual manifesting the dysfunction. However, the diagnostic remedial approach focuses on the individual's abilities that are assumed or demonstrated to be necessary in order for him to accomplish a specified educational task. The assessor strives to document deficit areas and to prescribe therapeutic activities that will strengthen or compensate for areas of weakness. For example, an assessor using the medical model may hypothesize that a neurological dysfunction is causing a student's reading problem. An assessor using the diagnostic remedial model would analyze the functional prerequisites of the reading process, assess the child's capacity to perform each of these, and recommend techniques by which the child could improve his reading ability by developing compensatory skills.

Rather than attributing a certain problem to a certain cause, Bateman (1967) uses the term *correlated disability* to describe an aspect of functioning that can be learned which then improves the child's success in an academic skill. For example, one need not prove that poor visual discrimination causes a child's reading problem, but instead, it is sufficient to demonstrate that the child's improved visual discrimination effects an improvement in his reading.

Thus three basic assumptions are implicit in the diagnostic remedial approach: (1) A deficit area in some way, either by association or cause, accounts for or represents the nature of the disability; (2) an individual can learn to compensate for or strengthen a deficit, and thus improve his achievement; (3) assessment measures are accurate enough to identify deficits and low scores represent low areas of functioning.

These last two assumptions have received the most challenge and criticism. Deutsch (1967) recognized a basic potential problem with this model early in the history of its development: "An important question raised by the decision to seek out the areas of retardation in development is: On what level does one seek deficits? If only the most complex areas, such as reading, are analyzed, then the factors which may contribute to deficits might be missed. On the other hand, if only the smallest definable components, such as visual perception of the diagonal, are measured, then a great deal of time might be spent in seeking procedures to train a skill that may not be too important to overall functioning, and that, perhaps, would develop as a byproduct of some other training procedure anyway" (pp. 382–383). And this is in fact what did happen—Deutsch correctly anticipated the problem. The idea, after all, is attractive. If the desire is to determine what the prerequisites are for learning a task, the end product of such speculation would be similar to the elements offered in the Frostig and ITPA approaches. It is not sufficient to say that knowledge of the alphabet is the best predictor of reading success when knowledge of the alphabet is a component of the task to be learned. How are pupils who do not know the alphabet to be helped toward reading mastery? The disappointment, however, need not be attributed to the hypotheses posed or to the train of thought generating these hypotheses. The disappointment has been more a function of the specific end products of such speculation and the manner in which they have been interpreted. Indeed, when researchers investigated whether remediation of the deficit areas, operationally defined in terms of the measures used, resulted in improved achievement (other than higher scores on the measures themselves), the results were at best equivocal (see Arter and Jenkins, 1977; Hammill and Larsen; 1974).

Mann and Phillips (1966–1967) criticized proponents of this model for "their often facile extrapolation of unsettled and controversial experimental and theoretical issues into educational and clinical dicta and practice; . . . their establishment of techniques of uncertain and, at best, limited validity, as prime diagnostic and treatment instruments; . . . their seeming disregard of the handicapped child as a unitary, though complex, organism; . . . their approach to him as a collection of discrete and isolated functions" (p. 311). Mann (1971) also criticizes this model for assessment as one in which "measures are confused with and identified as processes . . . [and] programs are established to develop or correct reified abstractions and metaphors" (p. 5).

The concept of *deficit* is obviously central to the diagnostic remedial approach. Practitioners typically define a deficit as the difference between a client's potential or expected score and his actual or obtained score on a particular assessment measure. Salvia and Clark (1973) note that "As a general rule, difference scores are less reliable than the scores on which [they] are based . . . . The variance attributable to any difference between norming groups is not determinable. An unspecified amount of error is attached to any difference score when the original scores come from tests normed on separate samples" (p. 305). These authors discuss the high frequency of both false positive and false negative assessments resulting from the use of deficit scores.

Several studies of the diagnostic remedial assessment model should be briefly noted. Lilly and Kelleher (1973) report success in demonstrating differential modality strengths in auditory and visual memory tasks, but they do not feel that their findings justify optimism in the attempt to match instruction to modality. Arter and Jenkins (1977) review thirty-two studies that sought to match instructional treatment and modality strength. They conclude that "no one has successfully demonstrated that beginning reading instruction can be improved by modality and instructional matching" (p. 281).

Hammill and Larsen (1974) review 38 studies of psycholinguistic training and conclude that this endeavor has not received research support. In 1978, Lund, Foster, and McCall-Perez challenge these earlier conclusions in their re-review of the majority of the 38 studies initially reported. Hammill and Larsen defend and continue to support their earlier conclusions in a 1978 point by point response to their critics, in which they concede some points, but not the essence of their position that "the effectiveness of psycholinguistic training is essentially nonvalidated" (p. 411).

Thus, despite the appeal of the premises of this approach and its promise of linking assessment to instruction, this model has not proved satisfactory. Its failure may reflect an overly simplistic, if not incorrect, concept of the learner, or a dependence on assessment measures that are inadequate.

Several researchers have challenged the Frostig and ITPA tests, two instruments used for diagnostic remedial assessment, arguing that these tests do not accurately measure the skills and aptitudes they claim to (Carroll, 1972; Mann, 1972b; Ritter and Sabatino, 1974; Sommers, Erdige, and Peterson, 1978).

While both the medical and diagnostic remedial models focus their attention on the learner, task analysis, a third model, analyzes the task to be mastered, isolating the sequential components of the task and the demands that the task places on the learner. Bateman (1967) points out the greatest difficulty with this approach: if the assessor relies on it to the exclusion of other models, he can say little about the child who does not respond adequately to the planned curriculum. Although this approach properly places responsibility on the teacher to plan a curriculum that the child can respond to, rather than expecting all children to respond to one curriculum, task analysis differs from the other approaches in its emphasis on the task instead of on the child. Because task analysis is closely aligned with criterion-referenced assessment, an approach we discuss at length in Chapter Four, we will not discuss this model at length here.

Testing and observing a child and analyzing the learning task alone do not enable an assessor to understand or predict the child's learning behavior. Behavioral psychologists remind assessors that external environment is assessable and can be shown to account for a good deal of behavior. The behaviorist approach to assessment is best explained in contrast to a trait concept of assessment. The basic assumption of a trait approach is that an individual has identifiable and consistent predispositions to behavior and thought which he maintains in all situations. One can thus attempt to predict an individual's behavior in a given situation on the basis of his previous responses. The basic assumption of the behaviorist approach, in contrast, is that behavior is specific to the situation and cannot be predicted, although individuals have some historical patterns of behavior. Readers interested in this approach may wish to consult Mischel (1968), a landmark work on behavioral assessment and interpretation in clinical psychology; Ekehammar (1974), a discussion of the historical precedents of this approach; and Bersoff (1973) and Bersoff and Grieger (1971), analyses of the application of behavioral assessment strategies in educational settings.

The potential effects of environment upon behavior are dramatically illustrated by Gump, Schoggen, and Redl's (1963) case study of a nine-year-old boy from a family of upper-low socioeconomic status. They recorded his behavior at summer camp and ten days later at home. At camp, he was "active, exploratory, construction-oriented, fantasy-tinged, and physically exuberant," while at home he was "passive, dallying, and competitive" (p. 179). Thus an observer of this boy at home would conclude that he had a trait of passivity, while an observer at camp might conclude that he had a trait of active exuberance.

The behaviorists' assumption that behavior is strongly influenced by environment leads them to question the generalizability of assessment results. Rather than attempting to identify a client's intrapsychic dynamics in a clinical setting, the behaviorist observes a client's behavior in a given situation, discerns the controlling aspects of the situation, and bases his assessment on the client's behavior in the situation. Specific behavioral observation strategies are discussed in Chapter Five.

Although Mischel (1968) dismissed the trait position, he (1973, 1977, 1979) and other researchers (Alker, 1972; Bowers, 1973) now advocate a view that posits an interaction between an organism's predisposition and situational factors. Interactionists argue that individuals have consistent response patterns to situations, more so to some than to others, and more so for some individuals than for others. Studies illustrate both a "considerable" consistency of behavior across situations (Roper and Hinde, 1978) and the differential effects of situational factors (Stoneman and Gibson, 1978). Bowers (1973) argues that research results are a function of methodology: experimental studies tend to support the behaviorists' interpretation, while correlational studies tend to yield results supportive of the trait position.

Bem and Allen (1974) cite another aspect of methodology that biases research findings. They criticize researchers who concentrate on large group, interindividual measures, rather than idiographic data. Because individuals differ in the traits they possess and in the relationship between those traits, the study of large groups yields "the conclusion that a sample of individuals is inconsistent to the degree that their behaviors do not sort into the equivalence class which the investigator imposes by his choice of behaviors and situations to sample" (p. 509). Thus, researchers are measuring their own cognitive processes rather than aspects of the individual subjects. Bem and Allen's idiographic study of "friendliness" and "conscientiousness" shows that individuals differ in the degree to which they are consistent in various situations and in their definitions of the traits under study. When the researchers used the subject's definition of the trait, the subject's behavior appeared consistent; but when the researchers used their own definition, such consistency was absent.

Current theoretical positions recognize that the assessor need consider the situation, the individual, and the nature of their interaction in order to either understand or predict behavior. Weiner (1972) reminds us, however, that the more complex the inferences an accessor must draw from assessment data, the greater the potential for errors in measurement. When an assessor symbolically interprets a client's responses to assessment stimuli, the high level of inference can lead to increased error.

Finally, we mention the ecological model, an interactional approach whose primary methodology is naturalistic observation of the child and his environment (Pastor and Swap, 1978). This model has not yet demonstrated its potential for contribution to assessment, although it has served as a model for research and consultation, with some negative data regarding the latter (Jason, Ferone, and Anderegg, 1979). This model also offers a conceptual label that can be used in both the design of an individual assessment program and the interpretation of the data.

As our brief review of models for assessment has shown, no one comprehensive methodology exists. In Chapter Two, we refine our description of assessment, describe optimal assessment procedures, and propose a comprehensive model for psychological assessment. An awareness of the problems and limitations of certain assessment procedures should not discourage us or prompt us to abandon assessment as useless. As Meier (1967) points out, the professional's failure to derive an appropriate diagnostic approach to a client's problem reduces program planning to "sheer guesswork" (p. 188). Thus our awareness of methodological controversies must serve as a motivation for us to improve our procedures and to refine our assumptions. In this book, we strive to inform the reader of approaches and strategies currently available and how these methods may be applied to the educational setting. Our goal is to help the reader conduct assessments that will be of optimal benefit in the planning of educational programs for school-age children.

Chapter 2

⧉⧉⧉⧉⧉

A New Model for Optimal Assessment

$\mathbf{I}$n this chapter, we present a comprehensive definition of assessment and propose a model for an optimal assessment process. Two central assumptions inform our discussion. First, we consider assessment as part of the broader consultation process. Second, we view assessment as a problem-solving activity whose objective is to contribute to decision making, a position also taken by Berger (1979), Sloves, Docherty, and Schneider (1979), and Sundberg, Snowden, and Reynolds (1978).

Rather than equate assessment with any one specific procedure or suggest that any one procedure is best, we believe that an array of alternatives is essential to the conduct of assessment (Mercer and Ysseldyke, 1977). To say that assessment is not equal to any one technique is to say that assessment is not merely the use of any particular tools of measurement, that assessment is more than a technique of asking questions and deriving scores. The mature assessor realizes that a client is not merely the sum of his responses or scores on any particular set of measures.

Thus, we can describe the general characteristics of assessment procedures that are optimal, appropriate, or desirable, but we will not endorse any one strategy as always good in and of itself. Rather, we seek to determine in which situations a particular strategy is useful. Our first step is to clarify a number of terms that are often used almost synonymously with assessment: *evaluation, measurement, testing,* and *diagnosis*.

The Terminology of Assessment

Although the terms *assessment* and *evaluation* are often used interchangeably in practice, an important distinction between the two exists. *Evaluation* implies some degree of judgment regarding goodness or worth (Merwin, 1969; Stake, 1969; Wittrock, 1967) and is mostly accurately applied to activities that lead to decisions regarding the survival or modification of a program. As Bloom (1967) points out, the primary concern of evaluation is to judge the validity of the content of a program, technique, process, or strategy.

Evaluation is accurately applied to individuals when one is considering an individual's ability to progress or respond to a specified procedure or treatment, or when one is determining the appropriateness of a program or a treatment for an individual. In the first case, the individual is evaluated in relation to the program; in the second case, the program is evaluated in relation to the individual. Venezky (1974) describes evaluation as "backward-looking" (p. 4), the asking of, How did we do? Assessment asks the forward-looking question, What do we need to do?

Evaluation is particularly sensitive to cultural values and issues (Glaser, 1967) because it poses questions of goodness or worth. One's responses to such questions are dependent on one's values, which are derived from implicit or explicit cultural values. In this sense, the criterion for evaluation reflects cultural mores and social values. For example, if the public is suddenly interested in developing scientists, a social criteria for evaluating an educational program would be its success in meeting this objective. A program that emphasizes foreign languages would not be likely to receive a high evaluation in such circumstances.

One component of the assessment process is measurement, the means or standardized procedures used to sample behavior and objectify observations. Measures include tests and psychometric instruments, systematic observation, structured interview, and projective materials. Measures vary considerably in their relative subjectivity or objectivity. Measures that rely the least on the assessor's subjective judgment facilitate comparison between individuals and between an individual and a criterion of performance.

The attempt to measure presents an inevitable difficulty because measuring imposes a static framework on a dynamic process and artificially separates interacting functional components. However, the need and desire to intervene and manipulate, taken here in the benign sense, requires such "handles" and categorization. Although artificial, measures can provide information useful to the assessor if the measures are carefully chosen, administered, and interpreted.

Testing refers to specific types of measures, those that seek to obtain "a sample of behavior under controlled conditions" (Maloney and Ward, 1979). Most tests are indirect measures that require the examiner to infer generalizations about the examinee's behavior. Because tests are most frequently administered to individuals in order to ascertain descriptive characteristics or traits, they usually ignore situational variables and interactional factors. Although assessment is not limited to these types of measures, as Wohl (1967) suggests, the traditional approach to assessment equates the assessment process with psychometry. Such an equation, however, is not advocated in such basic professional training texts as Bardon and Bennett (1974), Gray (1963), Magary (1967), or White and Harris (1961).

Tests sample behaviors that are assumed to represent a larger constellation of behaviors which interest the referral source and, therefore, the assessor. Some tests provide a means of comparing an individual's performance with that of others. A test's adequacy as a measure is determined by the extent to which it meets the standards of construction, administration, reliability, and validity, as described in the psychological literature. However, the adequacy of a test's contribution to the assessment process itself and the validity of testing as a process are, as indicated in Chapter One, issues rarely subjected to investigation (Cronbach and Gleser, 1957; Ysseldyke, 1979). Researchers have focused on the validity of discrete measures rather than on their contribution to assessment.

One goal of some assessment procedures is to identify a diagnosis. The medical model posits a close relationship between diagnosis and treatment as the diagnostician infers an intraorganismic condition which specifies a treatment. The diagnostician assesses the external manifestations of this condition, and such an assessment culminates in diagnostic inferences. Accurate assessment advances accurate diagnosis, which identifies appropriate treatment, and the validity of this process is confirmed by the patient's response to treatment.

Such a diagnostic process can be appropriate to the assessment of school children (Hutson, 1974), but one cannot and one need not obtain a diagnosis in all cases. Powell (1971) offers a broader definition and conceptualization of *diagnosis* that enhances the value of applying the term to the educational setting. For Powell, *to diagnose* means "to know something completely" (p. 251); diagnosis comprises the statement of an objective, the description of symptoms, the precise identification of problem areas, and suggestions for remediation. This type of diagnosis provides information about the factors that are hypothesized to account for the client's problem. Such a diagnosis may yield suggestions for remedial efforts, although such recommendations may not always specify factors that are manipulable within the classroom. Diagnosis as thus conceived is a relevant endeavor for the psychologist, but diagnosis is not a sufficient end in itself, particularly in the assessment of the child in school. We now consider this process in greater detail.

Assessment

There are several ways to discuss the assessment process: by defining it, by considering its components, by describing the phases of the process, and by delineating the criteria for an optimal assessment. Our discussion relies on each of these strategies in turn.

Sundberg, Snowden, and Reynolds (1978) characterize the traditional approach to assessment as response to the question, How much?. Wohl (1967) elaborates on the definition of a traditional approach by citing the psychometric view that "if something exists, it does so in some measurable amount" (p. 16). Traditional psychometric assessment is the attempt to derive a score that locates the client's characteristics on a particular dimension. The score represents the client's variance from a given norm, and the assessor attempts to account for that variance, attributing whatever variance he cannot account for to errors of measurement. The traditional assessor strives for objectivity, if not anonymity, keeping interaction during the assessment process to a minimum. The assessment focuses on the individual, not on the interaction between him and his setting. Wohl criticizes this approach as an overly restrictive process that fails to generate sufficient important information.

In this book, we view assessment as the phase of consultation during which the professional gathers data that inform a decision about the child's educational program. This type of scientist-practitioner attitude can help to raise the system above reliance on subjective intuition and momentary fads.

There is no necessary conflict or contradiction perceived to exist between assessment and consultation. In fact, Clark (1975) refers to the assessment process as "individual diagnostic consultation." However, consultation without the ability to determine and utilize the appropriate assessment procedures on which to base consultative input is viewed as insupportable. Gray (1963) suggests two major roles for the school psychologist, that of the "data-oriented problem solver" and that of "transmitter of psychological knowledge and skill" (p. 10).

Our definition of assessment stresses two aspects of the process that are of particular importance: problem solving and decision making. Problem solving both directs and organizes the assessment activities (Maloney and Ward, 1979); decision making addresses the specific actions to be taken within the educational setting. Problem solving and decision making also demarcate the beginning and conclusion of assessment. The posing of a problem by the referral source initiates the assessment process, and the decisions reached are the outcome of the endeavor. This series of events should include a follow-up to evaluate the effectiveness and appropriateness of the decisions, but the assessment process itself concludes when a decision is reached.

Ysseldyke (1979) lists five kinds of decisions that are typically made in a school setting. First, screening and identification respond to the question, Is the pupil different from the norm? Second, classification and placement decisions respond to the questions, Different in what way and to what extent? Third, decisions regarding instructional planning specify areas to which instruction should be directed and recommend methods likely to result in positive gains. Fourth, evaluation of the pupil's response to instruction provides information that enables educators to determine the appropriate next step. Finally, evaluation of the program judges the program's effectiveness for various pupils with regard to the accomplishment of instructional objectives.

Assessment thus is the process of collecting systematic, valid, reliable, and relevant data in response to the problems presented by the referral source for the purpose of making decisions for or about students. Assessment does not always require the collection of elaborate data and need not address issues beyond those mentioned in the referral, although sometimes an assessor will explore new questions that arise during the course of the assessment. Assessment is a dynamic process in that the determination of procedures to be used develops from the questions posed during the assessment and reflects the characteristics of the client and the issues involved. Assessment need not be limited to a narrow period of time; the assessor may follow a pupil over an extended period of time.

From this definition of assessment, we derive a set of criteria, shown in Figure 1, by which to evaluate a psychological assessment:

Evaluation of a Psychological Assessment

1. Were the measures and procedures used appropriate to the referral issues? Were multiple procedures and multiple sources of information used?

2. Were the measures used and interpreted in a manner appropriate to such characteristics of the assessed individual as age, race, sex, and socioeconomic status?
3. Were the measures and procedures employed within the examiner's competence to administer? Were issues not within the examiner's areas of expertise referred to other assessors?
4. Did the assessment yield recommendations for intervention? Were the recommendations judged for their feasibility?
5. Are the findings reported in a manner that is comprehensible to the referral source and other involved parties (parents, teachers, school administrators, guidance counselors)?
6. Does the interpretation of the assessment findings reflect the dynamic, interactional, and multidimensional nature of behavior?
7. Have the following questions been answered by the assessor:
   a. Who is the individual assessed? What are his or her most salient characteristics?
   b. What is the nature of the difficulty? What are the discrepancies between current and expected levels of functioning?
   c. In what situations and under what circumstances are problem and nonproblem behaviors manifested?
   d. How does the individual attempt to cope? What strategies are used? Which of these, and when are these, effective or ineffective?
   e. Why does the pupil have difficulties? How can the manifestations of the problems best be accounted for? Why are they occurring at this particular time?

These criteria reflect issues of concern in the current psychological literature regarding nonbiased assessment and professional accountability. The criteria also address the aspects of psychological assessment most frequently criticized by teachers. Our hypothesis is that if an assessment meets these criteria, it will fulfill professional standards of nonbias and accountability, will be judged as helpful and relevant by teachers, and, most importantly, will facilitate positive intervention for the referred pupil.

Having posed these standards for assessment, we now identify the steps in the implementation of an optimal assessment process. The first step is the referral of a pupil for assessment. Although the dynamics of the referral are affected by the role of the person who initiates the referral—a parent, the child, a teacher, or another concerned individual—for the sake of discussion, we assume the teacher to be the primary source of referral within the educational setting. In initiating a referral, the teacher becomes the consultee of the school psychologist or assessor.

A school's forms and procedures for referrals are an important aspect of the assessment process as referral is the first step. Teachers must know how and when to make a referral and what constitutes an appropriate referral. This information shapes the teacher's expectations of the possible results of the assessment process. Most basic school psychology texts discuss referral and suggest forms; in particular, Alper and White (1971) offer referral forms that elicit information most useful to the assessor.

After the assessor has received the initial referral form, he should review the pupil's records and confer with the pupil's teacher to further clarify the reason for the referral and the nature of the pupil's problem. From this conference, the assessor formulates hypotheses regarding what information he must gather to further define, identify, and remediate the problem and how these data are to be collected. Sometimes the resolution of a problem requires only that the assessor share psychological knowledge with the teacher, that the assessor use his knowledge of child development or learning theory to clarify the problem and guide the teacher to a simple strategy for resolving the problem in the classroom. If this is the case, the entire assessment sequence comprises a conference with the teacher and a follow-up interview. (See Grubb, Petty, and Flynn (1976) for a detailed account of the implementation of this approach.)

Other referrals, however, require the assessor to gather more information. Figure 1 illustrates five sequences for the assessment process. Each sequence represents a full, complete, and adequate assessment. The assessor's choice of sequence depends on the nature of the referral issues. Note that the administration of tests is only one possible response to a referral. As Ahr (1965) stresses, assessors must resist the referral-testing reflex.

Figure 2 illustrates the cognitive activities of the assessor as he proceeds to formulate and test his hypotheses about the pupil. At each

Figure 1. Five Sequences for Assessment

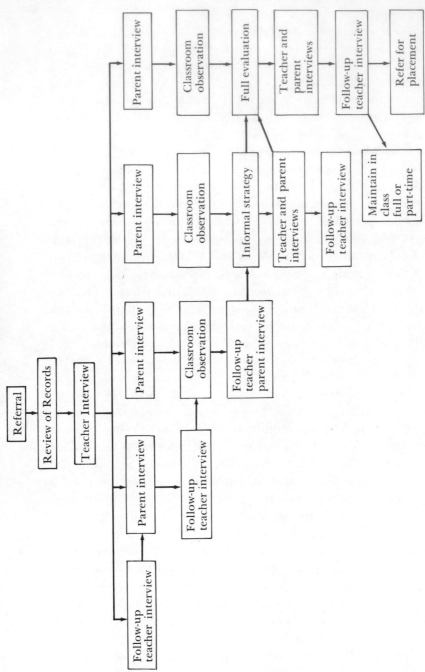

Source: Lidz, 1977b.

Figure 2. Assessor's Cognitive Activities

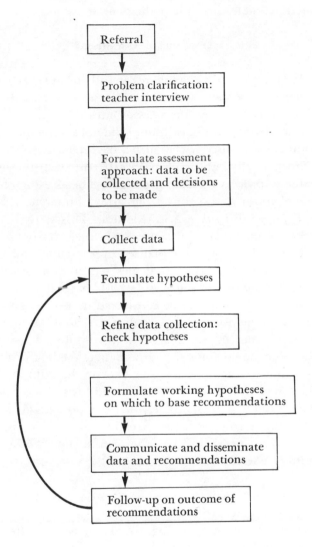

step in the assessment, the assessor asks, What do I need to know? What are the best means of deriving this information? The assessor gathers the information he needs, uses it to formulate hypotheses about the pupil, and then gathers information that will support or disprove these hypotheses. (See Shapiro, 1951, for a similar experimental approach to assessment.) Figure 3 details an example of the formulation and testing of hypotheses by an assessor.

Domains of Assessment

We must now consider more carefully what types of problems and behaviors a school psychologist or assessor confronts. In delineating a child's problem, the assessor must draw generalized inferences from observations like "Johnny did not succeed in adding one-digit numerals" to discern what such behavior implies about Johnny. Is Johnny partially sighted, mentally deficient, overcome by anxiety, or unable to process verbal instructions? The assessor's functional analysis of Johnny must consider an array of inferences that can be drawn from his difficulties with addition. This analysis would include genetic and organic influences, and situational or interactional qualities that have been internalized by the child and which are expressed in attitudes, styles, strategies, sets of responses, and so on. The first domain of assessment is the child himself.

A second domain to be considered in any assessment is the child's social and instructional situation in school. An analysis of the situation includes an examination of the pupil's teacher, his peers, and the educational content and pedagogic method of the pupil's classes. The assessor thus must quickly survey the child, the situation, and the interaction between the child and his situation in order to make an initial hypothesis about which components are most likely related to the referral problems. Sabatino and Miller (1979, p. 192) propose seven general areas that the assessor should consider in his preliminary assessment:

1. Educational functioning: achievement levels, learning styles, strengths, and weaknesses
2. Social-emotional functioning: social interaction, affective functioning, and self-help skills
3. Physical functioning: visual, auditory, speech, and motor skills, and overall health
4. Cognitive functioning: problem-solving skills in school and at home

Figure 3. Example of One Possible Assessment Sequence

Referral issues

1. Child answers questions inappropriately, seems bizarre.
2. Teacher must often repeat directions before child responds.
3. Child is not completing assignments and is achieving on a level at least six months below peers.

Preliminary questions

1. Can child hear?

No: Problem is hearing impairment: refer to appropriate professional resource.
Yes: Proceed.

2. Does child have normal cognitive level of functioning?

No: Possible mental deficiency; probe further.
Yes: Proceed.

3. Does referral problem occur in situations other than classroom, and how pervasive is problem?

No: Probe teacher and instructional approach.
Yes: Proceed.

4. Are there significant emotional stresses?

Yes: Refer to appropriate professional resource.
No: Proceed.

Means of assessment

1. Refer for audiometric evaluation.

2. Administer measure of cognitive functioning.

3. Interview parents; check records and developmental history; observe.

4. Observe with parents; interview child and parents; projective measures.

Hypothesis

Neither mental deficiency, hearing impairment, nor emotional disturbance appear primary; consider language processing problem.

Refine assessment

1. Compare receptive and expressive language abilities.
2. Analyze expressive spontaneous statements in relation to verbal input.
3. Analyze nature of errors and ability to follow directions.
4. Determine which strategies improve the child's comprehension.

5. Language functioning: receptive, expressive, and nonverbal skills and speech
6. Family: social interactions with family members, dominant language, social service and economic needs
7. Environment: at home and at school

The assessor should consider each of these areas in relation to the specific referral issue. For example, if a pupil is referred for inattentiveness, the assessor would ask, How could the child's educational functioning relate to this inattentiveness? His social-emotional functioning?, and so on.

In formulating a taxonomy of functions relevant to the educational setting, Quay (1968) postulates three basic parameters of the instructional situation—input, response, and reinforcement—which interact with seven learner modalities—visual, auditory, tactile, motor, verbal, social, and information—to yield a set of educationally relevant functions. For example, visual, auditory, and tactile input functions include: acuity, orientation, perception, and failure to store. Quay's taxonomy of forty-one measurable behaviors offers a means of delineating areas of a pupil's strength and weakness as well as a basis for grouping pupils for instruction. Although Boeding (1976) and Ledford (1975) also present lists of accessible areas, their lists rely exclusively on learner variables, while Quay considers components of the learner, the situation, and their interactive qualities.

In contrast to investigators who stress the assessment of a pupil's functions, Glaser (1972) argues the need to assess "the different ways in which different students learn best . . . the basic processes that underlie various kinds of learning, [and] . . . the prerequisite performance capabilities required for learning a new task" (p. 7). He criticizes traditional measures of products or outcomes as being generally poor predictors of school performance; for example, IQ tests account for only a maximum of 35 to 40 percent of the variance of achievement.

Glaser specifies three areas of assessment that he calls the "new aptitudes." The first is mental elaboration: the pupil's ability to recode or transform materials presented to him by elaborating on their content. This activity is an aspect of what Piaget terms *assimilation*, the means by which new material becomes a part of and is acted upon by the individual. Second are the aptitudes of visual and auditory perceptual processes, which are "concerned with competence in organizing and extracting patterns of information" (p. 9). This category includes auditory and visual discrimination, figure-ground discrimination, and spatial orientation, as well as an individual's more active strategies for interacting and acting upon stimuli. Glaser's third group of new aptitudes includes "cognitive styles and personality characteristics related to learning" (p. 9). (Cognitive styles are discussed in Chapter Nine.)

Glaser holds that the assessment of these aptitudes seems more likely to predict a student's response to instruction than the traditional measures of achievement levels that provide only inferential information about how to improve the student's performance.

In an earlier study, Glaser (1967) delineates five categories of behavior that need to be assessed as the bases for decisions about instructional methods. These include "the extent to which the individual has already learned the behavior to be acquired"; "the extent to which the individual possesses the prerequisites for learning the behavior to be acquired"; "learning set variables, that consist of acquired ways of learning that facilitate or interfere with learning procedures"; "specific ability to make discriminations necessary in subsequent instruction"; and "general mediating abilities" (p. 78).

Glaser also discusses a variety of instructional variables that affect a pupil's progress: speed of presentation, amount of practice, amount of structure, type of reinforcement, distribution of practice, mediational mechanisms, stimulus and modality variables. However, no one has yet organized these variables in a systematic form that can be applied during assessment. Glaser's challenge remains unanswered: "the task is to determine those measures that have the highest discriminating potential for allocating between treatments and then determine their intercorrelations so that they can be combined in some way and all of them not be used" (p. 79). Until researchers have determined the skills prerequisite for specific learning tasks and the ways in which instructional variables affect learners, assessors cannot adequately decide which instructional method is most appropriate for a particular learner in a particular learning situation.

Table 1 synthesizes the preceding discussion of the functional analysis of the pupil and relates these areas to decision-making objectives. For each assessment question, we have suggested appropriate measures that will yield information necessary for decision making. These measures are described in detail in Chapters Three through Seven.

Decision Making

The model of assessment described in this chapter emphasizes the formulation and testing of hypotheses to arrive at decisions about treatment. We must now consider the bases for such decisions.

The assessment bases for making decisions must be taken into account when assessment concerns final decisions. In deciding which particular measures to administer, an assessor selects measures that enable him to assess those aspects of individual functioning, the task, or the situation that are relevant to the referral issue. For example, if the examiner wishes to know how inattentive the pupil is compared to his classmates during an independent reading activity, classroom observation would be an appropriate measure.

In making decisions about treatment, the assessor may first consider the discrepancy between the referred pupil's level of functioning and that of a criterion group. The determination of a significant difference aids the assessor in deciding whether to label an area as dysfunctional; this decision must often be made on the basis of such comparisons rather than on the basis of absolute identification.

Second, the assessor will want to establish the pervasiveness of the problem; that is, in which situations it occurs, how often it occurs, and the like. Obviously, one or two instances of difficulty do not necessarily indicate that a pupil has a problem. Determining the pervasiveness of particular behaviors helps the assessor decide whether a problem exists and suggests possible directions for intervention.

Pervasiveness and frequency are insufficient guides in some cases. One act of serious violence by a pupil, for example, warrants attention and intervention. Thus, the third basis of decision making concerns the problem itself, since some problems are inherently more serious than others. The assessor must also relate the nature of the

Table 1. Areas of Need and Recommended Assessment Decision

Academic	Behavior	Social	Family	Physical
What level of work can be expected? *Norm-referenced cognitive measure*	What is the nature of the behavior? *Referral form* *Interviews* *Observations*	What is the nature of the problem? *Referral form* *Interviews* *Observations*	What factors about the family may affect current functioning? *Referral form* *Parent interview* *Child self report* *Family observation*	What preexisting factors may be influencing current functioning? *Referral Form* *Parent interview* *Medical records* *School nurse*
What are the current academic achievement levels? *Norm-referenced achievement measure*	Under what circumstances is it likely to occur? *Referral form* *Interviews* *Observations*	Under what circumstances does it occur? *Referral form* *Interviews* *Observations*		
What are the specific areas of mastery and deficit? *Domain-referenced achievement measure*	What are the possible "causes" or maintaining conditions? *Observation interviews* *"Projective" procedures*	What are the possible "causes" or maintaining conditions? *Observation* *Interviews* *"Projective" procedures*	To what extent is the family modifiable in the area(s) requiring change? *Parent interviews* *Observation* *Trial intervention*	What is the current physical status? *Same as above and individual and classroom observation*
What are the patterns of asset and deficit? *Task and error analysis* *Observation of test performance*	What conditions have potential for modifying the behavior? *Observations* *Interviews* *Testing the limits* *Role-playing* *Self-report*	What conditions have potential for modifying the behavior? *Observations* *Interviews* *Role-playing* *Self-report*		To what extent do current factors affect functioning in the referral area? *Individual and classroom observation* *Interviews*
How does the child learn best? *Trial teaching* *Other informal procedures*				

Note: Assessment procedures are in italic.

problem to the pupils's age and development; a twelve-year-old who reverses letters is quite different from a six-year-old that reverses letters.

Fourth, the assessor should note intraindividual discrepancies, which are most often apparent in a profile of the pupil's scores. Such discrepancies alert the examiner to specific areas of difficulty and are suggestive of the pupil's experience, as such discrepancies are likely to confuse him and provoke anxiety. However, the assessor must remember that the subtests on which profiles are based are often considerably less reliable than the overall measures from which they derive, and they often do not assess what they purport (Ysseldyke, 1979).

Fifth, the assessor's decisions should reflect observations of which aproaches are effective with the pupil and observations of pupil-teacher interactions.

As we have noted throughout this and the preceding chapter, making assessment decisions requires the professional to exercise judgment, draw inferences, and formulate educated hypotheses. Although one strives to obtain the most complete and accurate information relevant to the referral issue, one faces the limitations of current knowledge of child development, child psychology, psychometry, pedagogy, and learning theory. The assessor must acquaint himself with a large variety of assessment procedures, which will be presented in Chapters Three through Seven, while remembering the intrinsic limitations of these procedures.

Chapter 3

⚛⚛⚛⚛⚛⚛

Methods for Estimating Children's Full Learning Potential

Dynamic assessment strategies embody two basic principles: First, the examiner's interactions with the client are considered an integral part of the examination; the examiner does not remain aloof or neutral, he actively relates to the client. Second, the examiner does not necessarily accept the response a child gives to an assessment task "as is." The examiner may investigate the basis for the response, seek to identify factors that would enable the child to make a better or more appropriate response, and investigate factors that inhibit the child from making a better response. These two principles distinguish dynamic strategies from traditional approaches that mandate the examiner's neutrality.

Dynamic approaches are not new, but the last twenty years have witnessed the greatest activity in this area of assessment. Dynamic approaches were developed primarily for two purposes: to improve the classification of exceptional children, and to produce more effective remedial strategies for classroom instruction. Although our primary interest iş not classification but the remedial educational recommendations that assessment yields, we discuss in this chapter dynamic strategies that have been developed to improve classification. These strategies are not widely known among psychologists, yet they provide a unique, iconoclastic, and interesting approach to psychological assessment. Furthermore, distinctions between dynamic approaches for the purposes of classification and those for the development of remedial strategies are often minor, and the former often have strong implications for the latter, even if not explicitly devised for that purpose.

Dynamic Assessment for Classification

Traditional, static assessment procedures have been criticized for providing inadequate information regarding the degree to which a child can profit from instruction, a characteristic that researchers consider a more significant basis for diagnosis of mental deficiency than standard cognitive measures (Kratochwill, 1977). These static approaches have also been criticized as inadequate for assessing the learning ability of ethnic minority children and children from culturally disadvantaged backgrounds (Budoff, 1974; Feuerstein, 1979; Jensen, 1961; Kratochwill, 1977). Children from such backgrounds often lack the cognitive strategies necessary for success in both these traditional cognitive measures and in the traditional instructional situation (Feuerstein, 1979). Because even the use of special norms for interpreting these measures still does not enable one to determine which low scorers are deficient and which merely need more opportunity to develop the appropriate problem-solving strategies, Jensen (1961) argues that "a battery of learning tests will have to be developed in order to achieve the kind of diagnostic instrument we would desire for use in schools with children of ethnic and cultural backgrounds for whom the usual intelligence tests are of limited value" (p. 158). Until new tests are devised, culturally disadvantaged pupils are best evaluated after they have received instruction in problem-solving strategies. Those who do not profit from such instruction may then be examined for organic deficiencies. The performance of children from disadvantaged backgrounds is more likely to be underestimated by static procedures.

Poor test performance that reflects an individual's inexperience in taking tests rather than the individual's mental acuity is not a phenomenon particular to school children from disadvantaged backgrounds. Studies by Fleishman and Hempel (1955), Mackay and Vernon (1963), Ortar (1959), Simrall (1947), and Woodrow (1938, 1939) on various subjects show that practice can influence an individual's performance on static measures, that individuals respond differently to such practice, and that therefore traditional static measures do not adequately distinguish between individuals who merely lack experience and those who have actual deficiencies.

Many dynamic assessment procedures use a test-teach-retest paradigm, rather than a static measure, to gauge a student's ability to learn. Rather than measure what the student already knows, these procedures seek to ascertain how and how well the student learns new material. Two of the best-known dynamic strategies have been successful in differentiating among pupils with low IQ's those who are inexperienced and those who are truly deficient. Let us now consider each of these strategies in detail.

Budoff's Learning Potential Assessment Strategy

Budoff and his associates have devised an alternative assessment of cognitive functioning in an attempt "to obtain the estimate of general ability in a context that minimizes the possibly adverse effects of the child's prior experience" (1968, p. 297) that will "enable us to distinguish the low IQ child who is relatively unintelligent from the child who is relatively competent in nonschool-related areas of his life" (1974, p. 75).

Rather than assessing the consequences of past achievement, Budoff seeks to assess the child's capacity to profit from experience. He uses the Kohs Block Designs, a measure that has been traditionally considered relatively culturally unbiased, in a test-teach-retest sequence. His methods have been used primarily to assess disadvantaged adolescents, classified as educable mentally retarded (EMR) according to traditional procedures.

The Learning Potential Assessment Strategy incorporates both practice and coaching, as follows: Fifteen designs (enlarged stimulus cards from the Kohs) are individually administered three times before coaching, the day after the coaching session, and one month after the coaching session. The coaching is intended to present the pupil with the necessary problem-solving strategies that practice alone may not assure. The Coaching includes praise and encouragement, and instruction to check the subject's design block by block with the stimulus design. The pupil proceeds from undifferentiated designs (blocks not outlined) to one row presented at a time, still undifferentiated, to one row of outlined blocks.

Studies of institutionalized EMR adolescents show that the coaching does affect performance; subjects exposed to the designs used for coaching but who were not coached did not improve their scores as much as subjects who were coached. Subjects tended to maintain their gains over a month's time, and many succeeded on designs not originally included in the coaching (Budoff, 1968). Furthermore, the coached subjects achieved significant gains on the Raven Progressive Matrices and WISC Performance IQ measures, with the Block Design subtest omitted, but not on the WISC Verbal IQ or the Stanford-Binet. Those subjects who profited most from coaching had initially larger discrepancies between their WISC Verbal and Performance IQs, with the latter being higher and often out of the retarded range (Budoff, 1968). Similar findings are reported for younger adolescent EMRs in public school special classes.

Using this approach with high IQ subjects, Babad and Budoff (reported in Budoff, 1974) report that although subjects with high IQs made gains, the dispersion of scores was narrower after coaching than before. In contrast, the postcoaching scores of EMR subjects increased in variability after training, with some scoring above the EMR range. Pupils from middle-class backgrounds rarely made significant gains following coaching; the authors conclude that these pupils' level of ability is accurately estimated by the pretest assessment. Jensen (1963) notes that students who initially achieve high scores are likely to show small gains, while those with initially low scores will show greater gains merely because the latter did not reach their optimal performance on the first test. Jensen's point does not negate the usefulness of Budoff's approach in discriminating among low initial scorers who are deficient and those who are inexperienced, but reminds us that computing gains is not useful in assessing pupils who do achieve high initial scores on cognitive measures.

In later studies, Budoff added the Raven Progressive Matrices and a Series Learning Potential Test (elaborated in Babad and Budoff, 1974) to the Kohs Block Design Test. The later research also provides data indicating which subjects are more likely either to make significant gains or to obtain initially high scores on the learning potential procedures: Subjects who are "white, over fifteen years, male, from the lower socioeconomic groups or living in situations that have been classically associated with poor school performance, for example, if one is a member of a family of recent immigrants, or one's parents do not speak English, or one's family is large" (Budoff, 1974, p. 80).

Sewell (1979), comparing the predictive success of Budoff's procedure with IQ and a paired-associate learning task for urban white, middle-class and black, lower-class first graders, finds IQ to be a significantly more successful predictor of reading and math scores for the white middle-class children. The best predictor for the lower-class blacks is the posttest score on the Raven Coloured Progressive Matrices, administered using Budoff's instructions.

A critical issue in the estimation of EMR subjects' learning potential is the criterion of their ability to function in a noninstitutionalized setting. Budoff's (1974) data show that, among adolescents institutionalized at the time of initial assessment, gainers usually leave the institution, either without permission or by discharge; nongainers tend to continue their institutional residency. Of pupils who attended public school special education classes at the time of assessment, gainers tend to be better employed and more independent than nongainers at the time of follow-up.

Budoff's data challenge the adequacy of traditional assessment measures to estimate the disadvantaged adolescent's ability to profit from instruction and the criterion of success in school as an adequate assessment measure. Budoff has not, however, adequately demonstrated whether his Learning Potential Assessment Strategy is a significantly better predictor of learning ability than WISC Performance IQ scores or initial scores on the Raven or Kohs Blocks. Budoff's strategy does not appear to contribute significant information about subjects whose initial scores on these measures are above the EMR range and are discrepant with a lower Verbal IQ.

Feuerstein's Learning Potential Assessment Device

Feuerstein's (1979) concerns about assessing the disadvantaged adolescent's cognitive capacity and ability to respond to instruction are similar to Budoff's. Feuerstein, however, more explicitly discusses the dynamic basis of his approach, attributing other theorists' "failure to create appropriate methods to assess the deprived individual" to the static quality of psychometric theory, which "confines the search to the most stable characteristics of the individual and totally neglects . . . any evidence which may point to the modifiability of the organism" (Feuerstein, 1971, p. 266). Feuerstein and his associates use a test-teach-retest sequence and encourage interaction between the examiner and pupil in order to optimize the pupil's motivation and performance.

The Learning Potential Assessment Device comprises the Raven Coloured Progressive Matrices, variations on this measure, and three other measures of "representational, internalized, abstract thinking" (Feuerstein, 1971, p. 271) that place minimal demands on verbal expression. Although Feuerstein (1979) describes these procedures, he does not provide sufficient detail to prepare the professional reader to administer the measures.

Feuerstein urges the assessor to intervene during the testing to "induce skills, learning styles, and attitudes considered prerequisite to appropriate problem-solving behavior" and to teach "content directly related to the problem at hand" (1971, p. 272). Feuerstein and Krasilowsky (1972) characterize the testing session as the continuous interaction of examiner and subject, with the examiner frequently intervening to modify the subject's level of response.

Feuerstein (1971) reports that eleven-year-old pupils with initial scores in the EMR range received average scores on retests and improved further on follow-up retests. Feuerstein believes that his approach can be used to generate remedial strategies for the pupil, as well as to accurately label a deficient pupil, because his dynamic strategies help the child who has not had the opportunity to develop problem-solving skills.

Severson and Associates' Process Learning Assessment

Severson and his associates have developed procedures to identify children with learning disabilities and to measure the relative effectiveness of various remedial methods for a given child. Process Learning Assessment does not use a test-teach-retest sequence; rather, the child is given a reading task, while the assessor manipulates certain variables—reinforcement, print size, loudness, and rate of presentation—and notes which conditions affect the child's performance. Severson (1976) reports that print size and loudness correlate with the rapidity with which children learn the experimental words. Unfortunately, the entire procedure is not fully described in available publications.

This assessment system also examines affective and environmental influences. The assessor defines the critical elements of the teaching situation, determines variations of these, and systematically assesses the child's response to these variations (Kratochwill and Severson, 1977; Sewell and Severson, 1974). The assessor then recommends a program that incorporates those variations that promoted successful responses on the assessment tasks.

Sewell and Severson (1974) compare their strategy with both Budoff's approach and a paired-associate task of learning to match a picture with a printed word (for details, see Rohwer and others, 1971). Their subjects were urban, black, first-grade pupils. Although they found the Full-Scale WISC IQ to be a highly significant predictor of these pupils' achievement, the researchers' diagnostic teaching procedure was a better predictor than either IQ or gain scores from Budoff's technique, and the paired-associate task was the weakest predictor.

As Kratochwill (1977), who has worked with Severson, points out, "these new approaches are all in their formative stages of development and cannot readily be identified as assessment 'models' in the generic sense" (p. 300). He notes the difficulty of generalizing the findings from this approach because the tasks used in the procedures differ from the school curriculum and thus measure skills only indirectly related to classroom learning.

Dynamic Approaches for Programming

Several dynamic strategies have been devised to aid the assessor in making recommendations for a referred child's educational program. The two approaches that we discuss here in the greatest detail are among the few currently available for use: Mills' *Learning Methods Test* (1970) and Jedrysek and others' *Psychoeducational Evaluation of the Preschool Child* (1972). At the end of the chapter, we provide case studies to illustrate these methods.

Mills' Assessment Methods

Mills' *Learning Methods Test* measures a child's word recognition skills using instructions that emphasize each of three modalities—visual, auditory, and kinesthetic—and instructions that combine all three. (Rivkind, 1959, presents a similar procedure to be administered to groups.) The procedure is a test-teach-test-delay-test sequence for each of the modalities and requires several days to administer. The procedures, however, may be combined with other procedures during a long assessment session. The measure provides evidence regarding the comparative success of the different modalities in affecting the child's mastery of word recognition.

The materials include a box of graded stimulus cards with words grouped by grade level: primer, first, second, and third grade. The manual reviews the literature on the teaching of word recognition and provides directions for the assessment procedure. The basic strategy is to establish a list of forty words that the child does not know, divide this list into four groups, and instruct the child using one modality for each group of ten words. Each instructional session lasts about fifteen minutes; after a half-hour delay, the child is tested for mastery of the words. During the next testing session, the child's mastery of the words is again assessed. The process is repeated for each modality.

Mills himself notes several difficulties with his test. First, the assessment procedure determines only which modalities appear to be effective for the individual at the time of assessment; this investigation resembles an experiment with a sample population of one. Mills also recognizes that the instructional procedures used are not equally "pure" examples of a given modality. Mills does not clearly explain the derivation of the particular procedures chosen; he cites only "frequency of mention in the literature" (1970, p. 46) as the criterion for categorizing instructional procedures by modality. It is debatable whether most psychologists would agree that his instructional procedures are the best examples of the particular strategies. Mills does not discuss whether the procedures that compose a modality form an integrated pattern of cognitive behavior.

Whether one can generalize the results of Mills' test to predict a student's classroom performance or to make valid recommendations for the student's educational program has yet to be established. A test-retest reliability study of thirty public school pupils yielded coefficients above .90 for the four instructional procedures, despite a long period between testing sessions (up to twenty-five weeks) and the large range of pupils' WISC IQs—(64 to 115) (Mills, 1970). The summary of research studies offered in the manual, however, is insufficient to show that the differences in pupils' performance effected by the procedures are real.

Mills designed his procedures at a time when hypotheses positing the validity of modality were in their ascendancy. Several researchers have recently challenged the concept of modality preferences, the effects of modality on instruction, and the value of prescribing instructional methods that match the student's modality strength (Arter and Jenkins, 1977; Tarver and Dawson, 1978). Mills' approach, however, is a valuable model for future research. Mills' attempt to standardize instructional strategies in the framework of an assessment procedure is an important contribution to the field.

Jedrysek and Associates' Techniques

Jedrysek and others' *Psychoeducational Evaluation of the Preschool Child* (1972), based on the work of Else Haeussermann, focuses on the moment at which the child makes an error on an assessment measure. The authors present a series of standardized probes that the examiner uses to establish the level at which the child can succeed. The expressed intent of this procedure is to explore "how the child has arrived at a solution and whether he has had to detour impaired areas of functioning in order to respond successfully" (p. 2). However, the procedure seems to provide normative information about the child's highest level of response, rather than information about the child's cognitive process. Although the procedure yields information about a preschool child's performance in a large number of areas, it does not satisfy the authors' stated goals of "exploring how the child has arrived at a solution." An assessor may be able to derive such knowledge from observation and conversation with the child during the assessment, but the measures themselves do not elicit this information.

The items of this procedure sample five areas: physical functioning and sensation, perception, short-term memory, language competence, and cognitive functioning. The "main items" of each section sample those skills that an average beginning first grader is expected to have mastered. For a five- or six-year-old, the examiner begins with these "main items," and, with each error, descends through a series of probes until the child is successful or the examiner exhausts the probes. For a three- or four-year-old, the examiner begins with the probes and ascends, as the child succeeds, to the "main items." The lowest level of probe approximates the performance of an average three-year-old, thus the procedure measures the span of achievement of three- through six-year-olds. The test's content resembles a typical preschool curriculum, and the subtests may be administered in part or whole, in one session or in several. Because the procedure is intended to yield information about the child's functioning, the authors offer no norms or standard deviations, and the examiner cannot add or average a child's scores to derive one comprehensive score. However, the examiner can estimate the child's developmental level in the areas sampled, identify areas for special instructional attention, and specify the instructional methods most likely to be successful.

One major limitation of this procedure is the difficulty in administering it. Preparing the materials involves pasting the pictures and drawings provided onto a durable surface and purchasing various three-dimensional objects. More importantly, the procedure is more difficult to administer than most infant scales; the examiner must be organized and experienced in order to smoothly execute the testing.

The procedure's second major limitation is a structural one. Although the probes purport to sample the same area as the main item, the nature of the probes varies across the main items. Strategies of the probes include simplification, reduction of choices, increased concreteness, addition of tactile-kinesthetic cues, among others. Because these probes are not identical for all tasks, the examiner faces difficulties in deciding which modifications increase the probability of a child's success. In addition, further research on the authors' ranking of the probes in order of difficulty is needed to confirm its validity. Similarly, only further research can confirm the reliability of the procedure and the usefulness of the subgroupings.

The *Psychoeducational Evaluation of the Preschool Child* provides some standardized means for exploring areas not covered by other measures, and its focus on the child's errors as a primary locus for assessment and exploration constitutes a noteworthy contribution to dynamic strategies. Although the procedure can be lengthy and complex, and inappropriate for children with short attention spans, administration does elicit a large pool of participant-observer information.

Ozer's Collaborative Service System

Ozer and his associates at Childrens Hospital in Washington, D.C. developed and modified a neurological evaluation model (Ozer, 1968a) to assess a child's behavioral and functional strategies that are relevant to classroom performance. Their interdisciplinary Collaborative Service System (Ozer and Dworkin, 1974; Ozer, 1980) advocates that professionals from education, social work, and medicine collaborate to elicit information from the child, his parents, and teachers, in order to prescribe an educational program that would enhance the child's success. The goal of this collaboration is to determine "the conditions under which the child can be brought to change" (Ozer, 1969, p. 39). During the half-day assessment meeting, the professionals, the child, the child's parent, and the child's teacher all participate. Interview, questionnaire, observation, and direct assessment are used to elicit information that will enable the professional team to recommend appropriate learning strategies (Ozer and others, 1970).

The neurological evaluation uses traditional procedures and three dynamic measures: (1) the means by which the child learns new information, for example, discrimination of left and right; (2) the means by which the child increases his attention span and focusing abilities; and (3) the amount of demonstration required for the child to achieve success on a task. At another time, the parent is asked to teach the child a skill, and the professional team notes how the parent attracts and maintains the child's attention, the instructional approaches the parent uses, the responses the parent gives, and the relative effectiveness of each of these.

Another aspect of the procedure is an assessment by the educational diagnostician that addresses five primary issues: "(a) Through what channels of input, by what processes of learning, and under what schedule of reinforcement is the child gaining information from his environment? (b) At what developmental levels is he currently able to use the information he has gained? (c) Under what conditions can the child be expected to correct, to circumscribe, to compensate for or adjust to deviations in his development or in his mode of learning? (d) Under what conditions can his repertoire of behavior be modified? (e) What are the available resources for providing the conditions under which the child can learn successfully?" (Ozer and others, 1970, p. 171). The procedure's relevance for educational assessment consists of the attempt to teach the child a task that requires abilities in the child's deficit area and the identification of means by which the child can succeed. The assessment yields no numerical scores but descriptive information about which methods seem to work (Ozer and Richardson, 1974). By involving the teacher and the parent, the assessor not only benefits from their perceptions but also induces them to consider the child's abilities as well as his deficits.

Kratochwill (1977) summarizes three criticisms of this assessment approach: "there are still the same issues of reliability and validity to be considered . . . it is heavily dependent on the child's verbal skills . . . many of the behaviors being assessed may be situation-specific and may not generalize" (p. 306). This third criticism applies primarily to the neurological part of the assessment. The educationally diagnostic component, in contrast, samples actual classroom tasks and should therefore have a high degree of generalizability, certainly more than most other procedures.

Ozer's procedures are not intended to be definitive diagnostic measures that contribute to classification or identification; they provide information to supplement an initial diagnosis or classification and to guide remedial prescriptions. The approach may also be used with children who do not require definitive classification, but who present incipient signs of learning dysfunction and may respond to minimal intervention strategies.

Before we discuss the last major assessment effort, which, under optimal conditions, would be describable as "dynamic," two other efforts at dynamic assessment deserve attention. Hutson and Niles (1974) outline a trial teaching approach for basic reading decoding which compares the child's response to instruction which emphasizes a "whole word" versus a "component analysis" approach to reading acquisition. These authors see trial teaching as a means of "learning why the child has difficulty" and to yield "insights (regarding) . . . how the child can be taught" (p. 189). For the "whole word" approach, the examiner selects at least five words that the child has not yet mastered; at least two of the words begin with the same initial consonant (the reason for this is not made clear; it appears contradictory as it stands). The examiner then has the child say the whole word several times, correcting errors, until memorized. Retention is assessed at varying intervals during the evaluation process. In the "component analysis" instruction, the focus is on determining whether errors are attributable to the discrimination, identification, or association aspects of the analysis. Discrimination might be visual or auditory, association concerns the sound-symbol match, and identification may concern the naming of letters. The examiner is interested in determining the area of greatest difficulty as well as the kind and amount of instruction required to help the child reach mastery. Lambert, Wilcox, and Gleason (1974) present and describe their Berkeley Paired-Associate Learning Test in a form that is readily administratable. They also offer norms for children ages four, five and seven years for this measure of improvement with repeated exposure.

Diagnostic-Prescriptive Teaching

"*Diagnostic-prescriptive teaching* is a currently fashionable phrase for attempts to design instructional programs for students based on test performances" (Salvia and Ysseldyke, 1978, p. 445). Most diagnostic-prescriptive teaching techniques are designed by special educators for use within their own programs; thus, in essence, these are trial teaching measures that may be used by diagnosticians and teachers. In the literature, such techniques are often labeled *informal assessment, analytic teaching, precision teaching, and responsive teaching.* Hammill and Bartel (1975), Salvia and Ysseldyke (1978), and Wiederholt, Hammill, and Brown (1978) offer compendiums of such approaches for each curriculum area.

These approaches urge assessors to direct their attention to recommendations for a student's classroom instructional program rather than to labeling the student's difficulty. While a psychologist who administers a formal assessment would attempt to identify a student's reading level and areas of strength and weakness, the educator who administers an informal assessment wants to identify the exact skills and concepts that the student now needs to master and an effective strategy for mastery. Salvia and Ysseldyke (1978) describe three goals that characterize a diagnostic-prescriptive approach: "identification of students who are experiencing learning difficulties, diagnostic delineation of their strengths and weaknesses, and prescriptive intervention (specification of goals, methods, strategies, materials, and so on) in light of these strengths and weaknesses" (p. 445). This emphasis on curriculum and materials differentiates diagnostic-prescriptive assessment from other approaches. The psychologist relating to a special education program should not only include elements of a diagnostic-prescriptive assessment within the "formal" evaluation but also be available to advise the teacher regarding how to be a good assessor both in attitude and function in order to use the materials of the classroom situation within an assessment framework (Cartwright, Cartwright, and Ysseldyke, 1973). The assessor and the classroom teacher must work together to assess the strengths and weaknesses of the pupil and to analyze the demands of the curriculum. Since learning results from the interaction of a pupil and a task, diagnostic-prescriptive teaching relies on a psychological profile of the learner and an educational delineation of the task to yield a prescription for a pupil's program.

Advocates of diagnostic-prescriptive teaching have thus far offered little evidence to support the validity of their informal assessment measures (Ewing and Brecht, 1977). Pikulski (1974b) asserts that the primary strength of "informal" diagnostic assessment instruments lies in their "close correspondence between the test material and the teaching material" (p. 142). Although this correspondence increases the validity of assessment results as predictors of classroom behavior, one must question the choice of informal instruments over better researched standardized instruments. Further, there is insufficient evidence that these procedures comply with basic measurement standards. It is also disappointing that many diagnostic-prescriptive approaches use traditional static measures, the shortcomings of which were discussed earlier in this chapter.

Case Studies

We now present three case studies that illustrate assessments in which dynamic procedures were used. The first case exemplifies Jedrysek and others' (1972) psychoeducational evaluation; the second, the Mills Learning Methods Test; and the third, a nonstandardized dynamic instructional procedure.

Case One

Mark, a five-year-old boy, was referred for assessment by his daycare center to "determine his level of functioning and assist in determining realistic goals for possible placement." He had a history of slow development but was not thought to be neurologically impaired.

Assessment. Mark is a small boy, whose glasses appear too small for his face and give him an unusual appearance. His speech is very difficult to understand. He is very active, frequently gets out of his chair, and his attention easily wanders from the test tasks. Although his attentiveness did improve during the two weeks of testing, his activity level remained high throughout. Mark relates well and warmly, but he can be a tease, which at times interferes with attempts to encourage him to complete tasks.

No test scores were obtained for Mark. He completed only the perceptual functioning section of the Psychoeducational Evaluation of the Preschool Child. On this measure he completed some tasks at about a four-year-old's level; however, this level is above other aspects of his functioning, such as his fine motor and language abilities.

Mark often imitates or echoes what is said to him. He has particular difficulty answering questions, regardless of how they are phrased. His expressive language appears to be better than his comprehension in that he is able to express basic wishes, but his poor articulation often makes him incomprehensible.

It is very difficult to make Mark understand the nature of tasks that require more than a matching response. On the Animal House task of the WPPSI, despite several and varied attempts, he never seemed to comprehend the instructions. He was able to match the colors of the pegs, so he is not color-blind. He seemed to have difficulty both matching and identifying pictures of the animals, which at first appeared to be a visual problem. However, when administered some Peabody Picture Vocabulary Test pictures, he was able to select pictures named for him. Thus, he is either unfamiliar with the animals depicted in the Animal House pictures, or the pictures themselves are too small or poorly articulated.

When Mark comes up against difficulty, his expression becomes sullen, he looks away, and says, "I don't know." Once this occurs, he resists encouragement to try another task. He needs to work on tasks he can easily accomplish, moving very slowly to more difficult ones. Modifications of the approach or the material are insufficient to reengage his attention after a failure.

Mark's initial copies of geometric figures were horizontal scribbles, regardless of the shape of the figure. The examiner first moved Mark's hand around the design so he could trace it with his finger and then make the same movements with his finger on the blank paper; this did not work. However, when the examiner gave verbal clues—"around and stop" for the circle—and helped Mark trace the figure, he produced very good circles. But his arm movements are very stiff and resistant, and it is difficult for him to change his horizontal predisposition and make a smooth circular movement. This copying task also revealed Mark's occasional perseveration. When a new stimulus was introduced, he continued to verbalize "around and stop" and was slow to adapt to the new shape.

Mark accomplished, with little difficulty, most of the tasks on the perceptual functioning section of the Psychoeducational Evaluation of the Preschool Child measure. He matched colors easily, but could not name any of them. When instructed, for example, to "give me red," he only echoed the phrase. He also readily matched geometric forms, but, again, did not name any. On the small geometric forms, he matched all but the square and was clearly using visual clues to do so. He did not succeed on the tasks of matching numbers of dots or on number and word configurations. When given three choices, he could match the cards with one dot, but could go no further. When given only two choices, he matched the number configurations. Mark easily constructed a circle from two halves; he had a little more difficulty with the square, but was easily guided to success by verbal cues. He was not able to construct a square from four pieces.

Mark works well if given short, structured tasks, followed by activities of his own choosing. Depending upon his level of interest, he can work well for five to ten minutes. The activity he chose during the assessment was to play with the examiner's umbrella. This activity dominated his interest, but he would allow it to be postponed for short periods of time.

Conclusions and Recommendations. It is not possible at this time to determine more than a very limited area of Mark's level of functioning. He appears at or close to his age level on the measures of visual perception, but is particularly low in fine motor and language functioning. His difficulty in comprehending the nature of many tasks and his level of spontaneous play are suggestive of mental deficiency, but further evaluation is required for diagnosis. Such evaluation would be profitable ony after some attempts at instructional intervention.

Specific instructional goals for Mark include: developing his ability to copy simple shapes and lines, according to the procedure described earlier; increasing his picture vocabulary by reading illustrated stories to him and playing games that require the identification of pictures; and developing his number concepts by using his well-developed ability to match.

His occasional tendency to perseverate may be reduced if he has many successful experiences, is warned that he is about to start a new task, and is given a kinesthetic introduction to the new task when possible.

Mark could profit from another year in his current daycare setting. He should be reevaluated before being placed in an elementary school.

Case Two

Don is a nine-year-old attending a special education program for learning disabled children. He has made little progress in developing reading skills, and recently his behavior began to cause him problems in school. His parents requested that he be evaluated to determine his learning difficulties and devise an educational plan for him.

Assessment. Don is a good-looking boy of average size. During the first session he kept his hat and jacket on, slumped down in his chair, and looked very disgruntled. He gradually warmed up and responded well to a straightforward explanation of what was being done and why. He expressed interest in becoming either a doctor or architect, and he seemed particularly aware of and knowledgeable about details of construction. He showed curiosity and asked polite, concerned questions about the assessment procedure. He cooperated with all requests, but found it difficult to remain seated beyond an hour; he had to get up and move around before doing any more work. Don assumes that he is in the special education program because of his behavior rather than any learning problem. He does not like his current placement, adding that he particularly dislikes the teachers' yelling.

Don's test results depict a classic picture of learning disability. His level of cognitive functioning is estimated to be generally well above average, and a discrepancy between verbal and nonverbal functioning favors the nonverbal. On the cognitive measure, his scores fell below average only in the areas of visual-motor speed and short-term memory. Further tests of Don's short-term memory showed that he has difficulty retaining both meaningful and non-meaningful content. His responses to visual or auditory presentations are similarly weak, but he remembered considerably more when an auditory and a visual stimulus were given simultaneously, for example, when a visual reference accompanied the oral directions he was to remember.

Don reads at about a mid-first-grade level. He is still struggling with the decoding process and thus cannot read for comprehension. Long latencies precede almost every word. He generally sounds out correctly the beginning and final consonants of the words, but misses the medial sounds. He seems to be searching his memory rather than using visual-auditory associations to sound out the words. When he pronounces consonant blends, he tends to insert a vowel between the two letters, for example, he pronounces *pl* as *pul*.

Don has difficulty associating sounds and symbols, a very basic problem that may underlie his slow progress in reading. Although he remembers meaningful auditory information better when he has a visual stimulus, he does not seem able to recall the essentially nonmeaningful associations of letters and sounds without a great deal of repetition. Thus, although visual stimulus may help his auditory memory, auditory stimulus does not seem to be an effective aid to his visual memory. In this way, Don functions as a classic dyslexic who appears to be almost "word blind." A trial teaching method was used with Don to compare visual and auditory emphases in instruction. His visual recall again appeared weaker, as he did much better with the method that emphasized auditory skills.

Don's math skills are higher than his reading level. However, his mastery of basic computation, which is at a mid second-grade-level, is low for his age. His mastery of basic number concepts is considerably higher, at a low fourth-grade-level. He can do easy addition problems that require carrying, but not subtraction problems that require borrowing.

Don appears to be experiencing a good deal of stress in that he shows some desire to regress to a more dependent stage. When he was younger, he was somewhat precocious, and his troublesome behavior may reflect his response to his lowered self-esteem.

Conclusions and Recommendations. Don continues to require a learning disability program. However, a change in his current placement is advisable, and his parents are currently investigating alternative placements.

Don needs an educational program that does not rely heavily on reading material. He could be a good learner in social studies and science if the classes use audiovisual materials. His reading skills may improve by instruction that has an auditory approach. Don would also profit from attending group therapy sessions with pupils who are, like he, bright but low achievers.

Case Three

Gary, a nine-year-old boy, was assessed at the request of his foster mother. She disagreed with the school district's recommendation to place him in a program for educable retarded and emotionally disturbed children.

Assessment. Gary is a nice looking boy of average size, who is generally warm and friendly and not unduly anxious. He is talkative, but his conversations deal with violence, and he strongly resists others' efforts to redirect the conversation. His conversations thus have a perseverative quality, and he often interrupts his work at a task to discuss violence. His attention to a task must be frequently and assertively reengaged. The violence he describes most often occurs at school, what the children have done to others or to him, or what he intends to do to them. He says the kids in school call him dumb, because he "don't know nothing." Despite this preoccupation, Gary has a rather nonaggressive, gentle demeanor. He says that he writes backwards.

When asked a question, Gary tends to repeat the question before responding. This repetition appears to serve as an aid to his processing, by facilitating his integration of the question and allowing him additional time to respond. At times he needs to have the question repeated to him. He cannot follow directions other than simple ones, even if they are repeated. He sometimes assumes that he knows things that, in fact, he does not.

Because this assessment was requested by Gary's foster mother to supplement the recent psychological assessment performed by the school district's psychologist, the measures previously administered were not readministered. Observations made during this assessment support the previous findings that Gary's performance falls in the educable retarded range. The consistency and pervasiveness of these findings suggest a mental deficiency of mild degree; since Gary only recently left a very difficult environment, the effects of his new homelife remain to be seen. His previous homelife seems to have impaired his cognitive and emotional functioning.

Gary's one significant success was his performance on a measure of manual expression. He was shown a picture of an object and asked to act out, without speaking, how the object is used. Gary tends to respond better to visual stimuli than to auditory stimuli. He will probably be more successful in following directions if he has a picture to look at, rather than only auditory cues. His spontaneous tendency to repeat verbal directions should be encouraged and supplemented by a visual stimulus.

Gary is particularly deficient in using visual imagery. He needs to develop the ability to paint mental pictures in response to what he hears. Such visualization may aid his weak recall.

Gary reverses his numbers and letters when he writes, although he is past the age where reversals are considered normal. He can match correctly when he has a model, but when he writes spontaneously, without copying, he reverses the figures.

Gary does not learn quickly from instruction. A great deal of repetition, practice, and simplification appear necessary for him to modify his behavior. For example, the examiner attempted to teach him to respond to an auditory-visual integration task. He was not able to match a pattern of dots to a tapped pattern; in fact, he may not have perceived a pattern either in what he heard or saw. Verbal cues and moving his hand through the pattern did not help. The only element of this task that he handled was clapping his hands in a simple imitation of the examiner's claps. Gary's slowness in learning new responses precludes an optimistic evaluation of his cognitive capacity and prognosis for achievement.

Gary is not ready for reading and number work. His language processing skills are particularly weak; further, more specialized evaluation of these skills is needed. His limited ability to develop concepts and his spontaneous attempts to compensate by repeating the question suggest a possible central processing disorder.

During an interview, his foster mother described his adaptive behavior. She describes Gary as above average in his physical development, self-direction, responsibility, and socialization skills; but far below average in independent functioning, economic activity, language development, number and time concepts. When compared with norms derived from an educable retarded population, Gary is below average in language and number and time concepts, average in independent functioning, and above average in economic activity.

Conclusions and Recommendations. This examiner supports the district psychologist's recommendation of placing Gary in a class for educable retarded and emotionally disturbed children. This placement appears to be the most appropriate educational program available to meet his needs. This program should be supplemented by occupational therapy and language therapy. Gary should also continue his individual therapy and family counseling. Gary should be reevaluated after one year of these activities.

Academic achievement instruction on a readiness level is appropriate in both reading and math. His spontaneous tendency to repeat questions and instructions appears to be helpful and should be encouraged. Gary is not likely to do well if asked to respond to verbal directions alone. His program should include concrete materials, visual stimuli, modeling, and repetition. He also needs to develop his visualization ability.

Gary's physical development, his ability to keep himself busy with activities, and his responsible behavior in running errands, doing chores, and carrying messages provide him with feelings of competence and success. His educational program should include opportunities for such activities.

Chapter 4

※※※※※※

Testing for Knowledge of School Subjects

Criterion-referenced tests are those "deliberately constructed to yield measurements that are directly interpretable in terms of specified performance standards. . . . Performance standards are generally specified by defining a class or domain of tasks that should be performed by the individual. Measurements are taken on representative samples of tasks drawn from this domain, and such measurements are referenced directly to this domain for each individual measured" (Glaser and Nitko, 1971, p. 653). At first glance, this procedure seems rather straightforward. The test constructor specifies the content to be measured, devises a sample of this content, and sets a mastery level that indicates which proportion of objectives must be accomplished to signify mastery of the domain.

However, controversies have arisen regarding almost every aspect of this process.

We devote this chapter to a careful examination of these controversies because psychologists, teachers, and assessment specialists are frequently called upon to select, administer, or interpret criterion-referenced measures. For example, many curriculums include measures to be administered by classroom teachers under the guidance of an assessment specialist. Literature on special education encourages teachers to perform informal diagnoses using variations on criterion-referenced measures (Hammill, 1971; Hammill and Bartel, 1975; McKenzie and Wendla, 1976; Vance, 1977). Criterion-referenced tests also play a large role in many schools' compliance with recent federal legislation regarding handicapped children. (See Chapter Eight for a discussion of this legislation.)

Psychologists in private practice and those working in programs in which the services of an educational specialist are not available may need to administer and interpret criterion-referenced measures. Those psychologists who coordinate or direct student services often are asked to advise other professionals about the selection and interpretation of measures. Thus professionals, regardless of their specialty, who are knowledgeable about criterion-referenced assessment can be highly effective in making recommendations about instructional content for referred pupils.

Three uses of the term *criterion* appear in the literature, the first of which—"criterion of comparison"—does not apply to criterion-referenced assessment. A researcher or test designer who wants to demonstrate the validity of a norm-referenced measure selects a second measure as the criterion of comparison. For example, most IQ tests are correlated with Stanford-Binet scores; the Binet serves as the criterion measure of IQ.

Second, *criterion* appears in the phrase "criterion of mastery." Test designers and interpreters specify a criterion of mastery, or mastery level, which the student must fulfill in order to show himself ready to progress to the next task. A test's criterion level is usually between 85 percent and 100 percent, depending upon the subject matter sampled by the test. The criterion level is an absolute line: A student cannot be "a little bit" of a master; all those above the line are masters, and all those below, nonmasters. Some researchers, however, consider mastery as a continuum and describe higher and lower masters (see Meskaukas, 1976).

Although criterion-referenced measures do specify a criterion of mastery, they derive their name from the third meaning of *criterion*, which is a reference for *domain*. A criterion-referenced measure samples a larger domain of objectives that are considered to define the task to be learned. Because this domain of objectives is the criterion to which the test items are referenced, performance on the test is expected to accurately predict performance in the domain. To avoid confusion, some writers recommend that *domain-referenced* be substituted for the term *criterion-referenced* (Hively, 1974b). But since "criterion-referenced" is used more frequently in the literature, and is thus more familiar to professionals, we use that term in this chapter.

Characteristics of Criterion-Referenced Measures

Two terms are closely associated with criterion-referenced measurement: *task analysis* and *behavioral objectives.* Task analysis, synonymous with *domain analysis,* is the description of a particular domain—for example, multiplication skills—in terms of its component parts. This precise specification of the domain distinguishes criterion-referenced assessment from other types of referenced assessment, such as content-referenced, objectives-referenced, and construct-referenced approaches (Anderson, Ball, Murphy, and Associates, 1975).

The analyst must state a behavioral objective specifying the precise skills and mastery level that the learner is expected to be able to perform following instruction. Advocates of objectives-referencing further stipulate that the statement include the manner in which the objective is to be assessed. After specifying the behavioral objectives, the analyst devises a random or stratified random sample of the objectives. This sample is the criterion-referenced assessment instrument. The analyst evaluates the assessment instrument by attending to how well it samples the domain. The level of the measure's difficulty is irrelevant; the measure need only be a valid sample of the domain. The analyst may then order the objectives to show which skills are basic and prerequisite for success at the next level. If the skills cannot be so ordered, the analyst may construct the test so that it follows the most logical sequence of instruction. Finally, the analyst sets a mastery level, a somewhat arbitrary decision, as mentioned earlier, although related to the particular domain.

These, then, are the basic steps in constructing a criterion-referenced assessment measure. These general characteristics of criterion-referenced measurement are summarized by Pikulski (1974a):

1. Clear definition of task objectives
2. Items chosen with the criterion of mastery rather than normal distribution
3. In-context evaluation (objectives embedded in the instructional content)
4. Items listed either hierarchically or in accord with the sequence of the instructional program

Norm-Referenced Measurement

Norm-referenced tests are designed to give the assessor information about an individual's standing in relation to a population of other people with whom he presumably shares some important characteristics. The tests yield scores that are distributed along a normal curve, guaranteeing that some individuals will score low and others will score exceptionally high. Thus the test items are selected to maximize individual differences and variability. Items that do not contribute to such differentiation are thrown out. An individual's score on the test indicates that he knows more, less, or about the same as his peers, but it does not necessarily reveal, in detail, what he knows or his patterns of error. A criterion-referenced test, in contrast, provides information about the individual's mastery of the domain and about his readiness to address the next level of instructional objectives. Some criterion-referenced measures profile the individual's patterns of error, others do not.

Although norm-referenced tests and criterion-referenced tests are designed to measure different phenomena, many norm-referenced tests can be interpreted with reference to criteria, and criterion-referenced measures are always constructed with some reference to a norm in that the domain be considered appropriate to the population who will take the test. Furthermore, normed tests that have a high

degree of construct and content validity do yield information about
what material the pupil knows, although the domain is not likely to
be as well specified and delineated as that of a criterion-referenced
measure, unless the test is both norm- and criterion-referenced.
Norm-referenced tests are often expeditious in that one need not
measure a pupil's mastery of the entire domain in order to find out
what level of instruction he requires. A normed test can indicate that a
pupil is at the 4.5 grade level or at the 16th percentile for grade five,
and the teacher can design objectives to match that level. Crocker and
Benson (1976) compared students' achievement, guessing, and risk
taking on normed and criterion-referenced tests. Their subjects,
graduate and advanced undergraduate students in an introductory
testing and measurement course, demonstrated higher achievement
on norm-referenced tests than on criterion-referenced tests. Students
taking the criterion-referenced test omitted more items and scored
lower than those taking the normed test. Although both groups'
knowledge were presumed equal, students taking the criterion-
referenced test were less willing to answer on the basis of partial
knowledge.

Thus assessors should not consider criterion-referenced measures and norm-referenced measures as inimical approaches. Rather,
one must decide which type of measure is most appropriate in a given
situation.

Item Analysis, Reliability, and Validity

Some professionals may claim that teachers have always prac-
ticed criterion-referenced assessment. This is not the case. Although
most informal classroom tests are content-referenced or even
objectives-referenced, they are not criterion-referenced and they are
not reliable, valid instruments. Criterion-referenced instruments, like
normed measures, must meet certain empirical standards.

Because the purpose of a criterion-referenced test is to distinguish between students who have mastered the domain and those who
have not, one must first judge the test by noting how well its items
sample the domain. Unlike norm-referenced tests, the criterion-
referenced test's degree of difficulty is a rather irrelevant measure of
the test's construction. Thus the second standard by which one judges

a criterion-referenced test is the test's ability to distinguish masters from nonmasters. Ideally, the pupils' scores on a criterion-referenced measure reflect the extent to which the pupils have responded to instruction (Payne, 1974); theoretically, all pupils should achieve a zero score before instruction and a mastery level score following instruction (Cox, 1971). The test scores should also provide information about how individuals responded to the test problems; that is, all those who achieved the same score should have arrived at their answers in the same way (Popham, 1971). These ideals, however, cannot be fully realized by any actual measure because any group of students tested will be at least somewhat heterogeneous in their prior knowledge of the domain and their response to instruction.

Thus the assessor or examiner who wishes to evaluate the quality of a criterion-referenced measure should first ask, How were the objectives of the domain generated? The two methods most often used by developers of criterion-referenced tests are logical methods and empirical methods (Ivens, 1970). In the logical, or a priori, approach, an "item form" might be used (Popham, 1971) to describe the parameters of an objective that would be considered acceptable. Objectives would then be proposed by curriculum specialists to fit these specifications. In the empirical, or a posteriori, approach, a large pool of items would be generated by whatever means the test developers chose, and these would then be submitted to empirical investigation to determine which items do in fact respond to instruction.

The next question to be posed in evaluating a criterion-referenced test is, How were the specific items of the assessment measure selected? The items of the test are either a random or a stratified random sampling of a given domain's objectives. Ideally, the measure should sample and represent every objective in the domain (Shoemaker, 1971). To the extent that each objective is sampled by more than one test item, the test's reliability is increased; however, the more items a test has, the longer it takes to administer. Every test thus represents a compromise between reliability and demands on testing time. The items may also be analyzed by means of an "item difficulty index" (Gorth and Hambleton, 1972) to ascertain whether items representing a single objective have the same level of difficulty. Item difficulty for criterion-referenced measures differs, however, from item difficulty for norm-referenced measures. In the latter, each item contributes to a varying degree to the difficulty of the entire measure.

The assessor must then ask, How reliable is the assessment measure? The reliability of a criterion-referenced measure is determined by the extent of its internal consistency—the extent to which the items are measuring the same thing—and by the stability of decisions made on the basis of test scores (Hambleton and Novick, 1973; Popham and Husek, 1969). Test-retest stability and equivalence of forms are relevant as well (Hambleton and Gorth, 1971), but these standards are not as important here as they are in judging norm-referenced measures. Cox (1971) advocates that researchers develop a new standard for evaluating the reliability of a criterion-referenced measure: a "coefficient of reproducibility" that would indicate "How well an individual's response pattern can be reproduced from a knowledge of his total score" (p. 73).

Cox's innovative standard aside, most standards of reliability for criterion-referenced measures differ in emphasis rather than in kind from those of norm-referenced tests, although users of the former tend to be more concerned about the reliability of decisions made on the basis of the scores. A difficulty arises, however, in that the statistical procedures developed to evaluate norm-referenced tests depend on test score variance. Most researchers agree that criterion-referenced measurement requires its own evaluation procedures. (See Hambleton and others, 1978, for a review of research in this area.)

The final question the assessor must ask is, How valid is the measure? As we have indicated, the primary standard of validity for a criterion-referenced measure is the adequacy with which the measure represents and samples the domain defined for measurement (Payne, 1974; Popham and Husek, 1969; Popham, 1971). In evaluating a measure's validity, one must specifically determine the adequacy of the measure's sampling of the domain for the particular assessment situation; that is, one must consider the extent to which the objectives of the measure coincide with the objectives of the examinee's curriculum (Ivens, 1970). A measure specifically developed for use with a given curriculum will, of course, coincide fully (Rosner, 1975), but the diagnostician who must assess pupils from various curriculums must judge a measure's appropriateness.

Such judgments are best made in consultation with curriculum specialists in the particular content area. Comparisons of preinstruction and postinstruction administrations of the measure (Hively and Reynolds, 1975; Ivens, 1970) or of administrations to individuals known to be masters and those known to be nonmasters can provide data about validity (Cox, 1971; Payne, 1974). A test's validity may also be judged by the degree to which the domain itself is specified, as this definition affects the adequacy of the sampling of the objectives (Krathwohl and Payne, 1971). A test based on fuzzy, global statements of objectives is likely to contain fuzzy, unreliable test items whose validity is difficult to determine. A final standard for validity involves the conditions under which the test results are valid, that is, whether the results are affected by the type of instruction, by timing, by characteristics of the examinees, and so on.

The validity of norm-referenced measures is also evaluated by standards of content and construction but, for those measures, predictive validity is of primary concern. Although an ideal criterion-referenced measure might predict which pupils will respond best to which types of instructional intervention, it would not successfully discriminate future failures from successes because it is designed so that all to whom the measure is appropriately administered can eventually be masters. We say "appropriately administered" because the examiner must, of course, judge the appropriateness of the domain for a particular pupil; no pupils can be expected to be a master of all content areas.

We may now summarize our guidelines on evaluating criterion-referenced measures by providing a checklist that assessors can use in appraising manuals that describe the development of a criterion-referenced measure.

Checklist for Evaluation of Criterion-Referenced Assessment Measures

1. Do the authors specify the manner in which the domain objectives were generated?
   What methods were used: logical? empirical? other?
2. Do the authors specify the manner in which the items on the assessment instrument were generated?

What methods were used: random sample? random stratified sample?
3. What methods of item analysis were used?
4. What is the evidence of reliability: internal consistency? reliability of decisions made on the basis of the scores? number of items representing each objective? other?
5. What is the evidence of validity?
How well do items represent domain?
Do scores discriminate between masters and nonmasters?
Methods used for determination of validity: judgment of experts? pre- and postinstruction test administration? other?
6. Is normative information regarding test provided?
For what level of ability or development is the measure appropriate?
7. Under what conditions, and for what population are scores valid?
8. Is there any attempt to systematize errors for diagnostic purposes?
Summary of conclusions regarding the measure:

Gronlund (1973) offers a helpful checklist for use with informal criterion-referenced measures designed by teachers or psychologists. Using these guidelines, an assessor or teacher should be able to make a prudent decision regarding the adequacy of criterion-referenced assessment instruments. Although statistical procedures for evaluation of these instruments still require further development, and those that have already been developed require further testing, an assessor who asks the kind of questions shown in the above list can judge whether a measure meets the essential standards of appropriateness, reliability, and validity.

Mastery and Hierarchy

As we noted earlier, the designer of a criterion-referenced measure indicates the standard of mastery, the score a pupil must receive to be judged ready to terminate work on the domain objectives and, if appropriate, to move to the next level. While some domains, by their nature, to some extent dictate a level of mastery, a certain arbitrariness in the selection of this level cannot be avoided. In the literature, the arbitrariness of the mastery level appears less frequently challenged than the issue of mastery itself; that is, whether mastery levels should always be set, and whether these levels, when set, should be the same for all students. Gronlund (1973, p. 4) notes that even the "most ardent advocates [of mastery levels] would agree that mastery of the more difficult and complex types of achievement would be unrealistic for many students," and that "at least for the present, it seems more defensible to require mastery of minimum essentials . . . and to set more realistic standards of performance for learning outcomes that go beyond the minimum essentials of a course."

An illustration from a particular domain should highlight the implications of Gronlund's criticism. For example, if the domain is mathematics, in its entirety, clearly it is unrealistic to require mastery, even at a 50 percent level, of this vast and complex domain. However, if the domain is multiplication, which is relatively easy to specify and delimit, it is difficult to attribute mastery to anyone who cannot do all the multiplicative operations. Still, it seems reasonable to set varying levels of acceptable performance for pupils of varying cognitive abilities. One must ask a normative question: Is it realistic to expect all pupils to reach a mastery level in this domain, or is mastery an inappropriate expectation for some pupils in some domains?

There is also some evidence in the literature (for example, a study by Block cited in Gronlund, 1973; see also Hambleton and others, 1978) that the level at which the standard of mastery is set affects pupils' performance. Some pupils are apparently motivated by high mastery levels, while others perceive these as unreachable and give up. Optimal mastery levels for pupil achievement have been deduced by experiment. Mastery levels also affect demands on the teachers' time: High levels create high demand. However, Reynolds and Gentile (1975–1976) report that university students prefer mastery learning (presumably when the level is not impossibly high) where those who fail to reach mastery receive more instruction rather than failing grades.

Hambleton and others (1978) raise the broader question of the appropriateness of mastery scores for any domain. In domains that have no inherent hierarchy beyond the initial levels—for example, reading comprehension—what does a cutoff score or percentage score say about a student's ability? If the domain's objectives are not hierarchically ordered or discrete, and there is no necessary sequence of levels, a student may answer 90 percent of the questions correctly and be considered a master, yet he may not have learned one major objective.

Ebel (1973) summarizes the argument against mastery learning by questioning the following assumptions of the method: (1) that there are unidimensional, discrete steps; (2) that there is a critical level below which the pupil cannot advance; (3) that this critical level is definable; (4) that this level is assessable. Such challenges are forcing defenders of mastery to verify their assumptions by experimental research.

An issue closely associated with that of mastery levels is that of hierarchy. Krathwohl and Payne (1971) describe a hierarchy as follows: "the lowest level of behavior in the hierarchy is believed to be the simplest and least complex, and its achievement is presumed to be the key to successful achievement at the next higher level in the structure;" (p. 29). While not all domains have objectives that can be organized into a meaningful hierarchy, Gronlund (1973) suggests that criterion-referenced assessment is most meaningful for domains that can be so ordered. He points out that measures whose mastery level is a percentage score are most relevant for hierarchical domains, as the score locates the learner on a continuum of increasingly complex information and thus indicates what the learner knows and does not know. For example, basic statistics is a more ordered domain than nineteenth century poetry. If a student of statistics masters 90 percent of the objectives, anyone familiar with the domain could fairly accurately determine what that student knows and the level of his skill. If a student of poetry, however, reaches the 90 percent mastery level, the student's score would not imply which poets or concepts the student had mastered. The score does not indicate which objectives the student has not fulfilled, because the domain lacks an inherent hierarchy.

White's (1973) investigation of research studies on hierarchies cites a number of problems in research methodology and notes that studies show that not all students learn in accord with hierarchical predictions. White posits that the evidence does not permit us to make a meaningful conclusion about how well proposed logical hierarchies match pupils' actual learning sequences. More recently, however, Airasian and Bart (1975) report that their data essentially confirm one of the rationally derived hierarchies proposed by Gagne, although their model is more complex than Gagne's.

Behavioral Objectives

The specification of behavioral objectives is an essential step in the construction of a criterion-referenced measure, yet it is the source of the greatest controversy among researchers in this area. The major criticisms of this procedure include: the lengthy amount of time required to formulate objectives; the possibility of oversimplifying educational goals and diluting educational quality if simplistic objectives, chosen because their mastery can be easily demonstrated, are used; the difficulties presented by content areas that are not easily susceptible to task analysis, insufficient evidence to demonstrate that the specification of objectives effects better teaching and learning; and a potential reduction in the spontaneity and flexibility of teaching approaches. (See Ebel, 1973, 1975; Joselyn, 1975; Ward, 1970).

Krathwohl and Payne (1971) suggest that researchers must define some standards of "goodness" for the evaluation of objectives. Studies are also needed to demonstrate the validity and reliability of objectives. Does a domain necessarily generate a standard set of objectives, or is the specification of objectives purely the product of the test designers' judgment? Ebel (1975) reminds us that objectives are not necessarily the product of objectivity.

Because developing objectives can be time consuming, many schools either adopt ready-made criterion-referenced measures, which may or may not be embedded in a curriculum, or assign the development of objectives to committees that convene infrequently. Either approach can easily effect a loss in flexibility, as the assessment procedure would determine the curriculum. Too, teachers might feel pressured to teach to the test, not because the test necessarily reflects their professional judgment of an appropriate curriculum, but because their skills and professional futures will be evaluated by their students' test scores.

Ebel (1975) criticizes some attempts to derive objectives as being motivated by the desire to avoid interindividual comparison or competition, a desire to prescribe all winners and no losers. Ebel says that this desire, when carried to the extreme, means "avoiding working to surpass anyone at doing anything" (p. 87), and he wonders if that is valuable. Ebel's criticism, however, implies that pupils are assessed only by criterion-referenced measures and that all such measures are interpreted in a purely ipsative manner.

Duchastel and Merrill (1973) review research studies of how pupils' knowledge of behavioral objectives affects learning. They report inconsistent results, with no clear pattern emerging from the data, and conclude that "objectives sometimes help and are almost never harmful" (p. 63). Although students who were aware of the objectives tended to spend more time studying, this did not result in a pattern of increased learning.

Krathwohl and Payne (1971) do offer some positive comments to recommend the specification of objectives: objectives can serve to guide learning; objectives allow one to judge whether pupils have reached certain goals and, in this way, provide a means to evaluate teaching and learning; and objectives compel those who use them to articulate their educational goals for their pupils.

As Hively (1975) recommends, assessors and teachers should question whether a criterion-referenced test can be easily changed to accommodate changes in the curriculum and how easily it can be adapted to different pupils' needs.

Applications and Limitations of Criterion-Referenced Assessment

As we mentioned earlier, an assessor selects a criterion-referenced measure or a norm-referenced measure to meet a particular assessment need. We now consider the means for determining which type of measure is appropriate. Gronlund (1973, p. 6) lists four types of assessment functions:

1. A pretest, that is, determination of entry level skills or readiness
2. Formative assessment, or the assessment of ongoing progress
3. Diagnostic assessment, or the elucidation of patterns, the nature of strengths and weaknesses
4. Summative assessment, or the assessment of learning outcomes at the end of instruction

For pretesting, a normed test provides information regarding the grade or age level at which the child is functioning in the particular area. A criterion-referenced measure provides information regarding what the child knows at that level; that is, whether the child has the skills presumed to be necessary to begin instruction in that domain. The ideal measure for a pretest, then, is both normed and criterion-referenced. Criterion-referenced measures would present difficulties, however, in areas in which the components of the entry level differ from those of the domain to be taught; for example, in the case of reading readiness, the components of the reading domain could not be used as the components of the assessment instrument. To assess a child's capabilities to learn to read, one cannot necessarily rely on either a norm- or criterion-referenced measure. One cannot use a child's familiarity with the alphabet to predict his mastery of first-grade reading skills unless one can prove that lack of familiarity necessarily results in inability to master the reading process or that lack of manifestation of the skill implies an incapacity to develop the skill.

For formative assessment, the assessment of a pupil's progress, a criterion-referenced measure is the most appropriate response. While a norm-referenced measure would indicate that a child's score has improved from 6.1 to 6.5 after two months' of instruction, a criterion-referenced measure would specify which of the objectives he has mastered and which he has yet to accomplish. A criterion-referenced measure thus would make a larger contribution to the assessor's ability to recommend an educational program for the pupil.

In diagnostic assessment, the criterion-referenced approach holds greater promise for yielding an evaluation of a student's patterns of error; however, the approach's potential is far from being realized. Certainly any measure that samples relevant content may be interpreted by an assessor to yield patterns of performance. However, since a criterion-referenced measure is, by definition, a thorough sampling of such content, it should yield more information about patterns of error than a normed measure.

Assessors who use criterion-referenced measures for diagnostic assessment must use their judgment and experience to select a measure appropriate to the curriculum objectives of the pupil's classes. Assessors working in a delimited setting know what educational programs are available and can build an experiential history regarding the relevance of information derived from assessment. Assessors whose experience in a setting is limited should consult with the pupil's teacher before selecting an instrument, in order to determine the objectives of the curriculum. If the assessor and teacher then find a disparity between the assessment findings and the pupil's performance in the classroom, they can always modify the initial recommendations.

Summative assessments, like pretests, are optimally performed using a measure that is both normed and criterion-referenced. Such a measure would demonstrate exactly what the child has accomplished and his ranking in relation to peers, useful information for placement decisions. Results from a criterion-referenced measure would allow the assessor to indicate appropriate instructional subgroupings in the placement recommendation.

In general, the strength of a criterion-referenced measure is its potential to respond to the assessment questions, What does the child know in the specified domain? What does he not know? (Payne, 1974). This approach does not necessarily respond to the equally important assessment questions, How does the child learn? Why does the child function this way? While the latter question is of interest to psychologists and parents, the former is of central importance to the educational setting. Assessors need to determine, as well as they are able, how the child learns, and how he optimizes and obstructs possibilities to master materials. Only the answers to these questions can indicate to the teacher how to optimize the child's educational mastery.

Although criterion-referenced assessment cannot explain how a child learns, it can be used to make decisions about individualized instruction (Reynolds, 1975). When pupils are to be grouped by their particular instructional needs, a good criterion-referenced measure is probably the best single source of information for decisions about the groupings. Criterion-referenced assessment also allows one to make a continuous assessment of a pupil's achievement in a domain (Proger and Mann, 1973). While it is possible to periodically administer normed measures to evaluate progress, a criterion-referenced measure provides more precise and relevant information to guide educational planning.

Some researchers contrast criterion-referenced assessment with approaches that attempt to assess a pupil's underlying mechanisms or skills. For example, if one determines that a child does not know how to pronounce the letters of the alphabet, should the child be taught how to pronounce the letters or should he first be taught visual discrimination or other basic skills in which he is thought to have deficits? This question of what should be taught will arise in various contexts throughout this book, and is one that will continue to plague diagnostic assessment until more definitive research is available.

Ebel's (1971) general opinion of criterion assessment is that it is an appropriate way to measure "basic intellectual skills that every-one needs to exercise almost flawlessly in order to live effectively in modern society" (p. 286), such as basic computation and literacy. But for other domains, Ebel (1973) wonders whether the time and detail required for criterion-referenced assessment are useful, necessary, or even appropriate, particularly since educators often disagree about what the objectives of education should be.

Critique of Popularly Used Criterion-Referenced Measures

Two measures that purport to be criterion-referenced are par-ticularly popular among psychologists (Mercer and Ysseldyke, 1977): the Woodcock Reading Mastery Tests (Woodcock, 1973) and the Key Math Diagnostic Arithmetic Test (Connolly, Nachtman, and Prit-chett, 1971). Our critique of these measures focuses on how well they guide a teacher in selecting precise instructional objectives for a child. Our analysis will follow the checklist presented earlier in this chapter.

The Woodcock Test appears more valuable in its norm-referenced rather than criterion-referenced aspects, contrary to the intent of its developer. In the test manual, Woodcock does not discuss how the domain objectives were generated; rather, he offers the five subtests—letter identification, word identification, word attack, word comprehension, and passage comprehension—as givens. He does not delineate objectives within these subtest domains. He casually refers to discussions with reading professionals, but does not document whether other experts in the field of reading agree with his analysis of the five subskills. We can surmise that some areas of disagreement exist among test designers, since not every diagnostic test has the same five subtests.

Woodcock offers a limited discussion of how he generated the items. The letter and word identification items were derived by a fairly straightforward sampling procedure, although the word identification subtest fails to yield any information about the patterns of error expected to occur at different stages in the reading process. The letter identification subtest would be improved by reproducing the types of script used in the test on the scoring sheet; in order to analyze errors, the assessor must either make notations during the testing or refer to the test itself.

Woodcock does not explain why he chose to structure the items in the word and passage comprehension subtests using analogies and a modified cloze procedure, respectively. He says only that multiple-choice items were not used in order to reduce guessing. But the solving of analogies requires reasoning, and this form seems less appropriate than others, for example, items that require a pupil to match a word with a picture. Woodcock does not explain why only one approach to passage comprehension is used or why he selected that approach.

The word attack subtest represents the test's best approximation of random sampling of potential error patterns. Interpretation of the results of this subtest can be very tedious, however, because one must analyze each item to determine its potential sources of error. If the manual specified which items sample medial vowel sounds, which sample initial consonants, and so on, diagnostic interpretation would be greatly facilitated.

Woodcock's procedure for item analysis resulted in the ordering of the test items according to their level of difficulty, derived by an estimate based on Woodcock's model of the reading process. However, neither the judgments of experts nor empirical methods were used to determine the suitability of the items included in the measure, contrary to Hambleton and others' (1978) suggestion.

The measure's reliability was assessed by methods traditionally used for norm-referenced measures, namely, split-half, test-retest (alternate form), and standard error of measurement. The measure was not evaluated by a standard of reliability for criterion-referenced measures, that is, the reliability of decisions regarding instruction made on the basis of the scores. Likewise, the measure's validity was evaluated by standards characteristic of norm-referenced measures, not by standards specific to criterion-referenced assessment, such as expert judgment of the extent to which items sample the domain, preinstruction and postinstruction testing, and external validation of mastery level scores. Thus, while the normative aspects of the Woodcock test appear well considered and executed, the test seems deficient as a criterion-referenced instrument.

Like Woodcock, the authors of the Key Math did not attempt a logical analysis of the domain, but generated a large pool of items from existing math programs of major publishers. They organized the subtests based on their judgment and their item analysis procedures were similar to Woodcock's. Unlike Woodcock, however, the designers of Key Math specify a behavioral objective for each item in the test. Thus the assessor can determine exactly what the pupil knows and does not know.

Although the specification of objectives fulfills one standard for a criterion-referenced measure, Key Math is not free of difficulties, particularly in the areas of reliability and validity. The manual does not clearly explain how the vast number of items generated were sampled to determine final objectives, and the final sample did not appear to have been submitted to expert judgment. Thus it is difficult to determine the adequacy of the sampling of the domain. The information about the measure's reliability and validity is even more limited than that for the Woodcock. Only split-half and standard errors of measurement are reported to substantiate reliability, and content, face, and concurrent estimates for validity. Although content validity is the central issue for a criterion-referenced measure, the authors did not rely on expert judgment, and one instance of preinstruction and postinstruction testing yielded negative results. They did not evaluate the reliability of instructional decisions made on the basis of the test.

The reviewer in the *Journal of Learning Disabilities* ("Key Math: A Review," 1978) cites the low reliability of individual subtests as a shortcoming of the Key Math. This deficiency results from the test's limited sampling of objectives, a limitation compelled by the designer's desire to restrict the test's duration. When interpreting the results, the assessor should remember that for objectives sampled by one or two items, any inferences regarding a student's mastery of that objective must be cautious ones.

Finally, Greenstein and Strain (1977) report that their factor analysis does not support the test's division of the domain into the three areas of content, operations, and applications. They judge the test to have great diagnostic value because its format allows analysis of error patterns and because it reveals systematic differences in error patterns between groups of normal and learning disabled adolescents. Key Math seems a somewhat successful attempt at criterion-referencing, despite its limitations and the need for further research.

Case Study

Carl is a four-year-eight-month-old boy who was referred for assessment by his family's therapist and his parents. The assessor was asked to estimate Carl's current cognitive functioning and to determine whether he needed a special education program.

Assessment. Carl is a cute, heavy-set boy with fair complexion and straight brown hair. His articulation is difficult to understand, but the quality of his linguistic expression appears appropriate for his age. He relates pleasantly, appears quite in touch with his social and material environment, and can sustain a meaningful verbal interaction. He was able to remain seated for an entire one-hour session.

Carl clearly prefers manipulative materials, and, when working with blocks and shapes, shows interest, imagination, and a good sense of design. In contrast, when presented with pictures, he whimpers and complains, although he complies with requests when given encouragement. He loved the fine motor tasks, but he reacted negatively to the gross motor activities. Carl's verbal expression is accompanied by a great deal of motoric expression; he is quite motorically expressive.

Carl's tolerance for frustration is low. He becomes angry and tearful when he does not succeed and tries to avoid tasks he anticipates as difficult. However, he is generally a willing worker, as long as he succeeds. Once he fails, he does not respond to encouragement.

The Boehm Test of Basic Concepts, a criterion-referenced measure, was administered to Carl. In no case did his level of functioning fall below the average range. His cognitive level is estimated to be high average, lowered by his relatively poorer quantitative knowledge. Despite his poor articulation, his language skills, particularly his passive comprehension and reasoning, are his highest areas of function. These skills suggest a potential for academic achievement that may be above average.

Carl's perceptual-motor skills are also well within average range, and, in the case of fine motor control, above average. He had some problems with figure-ground demands, and his difficulty in maintaining an image in the face of distractors suggests a mild problem with concentration. However, these relative low areas of function are not so low as to be termed deficiencies.

Carl's performance on the Boehm test reveals adequate knowledge of space and time concepts, but confirms the previously mentioned difficulty with quantitative concepts.

Impressions and Recommendations. The current assessment reveals no areas of cognitive deficiency in Carl's functioning. His interpersonal skills are improving, and he should be able to function in a regular kindergarten next year. Until then, he can continue to profit from attending a therapeutic nursery program, concentrating on increasing his tolerance for frustration and the use of verbal, rather than motoric, expressions of his reactions and feelings. His curriculum needs are highest in the area of quantitative concepts. He much prefers manipulative materials to two-dimensional ones, a preference appropriate for his age.

Chapter 5

꙳꙳꙳꙳꙳꙳

Observing Behavior in the Classroom

Interest in observation as a measurement technique has waxed and waned since the 1930s (Gellert, 1955). Most of the extensive literature on the subject discusses observation as a research method rather than as a diagnostic assessment tool (Withall, 1960). But many of the issues raised in the research literature are of interest to assessment professionals, and we review and discuss such concerns in this chapter. From this methodological base, we elaborate the application of observation to individual diagnostic assessment.

Observation of a child's activities in the classroom is often mentioned to assessment professionals during their training, but its techniques are rarely taught. Once in the classroom, many assessors uneasily wonder what they are supposed to observe. Brison (1967) notes that "most school psychologists are uncomfortable in the classroom in the role of an observer and get out as soon as they can" (p. 110). Observation can be a successful assessment strategy only if the observer enters the classroom aware of the theory and practice of this technique.

The rationale for using observation in assessment derives from the thesis that because behavior is a function of an individual in his environment, the direct observation of the individual in his environment provides data that have a great degree of generalizability (Adelman, 1970–1971; Bersoff and Grieger, 1971). Advocates of observation have tried to develop systematic procedures for the technique that meet standards of objectivity and reliability. In this chapter, we focus on such techniques of systematic classroom observation, omitting casual techniques such as rating scales and anecdotal narratives (Anderson, Ball, Murphy, and Associates, 1975; Gordon and Jester, 1973). Casual observation strategies do not adequately control the unreliability introduced by an observer's subjective interpretation. Systematic techniques, in contrast, are designed to limit such subjectivity, one of the greatest potential disadvantages of observation as an assessment strategy.

Behavioral psychologists are to be credited for much of the recent resurgence of interest in direct observation, particularly for individual assessment purposes (Boehm and Weinberg, 1977), as well as for many significant developments in observational research. Direct observation, however, does not require a behavioristic orientation. An assessor can record observations in a manner directed by ethological, psychodynamic, or any other theoretical or atheoretical source of hypotheses that enables him to draw inferences from his data. Objectivity, as measured by high interobserver agreement regarding what is observed, results from a high degree of behavioral specificity and a low amount of inference at the time of recording, as we will later discuss. An assessor's theoretical orientation will determine his choice of which behaviors to record and how to interpret the data collected.

The uses of observation as a measurement technique are many. As noted earlier, most of the literature treats observation as a research tool for studying behavior for the purpose of deriving hypotheses or investigating hypotheses derived from theoretical predictions (Bealing, 1973). Professionals can also observe teachers or parents to discern how they behave with a child in order to encourage them, train them in new strategies, and measure their progress. Observation can also be used to measure the outcome of program or therapeutic intervention (Anderson, Ball, Murphy, and Associates, 1975).

Definition and Procedures

Direct systematic observation is unique among diagnostic assessment approaches because it takes place in the setting in which the referral issue is said to occur. Therefore, data gathered during the assessment exemplify the actual referral problem, and the assessor need not draw complex inferences in applying the assessment data to the problem. This advantage of observation is highlighted in Jones, Reid, and Patterson's (1975) description of naturalistic observation as "the noting and recording [of] facts and events in accordance with, or in imitation of, the essential character of a thing. . . . The targets of naturalistic observations are signs, indicants, or behaviors, and these data may or may not be used to make inferences. . . . The defining features of a naturalistic observation system include . . . the recording of behavioral events in their natural settings at the time they occur, not retrospectively; the use of trained, impartial observer-coders; and the descriptions of behaviors which require little if any inference by observers to code the events" (pp. 45–46).

This definition of naturalistic systematic observation, with one modification, serves to define diagnostic observation. While naturalistic observation is intended to produce an exhaustive record, diagnostic observation is highly selective. Of course all observation is selective to some degree, but the diagnostic assessor's observations are guided by the issues delineated in the initial referral.

All authorities on classroom observation seem to agree that no one observation instrument is appropriate for all occasions. One must select or construct an observation system to suit a particular purpose. The assessor first decides what he wishes to observe and for what purposes these observations are to be made. These decisions guide the choice of sampling procedures to be used (Boehm and Weinberg, 1977). There are two basic types of sampling procedures:

event sampling and time sampling; other approaches represent variations of these.

Event sampling is the recording of every occurrence of the specified behavior or behaviors during the period of observation (a half hour, for example). This count of how often the behavior occurs is supplemented by notes about the context of the recorded behaviors. Behaviorists, for example, would carefully note the events antecedent to the behavior and the events immediately following its elicitation.

Time sampling is often the preferred method for recording behaviors that occur frequently or for recording large numbers of behaviors. The observer divides the session into segments and records the behavior only if it occurs during an "on" interval. For example, the observer may choose to record behaviors for three-minute segments separated by five-minute segments of not recording. The length and proportion of the intervals are determined by the observer's intentions and judgment. The information lost in using this method, however, may be sufficient to impair the representability of the data (Repp and others, 1976).

Either sampling approach is facilitated by an efficient procedure for recording behaviors. The use of abbreviations, like "OSneg" for "out-of-seat for negative peer interaction," helps the observer in his note taking. If the observer's intent is to record all the pupil's behaviors during a time sampled observation, a sign or category system can be used.

In the sign system, the observer observes without recording for a designated period of time; during the next interval, the observer records the behaviors that occurred during the previous observation interval on a prepared sheet that lists all the behaviors to be recorded. The observer notes only whether the behavior occurred, not how often or in what manner (Frick and Semmel, 1978; Lynch, 1977). The sign system is of little use to the diagnostician because neither frequency, sequence, nor context are recorded. The possible advantage of being able to record a large number of behaviors is rather irrelevant since most referrals mention a limited number of behaviors.

In the category system, the observer assigns to one of several categories every behavior to be observed during a recording interval, and records this category code with each occurrence of the behavior. Category systems have been criticized as being inflexible in limiting the particular behaviors to be recorded and as overemphasizing process at the sacrifice of contextual details (Brandt, 1975).

Both the sign and category systems require a precision and specificity in the definitions of the behaviors or categories to be recorded. The observer must be able to make an immediate decision regarding whether a categorizable behavior has occurred and to which category it belongs. Observers must be trained in this skill because it is critical to the objectivity, validity, and reliability of the measure. However, as Deno (1975) cautions, the definitions of the behaviors to be observed should not be so specific as to allow the observer to overlook or distort the more global issues that are of real concern.

Because observation measures have long been used in research, many specialists have recommended standards of acceptability for these measures. Unfortunately, the measures most likely to meet these standards are those least likely to be useful for individual diagnostic purposes. Nevertheless, assessors and diagnosticians should be familiar with these standards, as they are useful in evaluating all observational approaches.

Reliability and Validity

Clearly, the value of an observation measure is dependent on its reliability. Some researchers equate reliability with interobserver agreement, while others challenge that definition. The consensus is that interobserver agreement is one standard of reliability, but that additional standards must be fulfilled to assure a measure's reliability (Deno, 1975; Frick and Semmel, 1978; Greenwoood, Walker, and Hops, 1977; Haynes, 1978; Hollenbeck, 1978; Medley and Mitzel, 1963).

Stability is one of these standards. The measure must be designed such that one can determine if the observed behavior is consistent, at least within a similar context, from one period of measurement to the next. Verifying a measure's stability is difficult because a low coefficient of consistency among several periods of observation may result from the method of measurement or the nature of the behavior being assessed (Haynes, 1978; McGaw, Wardrop, and Bunda, 1972; Marshall and others, 1976–1977). Nevertheless, a researcher who develops a new instrument, after demonstrating that observers can indeed agree on what and how to score, must establish that the measure records a stable behavioral phenomenon. Until this stability is demonstrated, all other measurement concerns remain irrelevant.

Another standard for reliability concerns the generalizability of the scores derived from the observation instrument. A measure must sample adequately the universe of the pupil's behavior if conclusions based on the data are to be accurate statements about the pupil (Haynes, 1978).

Reliability, as measured by high interobserver agreement, results from measures that precisely define the behaviors to be recorded and have uncomplicated recording decisions; for example, measures that use a small number of behaviors or categories that are mutually exclusive. The more judgment and inference that observers introduce into recording decisions, the lower the agreement is likely to be (Weick, 1968). Too, observers differ in the amount of information they can adequately record. As this amount increases, differences between individual observers are correspondingly likely to increase, and the observation becomes a measure of the observer rather than of the situational variables.

Adequate training of observers and repeated visits to the observation setting also increase reliability and stability (Arrington, 1943; Bealing, 1973; Gellert, 1955; McGaw, Wardrop, and Bunda, 1972). The number of visits appears to be more significant than the length of any one visit. Rowley (1978), studying the relationship between observation time and stability, reports that "two hours of consecutive observation at best would be only marginally more representative . . . than one hour" and concludes that "reliability will be enhanced by a more representative sampling of occasions, and this is best achieved by using a larger number of shorter observation periods" (p. 172). Wright (1967) recommends a maximum of thirty minutes, but, as Wrightstone (1960) and Haynes (1978) suggest, the length of the observation should be chosen to suit the situation and the individuals involved. However, since some kinds of behaviors are specific to situations, samples should be gathered from similar contexts (Westbury, 1967–1968).

Most researchers agree that concerns about reliability have overshadowed research on the validity of observational measures

(Greenwood, Walker, and Hops, 1977; Heyns and Lippitt, 1954). All the traditional standards of validity apply to observational data (Gellert, 1955; Jones, Reid, and Patterson, 1975; Lynch, 1977), although there is controversy regarding the applicability of traditional statistical procedures to observational measures (Hollenbeck, 1978).

To supplement the traditional standards for validity, Lynch (1977) proposes three standards specific to observational approaches: context, process, and product (outcome). He defines these terms by proposing a question for each; for context, "How would the results of this observation measure differ when used in a different situation or context?"; for process, "Is the observation system sensitive to the processes that are occurring in the classroom?"; for product, "Do the observation data predict significant outcomes of classroom activities?" (pp. 18-19). Lynch's questions pertain to the standards of stability (as validity), content validity, and predictive validity for this particular approach to assessment.

In summary, the validity of a behavioral observation system is discerned by evaluating its "utility, applicability, accuracy, comprehensiveness, generalizability, and sensitivity" (Haynes, 1978, p. 167). This evaluation is conducted through correlational and experimental studies or, in the case of content validity, by consultation with experts in the content area.

The Presence of an Observer

In all measurement, the administration of a measure and qualities of the measurement itself can influence the results obtained. In the case of observation, the results may be compromised by the manner in which the behaviors are recorded and by the influence that the presence of an observer exerts on the observed setting. Haynes (1978) and Lipinski and Nelson (1974) suggest that the effects of an observer's presence are significant under some conditions, and many authors discuss ways to reduce such interference, but the evidence does not substantiate the existence or pervasiveness of an observer effect. The anecdotal impressions of assessors who have been observers describe such an effect, but note that negative or disruptive behaviors sometimes decrease with the presence of an observer, yet other times, increase. An observer's presence may affect both the frequency and variability of a pupil's behavior, but further research is needed to explore this phenomenon (Jones, Reid, and Patterson, 1975).

Arrington (1943) suggests that the presence of an observer who is a familiar, but nonparticipating, figure will have the least effect, but that the effects are greater with older subjects and in formal situations. However, Weick (1968) states the somewhat controversial point that an observer's nonparticipation exacerbates the observer effect; Wright (1967) recommends that the observer be active in an active situation and inactive in an inactive situation.

The only way to preclude any observer effect is to situate the setting to be observed in a room that has a one-way mirror (Boyd and DeVault, 1966; Gellert, 1955). The setting is thereby unaffected by an observer. Because this luxury is obviously not practical for the average classroom, classroom observers must learn to minimize observer effects. Gellert (1955) offers these suggestions to the observer: "ostensible disinterest, preoccupation . . . it is considered good practice to sit down, to change position and location as little as possible, to refrain from interacting with the children, and to keep silent" (p. 187). The observer should avoid doing anything that induces novelty. This injunction also applies to the number of observers: One observer is less intrusive than a team. However, as we mentioned earlier, there is little agreement among researchers about the degree of participation necessary or recommended to administer a valid observational assessment.

Masling and Stern (1969) hypothesized that the effects of an observer's presence in the classroom would decrease over time. They compared observation from the beginning and end of a two-day observation, but discovered no pattern. They conclude that either there were no observer effects or that, if present, they were of greater complexity than had been anticipated. We may add that their method of measurement may not have been adequate to detect such effects and that the period of observation may not have been sufficient.

Because individuals may react differently to the presence of an observer, some increasing and others decreasing socially desirable behaviors (O'Leary, 1975), studies of observer effect should not present aggregate findings that might cancel out individual differences (Yamamoto, Jones, and Ross, 1972). Furthermore, because observer effect may be specific to a situation as well as to the measurement method (Heyns and Lippitt, 1954), studies must specify the circumstances under which the observations were made. These circumstances include the degree and nature of novelty, characteristics of the subjects (for example, age), behaviors observed, the observer's behavior (passive or active), the length and frequency of observation, and the method of describing the observation to the subjects (Haynes, 1978).

Selecting an Observational Measure

The assessor must first decide what the targets of his observation are. This decision guides the choice of an appropriate observation measure. For example, if the assessor is to screen an entire class to identify children at risk for behavior or emotional disorder, a category or sign system that incorporates relevant behaviors would afford the assessor an instrument with a research history. For a diagnostic referral, a more specialized measure is necessary. The assessor would have to precisely define the behaviors to be observed so that all observers could agree that a specific behavior has occurred. If an observer's inference and judgment are required to make that determination, the measure has little chance of yielding high interobserver agreement.

The assessor should select behaviors that occur with sufficient frequency that they can be sampled by an outside observer. Chronically withdrawn behavior is not a meaningful target for a classroom observation measure. Next, the assessor should determine the context in which these behaviors occur: time of day, subject matter, and other situational variables. This specification allows the assessor to schedule a visit when the behaviors are likely to occur; subsequent observations should be scheduled at the same time to enhance stability (Marshall and others, 1976–1977).

The behaviors selected for observation should reflect the general areas of concern expressed by the referral source. The referral source and assessor should determine both general areas of concern and several specific examples of these concerns. For example, if "disruptive behavior" is the referral problem, the observer will need to know whether "speaking when not called upon" is to be considered disruptive or if only incidents of hitting or bothering other students are to be considered.

For diagnostic classroom observation, event sampling is likely to be more useful than time sampling (Forness and Esveldt, 1975; Forness, Guthrie, and Hall, 1976). If only selected behaviors are of interest, the criticisms of time sampling as not reflecting the natural span of classroom events and as possibly precluding the notation of infrequent behaviors (Biddle, 1967) limit its usefulness.

In selecting a predeveloped measure, usually a category system, the assessor should consult Herbert and Attridge's (1975) extensive list of evaluative criteria or Boehm and Weinberg's (1977) less detailed list. Lynch (1977) offers a very basic list that summarizes the criteria for selecting an observation instrument: (1) relevance to concerns (empirical, interpretive, and normative relevance); (2) feasibility (practicality); (3) reliability; (4) validity for purpose; and (5) constructiveness of resultant recommendations.

Advantages and Limitations of Observation for Assessment

The primary advantage of classroom observation is that the assessor can witness the context in which the referred behaviors occur and the complexity and interactional components of these behaviors. Observation is thus the assessment approach most likely to yield highly generalizable results (Payne, 1974; Randhawa and Fu, 1973). Depending on the initial referral concerns, classroom observation may be the only appropriate assessment measure, it may be used to supplement other measures, or it may be irrelevant. Because observation is time consuming, the assessor may prefer to use a teachers' verbal report, anecdotal notes, or rating scales. However, systematic classroom observation is one of the most direct assessment counter-responses to teachers' criticisms of psychological evaluation as being irrelevant or oversimplistic. Observation also provides a common frame of reference for a teacher and an assessor in their discussions about a pupil (Sitko, Fink, and Gillespie, 1977). Although they may offer different interpretations of a pupil's behavior, at least they can concur regarding the conditions under which particular behaviors occur.

The assessor's choice of classroom observation as an assessment measure indicates to the teacher that the assessor feels that what happens in the classroom is important and that his time is well spent in analyzing these events and confirming the teacher's impressions that a pupil has a difficulty worthy of attention. Cooperation between the assessor and teacher is enhanced if the assessor presents himself as open-minded and nonevaluative, and if the teacher is not defensive about being observed or about changing some of his approaches.

We conclude our discussion of the advantages of observational measures by noting several situations in which it is useful. To assess a very young child, for whom standardized tests may be too difficult, direct observation may be the only means of collecting data (Gellert, 1955; Lidz, 1977a). Systematic observation is also the only assessment measure that facilitates a teacher consultation model (Breyer and Calchera, 1971). Observation must be used when individuals cannot or will not adequately describe their circumstances during an interview (Weick, 1968). When used as an adjunct measure, observational data can enhance the reliability of IQ scores as predictors of academic achievement (McKinney and others, 1975). Finally, direct observation can be used to test hypotheses derived from other assessment sources, such as speculations about how a pupil functions in structured and nonstructured situations.

The major disadvantage of observation is that it is a slow and frequently inefficient strategy (Arrington, 1943; Haynes, 1978; Jones, Reid, and Patterson, 1975; Medley and Mitzel, 1963). In the time required to desensitize a class to the presence of an observer (Medley and Mitzel, 1963, recommend six to eight visits) and to gather sufficient data for an educated hypothesis, an assessor could administer a rating scale, several standardized tests, and an interview. Assessors must weigh the inefficiency of observation against its potential for yielding relevant information. Some information can be gathered only from observation, other information can be more efficiently collected by other means, with no loss of validity.

One cannot presume, however, that all necessary information can be gathered by observation. Organic conditions, such as a hearing deficit, may promote observable behaviors, but such conditions cannot be diagnosed in the classroom. Similarly, events in a child's life outside the classroom, such as the death of a parent, affect his behavior in the classroom, but they cannot be discerned from observation. Boehm and Weinberg (1977) allude to this limitation in their discussion of naturalistic observation: "the astute observer should not accept naturalistic observation methodology exclusively over other methods of inquiry. While feelings and attitudes underlie many classroom behaviors, it is often impossible to understand these dimensions through direct observation. . . . Moreoever, since certain behaviors rarely occur in naturalistic situations, it may be necessary to create an experimental or testing situation" (p. 75).

In interpreting their observational findings, assessors must understand that the generalizability of any findings is limited. Classroom behavior occurring in one context is not necessarily generalizable to another. Kowatrakul (1959), studying fifth- and sixth-grade pupils in varying classroom contexts, reports that behavior is related to the demands of the task; independent seat work elicits watching and listening behavior, while discussions elicit social behavior.

Although most of an observer's inferences need be of a low level—an advantage of observational measures—the recording of behaviors requires some exercise of interpretation and judgment, no matter how precisely the behaviors have been specified. Not all occurrences of a behavior are equal in their motivation and implications. Boyd and DeVault (1966) cite laughter as an example of a behavior that is appropriate or inappropriate, depending upon the context, the laugher's intentions, and characteristics of the laughter (frequency, intensity, and duration).

Another limitation of observation is that individuals differ in their ability to become adequate observers (Flanders, 1967). Flanders identifies the following difficulties: "The problem of observer training is two-faced: first, converting men into machines, and second, keeping them in that condition while they are observing" (p. 158). To these we add a third problem: Observers must be able to negotiate a series of transitions from sensitive clinician to recording machine. Observers' reliability tends to decrease as time elapses since their initial training sessions (Frick and Semmel, 1978; Jones, Reid, and Patterson, 1975; Reid, 1970). Accuracy of recording appears to be influenced by whether the observers think their records will be checked. Assessors should be aware of such phenomena that affect the correctness of observational measures.

Weick (1968) describes a number of human perceptual processes that introduce bias into an observation. The human mind tends to reduce the details of an event, to abbreviate the event, and to enhance contrasts to make the information more coherent and comprehensible. The mind's tendency to seek closure and symmetry reduces ambiguous acts to commonplace explanations. Concentration and focus are usually stronger at the beginning and end of an event than in the middle. Weick suggests that these sources of bias can be reduced or eliminated by reducing the demands on an observer's memory and vigilance. He recommends short but frequent observation periods, clear definitions, opportunities for rest, and adequate training.

Finally, an observer's analysis may disagree with that of the classroom teacher's because their definitions of problem behavior are quite different. An observer may note that children other than the referred child are exhibiting more problem behaviors than the referred child, or that the referred child or others exhibit behaviors other than those identified by the teacher as problematic. Brison (1967) and Nelson and Bowles (1975) suggest that the observer take normative samples of nonreferred children in the same class, using the same observation measure. Although such sampling requires time, it can help the assessor determine whether the pupil referred by the teacher is truly behaving unusually for a child of his age in his class.

Psychosituational Assessment

Most category, sign, and rating observation systems are "closed" (Hunter, 1977); that is, they provide a set list of behaviors to be recorded. While closed systems offer objectivity, reliability, and validity, they are of limited use for diagnostic assessment because the behaviors of interest to the observer may not be included in the system or may be embedded in a series of other behaviors that are not of interest.

Observational approaches for individual diagnosis must provide a valid structure that allows the assessor to incorporate behavioral targets that reflect the referral concerns (Hanesian, n.d.; Lovitt, 1967). One such approach is psychosituational assessment, an event-sampling strategy derived from basic behavioristic principles, but adapted to a school setting by Bersoff and his associates (Bersoff and Grieger, 1971; Ellet and Bersoff, 1976; Grieger and Abidin, 1972; also described by Dickinson, 1978).

Bersoff and Grieger (1971) define psychosituational assessment as "the investigation, measurement, and interpretation of behavior as it is elicited through interaction with stimulus situations. Its major aspects are (1) behavior, (2) environments and situations, and (3) attitudes, emotions, and expectations" (p. 484). The first two aspects are assessed in the classroom situation; the third is gleaned from an interview with the teacher and, presumably, guides the interpretation of the data to the teacher, although this aspect tends to receive the least attention by the authors.

Once an assessor receives a referral from a teacher, he schedules an interview with the teacher. During the interview, the two try to define target (undesired) and terminal (desired) behaviors; describe the situation in which these behaviors occur; and identify the contingencies that appear to stimulate and perpetuate the behaviors (antecedents and consequences, respectively). The assessor must also try to determine how the teachers' expectations, behavior, and teaching strategies are affecting the referred pupil.

If the interview yields information sufficient to suggest prescriptive action, further assessment intervention may be unnecessary. In the more likely situation in which the context and contingencies cannot be specified in the interview, the primary interview tasks are to define the target and terminal behaviors and to derive some hypotheses regarding the teacher's attitudes, emotions, and expectations.

The definition of the target and terminal behaviors includes their frequency, intensity, duration, and context; that is, how often, how much, how long, and under what conditions (Bersoff and Grieger, 1971; Ellet and Bersoff, 1976). An additional useful parameter is latency, the time lapse between the occurrence of a behavior and the response to it. The context includes antecedents, what happens just before the target or terminal behavior occurs, and consequences, what happens just following the occurrence. In preparation for the observation, the assessor can devise a list of abbreviations to facilitate recording. A form similar to the one shown in Figure 4 can be used to summarize the observations.

After the observation, the observer summarizes any patterns evident in the data regarding what conditions tend to elicit and

Figure 4. Summary of Psychosituational Assessment

Name of Pupil: School:

Date of Observation: Teacher:

Time Begun: Grade:

Time Terminated: Locus of Observation:

Observor:

	Target Behaviors	*Terminal Behaviors*
Definition		
Frequency (number of times emitted)		
Duration (how long it lasted)		
Intensity (force or strength of behavior)		
Latency (time between behavior and consequent event)		
Antecedent situations (what happened just before behavior)		
Consequent situations (what happened just following behavior)		

Additional Observations:

Recommendations:

_____

(Signature)

perpetuate the target and terminal behaviors. The observer's recommendations suggest ways to modify conditions such that target behaviors will be reduced and terminal behaviors increased. Neither Bersoff nor his colleagues discuss how much observation is necessary to obtain adequate data; although several visits are preferable, the technique can be used for a one-time visit. That patterns will emerge cannot be guaranteed by this or any other strategy.

Like any observation system that focuses on the immediate antecedents and consequences of observed behavior, psychosituational assessment excludes observation of delayed effects and responses (Weick, 1968). Clearly not all events that immediately precede a behavior are the effective elicitors, as not all events that immediately follow are sources of perpetuation. Patterns may emerge after several samples of observation, but these must be cautiously analyzed by the assessor.

Psychosituational assessment is particularly strong in the area of practicality, which Medley (1975) describes as "the most important characteristic of an observational record" (p. 104). The amount of training required appears minimal, and a few visits to the classroom may be sufficient for gathering useful data. The measure's reliability and validity, though to date unevaluated, appear high if the definitions of target and terminal behaviors are specific. The approach is adaptable to a variety of conditions and purposes.

A final advantage of this approach is that, despite the focus on the pupil's behavior, the assessor is cautioned not to assume the problem emanates from the student. The assessor searches for patterns of antecedents and consequences; these may reside in the student, the teacher, or the environment. If the observer finds no pattern, he then investigates intraorganismic or extraclassroom factors. Thus, although the teacher may refer the pupil as "the problem," the assessor need not accept this hypothesis as necessarily true.

Psychosituational assessment shows promise in the diagnostic assessment of individual pupils. Simon and Boyer (1967) present category systems for this approach, and Wahler, House, and Stambaugh's (1976) technique seems particularly promising. The diagnostician must judge whether these methods are sufficiently researched and adequate to a given assessment task.

Case Studies

Case One

Warren is a four-and-a-half-year-old boy referred for consultation because of his disruptive behavior in his preschool program; his teachers were considering placing him in a therapeutic preschool. His family therapist also requested a clarification of the extent and nature of Warren's difficulties, since his mother claimed to have no problems managing him, her only child.

Assessment. The examiner used a modified psychosituational assessment procedure, recording target and terminal behaviors; noting antecedents, consequences, and context; but not recording duration, intensity, and latency unless they seemed particularly important.

The target behaviors for Warren were: aggressive behaviors like punching or throwing (TG1) and running out of the room (TG2). The terminal behavior was appropriate response to a teacher's instruction, that is, obeying a request without an aggressive display (TM). The observation lasted one hour, spanning a free-play period, snack time, and a group activity. The examiner made the following notations during the observation:

TG1:   Warren throws pegboard at another child; teacher goes over and says to pick it up.

TG1:   Throws sponge at other child; teacher goes over to him (intervention is low-keyed, not corrective; tries to redirect activity; no clear precipitation to his behavior).

TG1:   Warren goes to hug a girl; she pushes him away; he hits her; another child comes over to hit him; Warren throws block at this child, then stands on top of table, and gets off. Teacher does not respond to the incident.

TG1:   Throws block at a boy; teacher yells at him and sits him down; (block was thrown at boy who attacked him previously); Warren spits, throws another object.

TG2:   Warren leaves room. Teacher runs after him.

Note: Warren is noticeably more provocative than others in his class; when he leaves the room, the class is considerably quieter.

Warren is carried into the room by a male staff member;

Warren has big smile on face. On his own, he sits in chair he had previously left and looks at the teacher, and then pops out of the chair to join a child to play with crayons. Teacher asks him if he wants to sweep the floor. (Teacher ignores Warren's having left his chair without permission; she had placed him in the chair with no explanation of why she did that, what he was to do, or how long he was to stay there.)

TG1:   Warren goes over to a child he wishes to play with, aggressively jumps in front of the child and scares him away.

Warren climbs up on table, looking at the observer and the teacher, seeking to be noticed, is not. New staff member enters the room and says, "You didn't give me a hug today," elicits Warren's help to clean up, and leaves room in search of dustpan.

TG2:   Warren leaves room.

TG1:   Warren reenters, saunters in, picks up block and throws it at a girl. The cleaning woman makes remarks to him.

TG1:   Slaps boy he was pursuing previously, claims that boy ripped his shirt. Cleaning woman asks if he wants to go into her room.

TG2:   Runs out of room and returns on own.

TG1:   Punches a boy who passes by, unprovoked; boy responds with punching back; Warren enjoys this and tries to provoke others. Another boy tells him he had better stop.

TG1:   Warren goes behind him and pushes him.

TG2:   Runs out of room. Teacher goes after him. Warren reenters the room from different entrance than the teacher; he joins a group playing at a table, and an aide goes over to caress him. Teacher tells group to put heads down; Warren does not; teacher goes over to give him physical contact.

TG1:   Warren goes over and pulls chair from under one of the girls; teacher returns chair to girl and tells Warren to get own chair. Aide comes in room and gives Warren the snack milk to pass out.

TG2:   Warren leaves room, going after aide.

TG1:   Warren spits on table during snack time. Members of class remark that he spit and bring the teacher over. No attention from teacher.

TG1: Warren hits each child who passes him, each time looking at teacher, who takes no note.

TG1: Warren goes to wash hands, and on way back, hits a boy in the face with a wet towel; boy reacts with a dirty look. Teacher does not respond.

TG1: Tears napkins; teacher takes napkins away.

TG1: Picks up chair and throws it.

TG1: Walks over to desk and throws objects on the floor.

TG2: Leaves room.

TG1: Throws objects in through the door. Returns to room on his own; stands at threshold of door (teacher pays no attention), mumbles to himself: "cops can't lock me up neither," and plays with electrical wire. Observer intervenes and begins talking, but Warren becomes increasingly disruptive.

TG1: Stamps foot against door, slams door, kicks file, empties trash basket: "Now, all the stuff on the floor; stink mess is right there." Aide comes down the hall, looks in and tells him: "Warren, be a good boy; go to your teacher, O.K.? "

TM: Warren spontaneously puts trash back in basket. Teacher ignores this.

TG2: Leaves room; returns on own.

TM: Gets broom and sweeps up trash on his own. Teacher sees him do it, but does not comment.

TM: Boy asks Warren to play with him and another boy; Warren goes over and speaks with him, with no aggression. Teacher makes no response.

Teacher directs group to sit on floor for an activity; Warren goes to table to have his snack; he eats, all the time keeping his eyes on the teacher, who says nothing.

TG2: Leaves room with cookie basket in hand; returns on own.

TM: Joins group and participates appropriately.

TG1: At end of activity, gets into tussle with classmates. Teacher immediately tells him he can play the autoharp.

Observations. Incidents of aggression clearly predominate Warren's classroom behavior. These incidents are usually unprovoked by the other children, at whom they are usually directed, but Warren's intention appears to be to elicit his teacher's attention, which she does not always offer. The attention he does get is usually in response to negative behavior, and it often comes from aides rather than from the teacher. Some instances of appropriate behavior elicited no attention. Thus, his negative behavior is highly reinforced. Warren also does not seem to know how to initiate positive social interaction with other children. He shows a desire to play and interact, but his attempts to become involved are aggressive and they repel the other children.

Recommendations. Warren needs to be told clear rules, and they should be repeated to him when he transgresses. For example, when he punches someone, he can be told, "Fighting is not allowed in this classroom." Warren needs to be rewarded for appropriate behavior because his teacher's attention is very important to him. When he complies, he could be rewarded with a compliment and physical attention. Warren needs a well-specified procedure that governs his "cooling off" periods. He needs to be told why he must sit still, what he is expected to do, and how long he is to sit. The teacher should monitor this procedure to assure that he complies. Warren needs help in developing alternative behaviors. If he wants to play with a child, but scares the child by jumping in front of him, the teacher could suggest to Warren that he walk up to the child and invite him to play. Warren's disruptive behavior should not be rewarded by attention. The auxiliary personnel should be counseled about this.

Case Two

Todd is a six-year-two-month-old boy recommended for a learning disability placement by a neurologist. He has a high activity level, and reverses letters and numbers. His parents requested the assessment in order to consider further the appropriateness of the recommendation for special class placement.

Todd's teacher reported that he did not exhibit learning or behavior problems in her class, and she would not have referred him for intervention had he not been brought to her attention. His parents were not concerned about his activity level until they were advised by a pediatrician that he appeared unusually active. His history includes his mother having experienced blackouts and numbness of her leg while pregnant, for which she ingested medication. His developmental milestones were recalled as late. He had tubes in his ears because of excessive fluid, and had suffered mild hearing loss prior to this. His father had experienced learning problems in his youth. A neurological evaluation noted hyperactivity and visual perceptual difficulty.

Assessment. Todd was administered a number of tests, and observed during three consecutive instructional periods in his class. Target behaviors included loss of attention and leaving his seat. Terminal behaviors included remaining in his seat during the lesson and following directions. The observer noted twenty-three behavioral sequences, eleven instances of target behaviors, and twelve of terminal behaviors.

1. Teacher asks him to read story title. He does not know where it is, although has the correct page. The teacher asks another child to do this. The teacher asks Todd if he needs help or if he knows the words. Todd says he needs help. The teacher writes on the board the words with which he needs help. The other children become restless and another child leaves his seat.
2. Teacher asks Todd to read a sentence and stands by his side. The other children are restless and talkative. Todd does not know the words. The teacher says that he needs help and asks another child. She asks Todd to point to the words as the other child reads, and asks him to read them again, which he does.
3. Teacher asks Todd to help another child spell a word, which he does successfully.
4. Lesson changes from reading to writing. Todd gets up out of his seat, reaches over to others nearby and chats pleasantly with them. The teacher does not notice, and Todd settles down on his own.
5. Teacher tells pupils to fold their arms. Most do, but Todd does not. No reaction from teacher.
6. Todd writes his name on paper as directed. (Two other children are out of their seats.)
7. Teacher gives instructions. Todd whistles to himself, eyes off the teacher. The teacher says she will ask someone to give a word name—many raise their hands. Todd sees others with hands raised and raises his—in response to classmates, not in response to teacher's instruction.

8. The rest of the class works on their papers; Todd leafs through his notebook. No reaction from teacher.

9. Teacher asks class to underline. Todd seems inattentive, may be doodling.

10. Todd follows direction to trace. Other children finish. Todd erases a great deal and continues working.

11. Todd follows teacher's new direction. No reaction from teacher.

12. Todd follows directions, but erases a lot and frequently looks to neighbors to check what to do.

13. Todd continues to follow neighbors rather than teacher.

14. Todd fails to follow direction.

15. Todd follows direction, but from cues from classmates; for example, when he sees other children turn their papers over, he turns his, regardless of where he is in the lesson.

16. Todd sits still with hands folded as papers are collected. He seems to be in a daze. Starts to twirl paper and looks at teacher for reaction. No reaction.

17. Teacher tells pupils to put their heads down. Todd follows; keeps his eyes turned to his classmates. (Many other children are more active than he; his primary problem appears to be absorbing instructions.)

18. Gets out of seat. Goes back on own.

19. Teacher says to take out math books. Todd does.

20. Todd gets out of seat to confer with neighbor; goes back on his own.

21. Teacher gives instruction regarding counting. Todd seems to follow, but doesn't complete assignment.

22. Todd thumbs through a library book when finished, as directed by teacher.

23. Todd gets in line to go out for recess, as directed by teacher.

Observations and Recommendations. In class Todd frequently does not absorb the teacher's oral directions; instead, or in addition, he tends to work from visual clues provided by his neighbors. In this way, he is usually able to keep up with the tasks presented in class; however, Todd often does not complete his work. This failure appears to result from his loss of attention when he is left on his own to work.

Todd's test scores, his early history, and his observed classroom behavior suggest that his ability to learn is average, but that he has difficulty with memory and concentration and, to a lesser extent, with verbal processing. Although he presents a picture of vulnerability to a learning disability, his teacher reports that the level of his work is appropriate. Todd should be reevaluated in one year. His tendency to look to his neighbors for help in understanding directions should be noted and encouraged.

Chapter 6

Modifying Traditional Methods of Administration

If assessment is to be more than the compilation of scores and hypotheses that attempt to account for them, assessors must often modify standard procedures to suit a particular case. Assessment as the imaginative application of technology distinguishes the professional from the technician. The assessment professional must know how to adapt procedures in ways that are effective, valid, and reliable. In this chapter, we discuss strategies that assessors can use to expand the usefulness of standard measures. Most of these modifications attempt to add a dynamic quality to somewhat static measures.

Dynamic manipulations and modifications of the assessment process are needed by examiners asked to make recommendations regarding educational or therapeutic treatment. Such modifications allow the assessor to discern the conditions under which a child may be able to succeed on a task. The modifications provide the examiner with detailed data about the child's performance, and thus enhance the examiner's ability to speculate on the difference between a child's capacity and his performance. The assessor can discover whether a child truly lacks knowledge or ability in an area, or whether his ability or knowledge merely has not been elicited by standardized measures. Modifications are absolutely necessary in the assessment of children with handicapping conditions, such as blindness, deafness, or motoric limitations.

If feasible, the assessor should first administer the standard measure and then the modified version. The assessor can then report the two sets of scores, alerting his readers that specific modifications were made and that the measure's norms do not apply to scores on a modified measure. In administering any modified measure, the examiner should analyze the nature and extent of cuing provided during the modification. Sattler (1974) reports some evidence that some cues effect improved performance on subsequent items and, thereby, prejudice total scores. Low-level modifications—for example, administering a larger number of questions than is necessary to establish a baseline—are less likely to prejudice results than such high-level modifications as changing the vocabulary of a question or correcting failed items.

Error Analysis and Task Analysis

Error analysis and task analysis of test responses are cognitive activities undertaken by the examiner to discover any pattern to the child's errors and to hypothesize what the child must learn to do in order to succeed on the task in which the error occurred. The assessor formulates hypotheses, searches the data to confirm or refute these hypotheses, and plans additional assessment to respond to these confirmations or refutations. This testing of hypotheses regarding deficit areas suspected to effect performance deficiencies by the administration of specialized measures is called *funneling in* (Aliotti, 1977).

Let us consider an example of this process. An error analysis of a pupil's reading reveals a pattern of medial vowel sound deficiency. A task analysis of the abilities required to identify and differentiate these sounds itemizes the following skills:

1. Normal auditory acuity
2. Auditory ability to discriminate between spoken vowel sounds (including discriminating among various long sounds, various short sounds, and between long and short sounds)
3. Visual ability to discriminate and identify the letters that represent the sounds
4. Ability to match a single sound with its letter symbol
5. Ability to match the sound of a word with its written symbol

All five skills are necessary to successfully complete the task of medial vowel sound reading.

Because the child is able to match letters with sounds in isolation and has visual discrimination adequate to name letters, the assessor hypothesizes that the child's deficiency may be caused by inadequate auditory discrimination of sounds in the context of words. The assessor can verify this hypothesis by administering an auditory discrimination measure, a finer analytic filter through which to identify the area of difficulty.

Task analysis is the attempt to locate the possible deficit area in terms of the parameters suggested by Chalfant and Scheffelin (1969): "(a) the stimulus which is presented; (b) the organism to which the stimuli are presented; and (c) the response which is required" (p. 57). The assessor tries to determine which of these to manipulate in order to promote competence.

In Chapter Four we discussed task analysis as a critical step in delineating the objectives of a criterion-referenced measure. If the task is multiplication, one analyzes the steps required for mastery of this task. In this chapter, the material for the task analysis is a pattern of errors made by the child. This analysis focuses on the demands a task makes on a child, on the interaction between the task and the learner. For example, a component of a reading task is the individual letter; the demands on the learner are visual acuity and visual discrimination. Valett (1972) combines the two applications of task analysis, discussing both the demands of the most common class-room instructional situations on the young child and individual pupil's deficits in terms of these demands.

When using task analysis for criterion-referenced assessment, one must determine whether each of the components assumed to be necessary for mastery is indeed a prerequisite. Similarly, when using task analysis to modify traditional measures, one must determine whether the area in which the child has an apparent deficit is essential for competency. Task analysis incorporates an informal research effort into the assessment process, as the hypothesis derived from the task analysis must be tested. The assessor does not accept the heuristic premise that "Unless all necessary subskills of performance are taught, dependency on specific performance conditions will be prolonged and the opportunity for deviance will be increased" (Towle and Ginsberg, 1975, p. 486).

Further research is needed to develop the theory and practice of error analysis; only a few researchers, including Blank (1973), Goodman (1970), and Sigel (1963), have seriously studied the topic. Assessors need to know how to intepret errors to yield information about developmental level, cognitive strategies, differential diagnosis, level of mastery, and so on. Although experts assume that error analysis can provide information, analysis is now an inexact procedure.

Blank (1973) discusses the analysis of preschool children's errors and proposes a number of specific instructional responses to their errors. Although intended for use by teachers, these techniques can be used by psychological examiners to assess a child's response to remedial strategies. The results can be directly applied to the child's classroom program. Blank recommends the following responses to common errors:

1. Delay: When a child's failure is thought to reflect an impulsive response rather than lack of knowledge, the examiner can tell him to wait before responding.
2. Focus for attention: When a child responds in terms of pre-formed habits rather than in terms of the current demands of the task, the examiner can ask him to recall (and repeat) the question or description of the task.

3. Repeat demand: Same as previous situation, but teacher or examiner, rather than the child, repeats the instructions.

4. Rephrase: When a child's error appears to reflect unfamiliarity with the vocabulary of either a word or phrase, the examiner can paraphrase the instruction.

5. Partial completion of task: When a child does not seem to know where to begin or how to start, the examiner can supply a partial response.

6. Dissect task into smaller components: When a child appears overwhelmed by the size of the task, the examiner can try to focus the child's attention on subunits or restructure the task using a verbal cue.

7. Offer relevant comparisons: If a child does not seem able to generate a response, the examiner can offer a choice of incorrect and correct responses, varying in degree of obviousness. With puzzles, the examiner can offer a correct construction to provide a model for the child.

8. Didactic teaching: When a child does not appear to have the necessary information in his repertory, the assessor can provide it and assess his retention at a later time.

9. Request for clarification of a response: If a child's response is ambiguous, the examiner can ask additional questions to elicit an elaboration.

10. Repeat demonstration for clarification: If a child shows bewilderment regarding how to proceed on an item that has been demonstrated, the examiner can repeat the demonstration.

11. Relate what is unknown to what is known: If the information requested does not appear to be within the child's experience, the assessor can attempt to relate the request to something with which the child is familiar.

12. Direct the child's action in order to aid recognition of the salient characteristics: If a child does not appear able to relate a concept to a concrete event, the examiner can provide concrete objects that represent the concept.

13. Focus on the relevant features: When a child seems to have difficulty differentiating details, or distinguishing relevant from irrelevant aspects, the examiner can ask a leading question to focus the child's attention.

These suggested responses to a child's errors enable an assessor to guide the child from an error to a more acceptable response. In the process, the assessor can observe what kinds of interventions improve the child's performance, what kinds of interventions promote his learning. The assessor, however, must be astute enough to determine the nature of the child's error so that he selects an appropriate intervention. The entire array of interventions should not be applied to each commission of an error.

Greenstein and Strain (1977) used the strategies of task and error analysis to compare the errors of normal achievers and learning disabled pupils between the ages of twelve and seventeen on the Key Math Diagnostic Arithmetic Test. Of six types of errors on the computation subtests, four occur significantly more often among learning disabled students, one is significantly more characteristic of normal achievers, and one does not discriminate between the groups. The errors that characterize the learning disabled adolescents are:

1. Use of an algorithm that "violates numerical logic and produces incorrect answers" (p. 280); for example:

$$\begin{array}{r} 47 \\ +2 \\ \hline 69 \end{array} \quad \text{or} \quad \begin{array}{r} 66 \\ +4 \\ \hline 1010 \end{array}$$

2. Incorrect alignment of numbers; for example:

$$\begin{array}{r} 34 \\ +31 \\ \hline 5 \quad 6 \end{array} \quad \text{or} \quad \begin{array}{r} 345 \\ +23 \\ \hline 3 \quad 6 \end{array}$$

3. Subtracting the minuend from the subtrahend instead of regrouping; for example:

$$\begin{array}{r} 14 \\ -6 \\ \hline 12 \end{array} \quad \text{or} \quad \begin{array}{r} 25 \\ -16 \\ \hline 11 \end{array}$$

4. Omitting such details as decimals and dollar signs

The use of defective algorithms may be attributable to a spatial error, as the numeral to be added is not being "held" in its place. In order for a pupil to make such errors, he also must fail to relate the numbers to the concepts they represent.

The error that occurred more frequently among the normal learners is the computational error, or mistakes in number facts, for example 86 + 23 = 119 or 94 – 42 = 42. The one type of error common to both groups is the student's failure to observe the signs indicating the process to employ, for example: 76 – 12 = 88 or 9 + 7 = 2.

Studies such as this and that by Hall and La Driere (1970) provide information that facilitates analysis of an individual's performance. The assessor can compare a pupil's pattern of errors with studies of errors to explore whether the pupil's pattern is similar to that of normal achievers or suggestive of some particular dysfunction.

Modifications of the Wechsler Intelligence Scales (WISC)

The modifications discussed in this section were devised for the administration of the WISC, but may be used with other measures. As Griffiths (1977) explains, intelligence scales can be analyzed for information other than that elicited by a standard administration. Griffiths' suggestions are applicable to the WISC, and other measures.

1. Ask the child how he arrived at a response to an arithmetic question.
2. Write out the child's full verbal responses and use the child's spontaneous vocabulary in future lessons.
3. Allow and even encourage the child to make spontaneous comments about the materials. Record these comments, as they provide a picture of the child's manner of thinking and his emotional behavior.
4. Record the strategies the child uses in nonverbal tasks, particularly those regarding spatial orientation and directionality.

The assessor can also note whether the child uses a systematic approach or a trial-and-error approach to solving problems and observe the flexibility of the child's thinking.

Shore (1962) implies that the use of the child-examiner relationship in the administration of the WISC "in order to explore certain aspects of intellectual and personality functioning and their interrelationships" (p. 239) represents a more sophisticated use of a measure originally designed for classification and clarification. In the early development of these measures, variability of response was viewed primarily in terms of stimulus error, yet just such individual variability offers an assessor information at least as important as the results of the standardized procedure. Shore suggests that, before the administration of the measure, the assessor and child engage in an "active exploration of the purpose of the testing and the child's previous experiences with testing" (p. 241). This discussion builds rapport, orients the child, and reduces the child's anxiety. Then, during the administration of the measure, the examiner must judge which of the child's responses he will accept as offered and which he will probe. Probing allows the examiner to explore four dimensions of the child's behavior:

1. Intellectual functions: The examiner can explore the processes the child uses in arriving at a response and the procedures that enable him to offer a higher-level response. Children referred for diagnostic assessment are often those who have been experiencing difficulty, not normal achievers on whom the measures were standardized. The assessor must have considerable clinical acumen to elicit optimal performance from such children.
2. Personality: The examiner can ask the child to elaborate on responses that differ significantly from those expected. The examiner can also ask the child to compare his behavior during the assessment—particularly his response to failure and frustration— with his behavior in other situations.
3. Interpersonal functioning: During the administration of even the most objective measure, the examiner can observe the child's manner of relating to a stranger, his need for support, search for help, degree of spontaneity, and other such characteristics.
4. Fantasies: The examiner can explore the child's willingness to move beyond the concrete givens of situations and his patterns of responses to less structured items. For example, themes of anger and expectations of hostility may recur in a child's responses to questions about vocabulary ("A knife is for stabbing") and comprehension ("Policemen are to beat up robbers"). The examiner can assess the child's general orientation and his reality-testing skills.

Shore's suggestions define an assessment procedure that is a clinical interaction which can be a therapeutic experience for the child; that is, the child not only gives responses, but also receives responses regarding his performance from the examiner.

Following Sattler (1974), we divide all modifications into two groups: *contingency reinforcement procedures* and *testing-the-limits procedures*. Contingency procedures most often involve the examiner's rewarding the child for a correct response. The reward can be verbal approval or a tangible object; for example, the examiner can say "Good" after each correct response, or he can tell the child that he will receive a token or some other concrete reward for correct responses. The latter method has been found effective primarily with children from low socioeconomic or so-called disadvantaged groups (Keogh and Macmillan, 1971; Sweet and Ringness, 1971). Remarks such as "You're doing well" and "That was good"—offered regardless of the correctness of individual responses—can effect significantly higher WISC scores for both normal pupils and the educable mentally retarded (Saigh and Payne, 1976).

Most procedures to test the child's limits represent variations of strategies for cuing, which we described earlier. Sattler (1974) offers two other procedures: allowing additional time and alternate scoring. Allowing a child additional time to complete a task is a useful and simple modification. The examiner can record the pupil's progress on the task within the allotted time without interrupting the pupil. By allowing the pupil to continue working, the assessor can discern whether the child's inability to respond quickly is the source of difficulty, or whether the child is unable to do the particular task. This modification is hypothesized to provide minimal interference with performance on subsequent tasks (unless the child gains some sudden strategic insights), and it helps the examiner distinguish between pupils who have deficits and those who are merely slow workers.

Sattler's suggestions for alternate scoring involve alterations of ceiling and baseline levels, another modification that must be implemented during the administration of the measure. The examiner may wish to administer more low-level items than necessary to establish a baseline to a child who is very shy, highly anxious, or insecure. (See Carrubba, 1976, on the negative effects of anxiety on

the Similarities, Digit Span, Picture Completion, and Mazes subtests.) The examiner can give the child greater experience with
success in order to increase his participation, cooperation, and motivation, thus improving his performance. If a child becomes very
anxious in response to repeated failures in the course of establishing a
ceiling level, the examiner can intersperse some easy items with the
more difficult. In this way, the examiner maintains rapport and
reduces the child's anxiety, both of which actions promote optimal
performance.

The examiner may continue beyond the standardized ceiling
level if the child's knowledge does not appear to be adequately
sampled by the particular items on a measure. For example, if a
child's overall performance is highly variable on the Information
subtest, or if he fails a number of low-level items, but succeeds on the
more difficult questions, the examiner can keep asking questions
until he senses that the child can really go no further. The examiner
can report two sets of results, the child's IQ calculated by the standardized score and an estimate or description based on the modified
score.

Sattler (1969, 1974) also discusses modifications that appear to
affect subsequent scores to a significant extent, such as asking a child
to verbalize as he works out the Picture Arrangement sequences and
Object Assembly constructions (see also Post, 1970), or demonstrating partial solutions of the Block Design items. Thus, these modifications should be offered to the child only after the standardized
administration is completed. In general, cues that provide a cognitive
strategy should not be offered until the standard administration has
been completed. Cues or modifications that influence the child's
affective functioning can be used during the administration, pending
further research, if optimal performance is of most interest to the
assessor.

Ellett and Bersoff (1976) advise modifications of WISC-R
administration based on their model for psychosituational assessment, which we discussed in Chapter Five. Although they do not
detail any particular modifications that can be systematically or
generally applied to the WISC-R, they discuss the administration of
the test as an opportunity for the assessor to elicit behaviors similar
to the target behaviors described in the referral. The assessor can

discuss these behaviors with the child, observe which interventions control them, and explore means of eliciting the terminal behaviors specified in the referral.

In our earlier discussion of error analysis, we mentioned Blank's (1973) general strategies to discourage impulsive responding. Margolis and Brannigan (1976) express the value of modifications specific to the WISC that encourage the child to make reflective, rather than impulsive, responses: "Not knowing to what extent impulsivity has interfered with an accurate assessment of a child's abilities can lead to spurious test interpretations resulting in instructional programs emphasizing the strengthening of areas that are not as deficient as test scores indicate" (p. 484). They discuss the possibility of establishing differential local norms on tests and the option of readministering "an alternate form of the test . . . using modified directions designed to increase the likelihood that adequate attention is paid to the stimuli" (p. 485).

Walker (1976), having documented that reflective pupils score significantly higher on the WISC than impulsive pupils, tested a strategy that required the pupil to wait for a prescribed period of time before answering. This modification, however, did not effect an increase in scores, perhaps because mere delay does not control a pupil's cognitive function and may simply distract the pupil from the task. Schwebel and Bernstein (1970), in contrast, report that delay appears to elicit spontaneous productive cognitive strategies for the Comprehension, Similarities, and Mazes subtests.

Hardy and others (1976) performed an error analysis of seven-year-old inner-city children's responses to the Information, Comprehension, and Vocabulary subtests. They report four types of errors other than lack of knowledge: failure to comprehend, failures attributable to enunciation, differences in frame of reference, and problems with verbalization of ideas. When the children are probed in response to these errors, their mean accuracy significantly increases for all subtests.

As Aliotti (1977) notes, many modifications that have been devised by psychologists have been incorporated into revision editions of the WISC. As in so many areas, methods once considered iconoclastic and revolutionary are now standard procedures.

Modifications of the Stanford-Binet Intelligence Scale

Most examiners have had the experience of having to subject a child to a large number of difficult items in order to establish a ceiling level on the Stanford-Binet. For some children, this experience is particularly prolonged and agonizing, particularly if they continue to succeed with one or two items at several age levels. Hutt (1947) proposed that modifying only the order of the presentation of items would improve both the qualitative and quantitative information yielded. Hutt hypothesized that a sequence of consecutive failures would affect the pupil's motivation and impair his performance. Six guidelines characterize Hutt's (p. 97) procedure:

1. Begin with an item that is "sufficiently below the anticipated mental level to insure the subject's success with this item."
2. Begin with an item that "does not require considerable concentration, rapid response, or prolonged and involved verbal directions."
3. Alternate easy and difficult items.
4. Administer serial tests serially; for example, all digit spans at one time, in order of increasing difficulty. Administer these as soon as the subject has warmed up.
5. Establish the basal and maximal levels as soon as possible.
6. In general, do not administer items below the presumed basal or above the presumed maximal levels.

Hutt compared 630 standard and modified test protocols. He reports no significant differences between groups regarding median IQ and interprets this as evidence that the normative aspect of the test was not disturbed by the modified administration procedure. However, the means of the group that received the modified administration were more consistently high than those of the standard group. Among pupils who were subgrouped as well adjusted or poorly adjusted, the modified administration resulted in significantly higher IQs for the latter. This finding supports Hutt's contention that motivation is negatively affected by repeated exposure to failure, at least for these more vulnerable pupils.

Sattler (1974) reviews some suggestions for testing the child's limits on the picture vocabulary items of the Binet. These include: (1) asking the child for a gesture response if he has difficulty saying or thinking of the word; (2) asking for another word "What else could it be?") if the first response is not exactly correct; and (3) having the child point to the correct picture from a set of alternatives. (This last technique requires either dismantling the book or having more than one picture book available.)

The Binet, even more than the Wechsler tests, requires the examiner to perform task and error analyses and to probe the child's responses because the test yields only one score and attributes no differential merit to varying levels of response (Sigel, 1963).

Modifications of Projective Measures

Although modifications that test the examinee's limits have long been used with projective measures such as the Rorschach, few studies of this approach are of specific use in the educational setting. In the context of psychosituational assessment (see Chapter Five), Ellett and Bersoff (1976) discuss modifications of the Thematic Apperception Test and a sentence completion task. They also mention the Rorschach as a measure that provides a context for the child's responses which is less structured and less obviously evaluative than that presented by the Wechsler tests. They suggest that assessors observe the occurrence of target and terminal behaviors within these varying contexts, noting how the context affects these behaviors.

For the Thematic Apperception Test, Ellett and Bersoff suggest a major modification. Whereas the standard directions allow for complete open-endedness, these authors propose that the examiner supply the beginning of the story. In this way, the examiner can modify the stimuli to reflect the context of concern. For example, Ellett and Bersoff present this opening for TAT card number five: "This is a picture of a teacher who is watching a little boy in her class. The little boy is supposed to be working alone and doing his writing lesson. The teacher is angry with the little boy because . . ." (p. 24). Although this modification is so significant a change that the literature for interpreting the measure cannot be used, the content elicited from the child may provide some insight into the referral behaviors.

Similarly, Ellett and Bersoff construct a sentence completion task that attempts to elicit responses relating to the referral issues. They suggest such incomplete sentences as "The thing I do most that makes my teacher angry is," "The thing I dislike most of all in school is," and the like (p. 27). In this way, the assessor obtains information about the pupil's perception of his classroom and about potentially effective reinforcers in the classroom.

Modifications of the Bender Gestalt

Most dynamic strategies in diagnostic classification are concerned with intellectual assessment, but Smith and Martin (1967) investigate strategies to improve the diagnosis of neurological impairment as measured by the Bender Gestalt. They developed a teaching strategy that focused exclusively on rotation errors on the Bender. The assessor would try to teach the child how to correct the rotation, and the child's degree of resistance to such modification (number of cues required) was compared with an independent neurological assessment of the child. Significantly impaired children made more initial rotations and required more cues in order to correct these rotations than children with insignificant or no apparent dysfunction. However, the response to the cuing was more discriminating than the initial number of such errors. The cuing consisted of a sequence of five cues; cuing was terminated as soon as the child corrected the rotation. The cuing sequence is:

1. The assessor asks the child to redraw the design.
2. The assessor reorients the card to match the child's drawing, and asks the child to redraw it. The assessor then reorients the card to its proper position and asks the child to draw.
3. The assessor asks the child to point to the top and bottom of the stimulus card and his own paper, and asks him to redraw.
4. The child traces over the stimulus design with his fingers and redraws.
5. The child traces figure onto tracing paper and redraws.

While the authors did not attempt to demonstrate whether practice alone or the nature of the cues effected the difference, they report that nine of the pupils judged as nonimpaired made rotations. Unlike the impaired pupils, however, none of these required more than a simple request to redraw the design in order to effect a correction.

Modifications of Cognitive Measures for Special Groups

In assessing pupils who have physical dysfunctions, those who are very young, and those from low socioeconomic backgrounds, the assessor should first explore the appropriateness of existing measures. Both the appropriateness of the population on which the test was normed and the appropriateness of the content of the measure for the individual pupil must be considered. The examiner must, of course, consider any instruments that have been specifically devised for specialized populations, such as the Hiskey-Nebraska Test of Learning Aptitude for use with the hearing impaired. If the administration of such measures is not within the competency of the examiner, he should arrange an appropriate referral.

In many instances, however, appropriate measures are unavailable, and the assessor must modify existing instruments. The most frequent modification of any measure to adapt it to a special population is to administer a selected portion of it; for example, only the WISC-R performance subtests to a hearing-impaired child, or only the WISC-R verbal items to a blind or motorically handicapped child. The extent to which such abridgment negatively affects one's ability to interpret the scores in terms of the norms depends on the test. For example, the omission of any one WISC-R subtest has apparently negligible effect on the full scale reliability. However, the greater the independent contribution of the particular subtest to the total test reliability, the greater the effect of its omission (Piotrowski, 1976); the Block Design, for example, is a poor choice for omission. The negative effect is compounded by increasing the number of omissions. Piotrowski also documents the greater seriousness of omitting verbal rather than performance subtests with regard to effects on total test reliability.

Many specialized publications discuss the assessment of handicapped children in greater detail than we will here. Particularly extensive is the literature regarding cerebral palsied, blind, and deaf children, for whom adequate assessment remains a controversial issue (Gerweck and Ysseldyke, 1975). Assessors should remember that no special population is homogeneous, that any selection of assessment measures must reflect the nature and extent of the individual child's impairment and those means that are available for exploring the child's functioning.

Modifications for the Hearing Impaired

If the child can lip-read or has partial hearing, Lutey (1977) recommends that the examiner speak slowly and repeat directions when necessary. The examiner must make sure that the child understands his requests, but he should not add information that would not be given to a child who can hear. This caution applies particularly to the use of gestures, the modification most frequently made for the hearing impaired.

Sattler (1974) describes several modifications of the WISC subtests, some of which are also presented by Neuhaus (1967). He suggests three ways to provide the child with instructions for the Picture Completion subtest. First, the examiner can show the child a picture, one not on the test, that has a missing part, which the examiner then draws in. The examiner then presents to the child another picture which the child is to complete. The child can draw the missing part onto tracing paper or onto transparent plastic or can merely point and indicate by gesture the location and nature of the missing part. Second, the examiner can present a series of pictures of a person with different parts missing. The examiner can point to the missing part on his body, and the child can similarly complete the subsequent items. Third, the examiner can present a picture, one not on the test, that has a missing part, followed by the same picture with the missing part filled in.

In order to explain the directions for the Picture Arrangement subtest, the examiner can present the child with a series of numbers and demonstrate how they can be arranged in numerical order. Then he could present a series of letters, and finally a series of pictures. Or, the examiner could pantomime the first item. Or, the examiner could give the child a paper having a series of three or four numbered squares. The examiner can show the child how to place the pictures in order by placing each picture on the correct square.

Sattler notes that the effects, if any, of such modifications have not been investigated. These two subtests are the most difficult of all the WISC performance measures to explain to a hearing-impaired child (Graham and Shapiro, 1953), but the revised WISC (WISC-R), which provides for demonstration of the Picture Arrangement items, makes administration somewhat less of a problem. Graham and Shapiro's (1953) study, despite its small number of subjects, does suggest that the substitution of pantomime for verbal directions on the WISC performance subtests is a significant enough modification to warrant further investigation.

One particular limitation in administering the Wechsler tests to the hearing impaired is that it is often difficult to communicate the need to work speedily to some deaf children, a factor that interferes with adequate assessment (Gerweck and Ysseldyke, 1975). The examiner could allow the child additional time, although this significant modification restricts one's ability to interpret the findings in terms of the test's norms.

A modification that deviates only minimally from the standard procedure is to type the instructions onto a card for the child to read (Sattler, 1974). This procedure is of limited use, however, since it requires the child to be a fluent reader, and good readers are not often candidates for psychological assessment of cognitive functioning.

Modifications for the Blind or Partially Sighted

A blind child whose language skills are high might be able to respond to a number of the available assessment instruments without significant modification, particularly if the child has some history of sight. However, the assessor would still encounter difficulties in deciding how to apply the norms to this child because visual experience does affect the ability to respond conceptually to some items on the tests. Blind children do not acquire information that sighted children daily obtain. For example, the WISC-R question "How many legs does a dog have?" is simple for most sighted children who have seen a dog and contrasted the dog's posture and limbs with their own. A blind child can gain this same information only if he has played with a dog while someone provided a verbal description of the dog's anatomy. Although the blind child can comprehend the meaning of the question, his experience may not provide him with an answer. For this reason, it is often considerably more difficult to distinguish between a blind child's ability and his test performance than to make this distinction for pupils with other handicaps.

Modifications of existing instruments or administration of alternative measures may be necessary for a blind child even if the measure appears to be within the child's capacity to respond. Lutey (1977) recommends that assessors not rely solely on verbal items in the assessment of a blind or partially sighted child because blindness may interfere with verbal development. Lutey offers the following suggestions for the assessment of the partially sighted:

1. Use enlarged materials with darkened lines when possible. (Photocopying allows for significant enlargement.)
2. Allow the child to hold the materials and select a comfortable reading distance.
3. Assure optimal lighting.
4. Do not begin timing until the child has had sufficient opportunity to see the materials.
5. Proceed beyond the specified ceiling level to allow the child an adequate opportunity to display his knowledge or skill.
6. Provide a thick primary pencil when paper-pencil work is required.

Margack and Kern (1969) disagree with those who recommend modifying materials for partially sighted pupils; they emphasize that the assessor verify adequate vision correction, illumination, and presentation distance of the materials.

Modifications for the Motorically Handicapped

The pupils who present the greatest challenge to assessors are those whose motor handicap affects their speech. The more pervasive the effects of the child's dysfunction, the more the examiner must modify and manipulate the measure. As long as the assessor can elicit a yes or no from the child, whether through articulation, head movement, or blinking, the assessor can explore some aspects of the child's cognitive functioning. The examiner can point to the choices for response (pictures work best), and the child can provide a yes or no to indicate the adequacy of each choice. By this method and by pointing, the assessor can administer such instruments as the Illinois Test of Psycholinguistic Abilities, the Peabody Picture Vocabulary Test, the Columbia Test of Mental Maturity, and the French Picture Vocabulary Test. Haeussermann (1958) discusses such procedures, and Sattler and Anderson (1973) report success with cerebral palsied children on a multiple-choice modification of the Binet.

Thus, the assessor can classify the child's level of cognitive functioning and, of even greater importance, he can explore such questions as, What are the paths of access to this child? How can his capability to respond be optimized? What are his strong and weak areas? What are the most important content areas for the child to work on? What does the child now know in these areas? As Birch (1958) comments, "the objective of the examination is to provide information about the positive qualities of a child's functioning; the difficulties he faces in mastering problems when they are presented in the standard manner; and information about the special circumstances which are needed to create appropriate conditions for learning" (p. ix). Excessive apprehension, low motivation and persistence, easy fatigue, and short attention span are often characteristic of children with cerebral palsy and other motoric handicaps (Jewell and Wursten, 1952; Lacey, 1962). Lacey offers several suggestions for assessors working with cerebral palsied children. First, since some of these children have had painful experiences with medical examinations and interventions, the assessor can calm the child's fears by explaining that the assessment is not a medical examination, that the assessment will not be painful. Second, the assessor can provide concrete rewards, begin with easy items, alternate easy and difficult items, and schedule the assessment for a series of visits. These actions are intended to increase the child's motivation and to preclude his becoming too fatigued to perform well. Third, the examiner should minimize extraneous distractors; the examiner's clothing and accessories and the room should be simple and plain. Similarly, the examiner should present the test materials one at a time. Fourth, the child should be given a chair that is comfortable for him and a pencil large enough for him to use easily. Fifth, the assessor should consider having the child's parent present to interpret verbal communication and to reduce the child's separation anxiety. The motorically handicapped, of course, are not a homogeneous population, and assessors must consider the individual child's functioning when selecting and administering measures.

Jewell and Wursten (1952) describe a method by which the WISC Block Design task can be accomplished without motor manipulation: "Blocks were placed before the subject in random fashion on a large piece of paper. Each block was designated by a number on the paper. The subject could then indicate 'start by putting block number 12 on space A'. By selecting the right blocks, no manipulation of direction of blocks was necessary" (pp. 632–633). These authors also describe a modification of the copying of bead patterns task that reduces the motoric demands of stringing. A book is opened in front of the child, and the child is asked to place the beads in the recalled pattern in the centerfold of the book, using whatever means he has to move or point out the bead.

While such modifications may change the nature of the task such that the assessor is not deriving from the handicapped child the information the measure elicits from the normative population, the information can be interpreted if the assessor uses task analysis to determine what skills are assessed by the modified measure. For example, the modified Block Design task allows the assessor to estimate whether the child has some spatial analysis ability.

Allen and Collins (1955) describe in detail methods of adapting the Ammons Full Range Picture Vocabulary Test, Columbia Mental Maturity Scale, Raven's Progressive Matrices, and Leiter International Performance Scale for the motorically handicapped. Holden (1951) cites some modifications that include pointing and scoring for intent; for example, on a vocabulary item that requires the definition of a *ball*, a child who approximates a throwing gesture but does not verbalize the definition would be scored as correct. Katz (1958) describes a pointing modification for the following items of the Stanford-Binet: three-hole form board, identifying objects by name, picture vocabulary, counting four objects, comprehension I, copying a bead chain from memory, and naming objects from memory.

In addition to having the child point to his responses, the assessor may use the child's eye movements as an indicator of his responses. Wamba and Marzolf (1955) have designed a box for this purpose and have used it successfully with the Ravens Progressive Matrices, noting that it can be applied to other measures.

In discussing the assessment of children with aphasia, Berko (1951) presents suggestions that apply to most children with handicapping conditions, particularly those characterized by neurological dysfunctions. Berko calls the test score "an incidental result of a good examination" and views the purpose of assessment as an "illustration of the child's mode of performance . . . that is, the way in which he approaches a problem" (p. 241). He suggests that assessors interpret perseveration as a signal that the child is stressed by the difficulty of the task. When perseveration occurs, the assessor should change the task, perhaps returning to the incompleted task at a later time. Because many children with brain dysfunctions are particularly upset by lack of order and need a sense of limits and structure, the examiner should keep the materials orderly and respond to the child's questions about time (for example, How much longer?) and the sequence of assessment events (What comes next?).

Similar procedures are recommended by Lutey (1977) for use with retarded and learning disabled children. In general, any modifications should be determined by the particular behavior the child manifests, rather than by his disability. If a child appears highly anxious and fearful of risk or failure, for example, the assessor should begin with items below basal level and alternate easy and hard items, regardless of the nature of the child's dysfunction.

Modifications for Preschool Children

Assessing children ages three through five can be a very unpredictable experience, at times fun, at times frustrating and always challenging. Critical elements in the child's response to assessment are his degree of separation anxiety, ability and willingness to respond to a stranger, activity level, attention span, language development, and general attitude toward responding to requests. Furthermore, the instructions of the major measures for preschoolers often include concepts beyond a particular child's capacity.

One cannot assess a preschool child in one session; a series of sessions is absolutely necessary. Not only is it difficult to quickly administer formal measures to preschool children, but the child's behavior often changes dramatically over a series of sessions. The examiner must yield to the child's pace and initiative. He should not rigidly adhere to a sequence of test administration, but must have a large enough repertory to capitalize on whatever the child spontaneously offers.

It is rarely necessary to have the child's parent present for the assessment session, unless the assessor specifically wants to observe their interaction. The child can be allowed to leave the room to check on the presence of his parent if he expresses the wish to do so, although the assessor should discourage this because he may then have difficulty getting the child to reenter the evaluation room. The assessor may plan the first session as a brief one to minimize the child's anxiety at the initial contact and separation from his parent.

One valuable modification for preschoolers is to allow the child some time to play freely with some of the test materials, either before or after the formal administration. The blocks for the McCarthy Scales or the Binet can be placed on the table, without comment, in order to attract the child's attention. Once he begins to play with them, the examiner can elicit test-related responses. Following the formal administration, the examiner can observe the child's imaginative abilities by asking him to "Make something else," or to "Make something that you made up." Thus the test material itself serves to attract the child and allows the examiner to sample the complexity of the child's thinking and his capacity for becoming involved with materials. Some children who resist verbal requests are willing to respond if they feel that they control the situation.

Not only are several sessions necessary for the young child, but multiple samples of responses, especially of drawings, are highly recommended. While it may not be possible to score the Draw-A-Child subtest based on other than the drawing requested on the McCarthy, an alternate, or capacity, score can be derived from the child's highest-level drawing.

Most of the techniques mentioned previously can be readily applied to children from minority and disadvantaged populations. The examiner must try to be aware of sociocultural differences and make efforts to reduce and ameliorate any related discomforts, including the postponement or cancellation of the assessment. If adequate rapport is not achieved, the examiner, rather than risking the misrepresentation of the child's abilities, should not report scores based on a normed measure. He can offer a behavioral description of the child's performance, but he should not normatively evaluate it.

Assessors can sometimes circumvent differences in language by using the methods recommended for the hearing impaired or by using an interpreter who is able to translate the questions without adding information or cues.

Case Studies

Case One

Pat is a seven-year-old boy, previously diagnosed as psychotic, who was making a poor adjustment to his regular classroom. The assessor was requested to diagnose his problem and recommend appropriate educational programming.

Description and Behavior. Pat's articulation is generally clear, but he mislabels, speaks in nonsequiturs and associations, and at times seems to make up words. These behaviors are interspersed with appropriate verbal expression. When he tries to give a lengthy description, it comes out jumbled; he has more success with short, simple responses. Pat often responds to tasks in his own way rather than following directions.

When observed in class, Pat stood out as seeking and requiring attention, behaving as though the situation concerned only him and his teacher. When the teacher gave an instruction, he responded only to a part of the phrase, usually the end, which was inappropriate to the entire instruction. At other times, when given directions for a task, he showed little comprehension of what was said and responded imitatively.

Assessment Measures. The discrepancy in Pat's ITPA test scores is unusually marked. On all the subtests requiring primarily visual perception without verbal expression, Pat's scores are within average range. On all subtests requiring auditory perception and verbal response, he is considerably below average. Possibly Pat's poor eye contact contributes to his illogical speech, since he misses the information provided by the expressions and reactions of others.

At times, one can interrupt Pat's perseverations and elicit an appropriate response. For example, a memory task on the McCarthy Scales consists of the examiner reading a story to the child and the child then retelling the story. Pat began to tell his own, totally unrelated story, repeating information from earlier assessment procedures. However, when the examiner said: "No, not your story; my story," Pat gave a very accurate account, omitting only two out of eleven details. He does have problems labeling and organizing, but he did absorb and recall what he heard.

Pat may have a central processing dysfunction. He needs further language evaluation and placement in a learning disabilities program. Specific recommendations for increasing his attentiveness and relevance include increased eye contact, particularly when he is being given an oral direction, but also when he is speaking. His teacher and parents should interrupt his verbal perseveration and modify directions to elicit an appropriate response. They should also use physical contact to increase his ability to focus; for example, placing an arm around his shoulders while directing his attention to a printed page.

Case Two

Terri is a seven-and-a-half-year-old girl whose perceptual-cognitive strategy involves focusing on a restricted portion of the larger field. Although she gains a great deal of information from the area that receives her attention, she sacrifices perspective and context. She does not respond to a new situation with a quick visual scan to size it up, but, instead, she focuses on a small portion. Within this selected segment, she demonstrates above average ability to extract and retain detailed information. This strategy appears to account for her low areas of function on the cognitive measure and her emotional reaction to frustration.

This analysis of Terri's error pattern suggests the following recommendations. One, present her with a page of pictures to memorize. Teach her to look quickly at all of them, giving her an orderly sequence for surveying the page, and having her repeat the names to herself as she sees them. This exercise can be done periodically to see if she can improve the number of items she recalls. The number of pictures, their placement, and their relationship can be changed to reflect her progress. Two, have Terri keep a daily log of tasks to be done, checking off items as she does them. A discussion of the log at the beginning and end of the day provide for review and perspective. Third, help Terri develop perspective on a stressful situation by encouraging her to talk to herself about it. Suggest that she talk about what she is afraid of, what it means if she gets something wrong, how well has she done so far, and so on.

Chapter 7

⚹⚹⚹⚹⚹⚹

Interview, Play, and Drawing Techniques in Assessment

The procedures discussed in this chapter present alternatives to standardized tests, but do not belong in the categories defined in earlier chapters. While some of these, such as interviews, drawings or play techniques, are not likely to be new to the reader, these approaches are often inadequately discussed in texts on psychological assessment in the schools. Other strategies, such as the Squiggle Game or Continuous Performance Testing, will be new to many readers.

Although these approaches are not psychometrically standardized, as supplements to traditional measures they aid the assessor in understanding a pupil as a dynamically functioning and interacting individual.

Self-Report and Interview

Both behaviorists and dynamicists in clinical psychology emphasize conversation between the client and the assessor as an important aspect of pretest preparation. Such conversations establish rapport, but they can also provide valuable information. The assessor may interview the child or other involved individuals. In deciding to interview the child, the assessor must consider the child's age, language facility, cognitive level, willingness to respond, and memory for historical details. That the predictive validity of guided and structured self-report during an interview with adolescents and young adults at times exceeds that of standardized tests is evidenced by Brodsky (1975) and McMorris and Ambrosino (1973).

Interviewing involves skills of observation, inference, and intervention, abilities not necessarily highly correlated in any single examiner (Richardson, Dohrenwend, and Klein, 1965). Interviews can also be therapeutic interventions in and of themselves. For many pupils, the experience of being talked with rather than at and being respected substantially enhances their self-esteem. The examiner can not only elicit information but also help the child to profit immediately and directly from the assessment experience.

In some assessments, no one clearly defined segment is devoted to an interview. Frequently, at the beginning, the assessor spends some time orienting the child, eliciting comments indicative of the child's comprehension of the situation, and gathering some basic biographical information. But much of the interviewing occurs between the formal tests, in conversations about the measures or in casual conversations that develop from the child's questions or comments. Although casual, such conversations allow assessors to examine the child's mental status, to make therapeutic interventions, and to note leads for remedial strategies.

The interviewer must pay attention to the stimulus value of the questions asked and of such factors as the interviewer's physical appearance, language, and interpersonal style (Richardson, Dohrenwend, and Klein, 1965). One cannot make assumptions regarding an individual child's reactions to the examiner's race or gender, despite research results based upon evidence from large groups. Children vary in their ethnic awareness and in the degree to which they apply such reactions to the assessment situation.

The assessor cannot avoid being perceived as an authority figure. Although professionals differ in their degree of authoritarianism, all pupils will respond to assessors as authorities. This response can be explored and analyzed during an interview. The examiner can compare a child's response to him with other children's responses to judge how the pupil interacts in a novel social relationship with an adult and how he relates to an authority figure. These behaviors are indicative of the pupil's expectations, perceptual sets, response readiness, flexibility, adaptability, and openness to experience. If the pupil's teacher has complained about the pupil's attitudes or disruptive behavior, the pupil's attitude toward the interviewer can suggest whether the teacher's behavior contributes to the child's disruptiveness and how the teacher could modify his own behavior.

When orienting the pupil to the assessment procedures, assessors should avoid any statement that implies that the session consists of playing some games. Children retain the phrase "play games," and manifest disappointment when games are not forthcoming. The examiner need not offer any explanation until he has asked the child about his understanding of the situation. More often than not, a child will greet this question with a shrug of the shoulders or its verbal equivalent, but any verbal response can be enlightening. At times, the child has been told that he is going to see a doctor, which conjures up images of shots and physical inspections. Frequently, the word *tests* has been mentioned to the child. The examiner should distinguish between classroom tests and assessment tests, explaining that he wants to find out if the child needs special help. The assessor can comment on the child's normal anxiety and provide some words of comfort and reassurance. Whatever the details of the introduction, children rarely absorb many of the actual words said at the beginning. They do respond to attitudes of friendliness and respect.

During the initial phase of the interview, the examiner can ask about the child's prior experiences with such situations, if any. Although one can obtain accurate information from the record or from a parent or teacher, the child's recollection of the experience influences his expectations and behavior in the current situation. As mentioned earlier, the examiner should ask the child what he has been told by his teacher or parents about the assessment. Parents frequently do not prepare the child at all, and teachers at times have threatened the child with referral as punishment for misbehavior. Even a straightforward explanation can raise a child's anxiety to the point of interfering with his performance. For example, a bright boy was told by his mother that he was being tested to see how smart he was. As a result, every time he made an error or did not know the answer, he responded with an anxiety-ridden, self-deprecating remark. Although he obtained high scores, the assessment was a needlessly anxious experience for him.

In conducting an interview, the assessor should phrase his questions in a manner that avoids influencing the child to respond as he thinks the examiner wants him to. Although this influence cannot be entirely avoided, since the assessor represents an authority, the examiner can analyze his questions to assure that they do not set particular expectations for the child. However, when interviewing a reluctant child, the examiner can deliberately ask leading questions. For example, the question, How do you like your teacher? may only elicit a one-word response. The question, What don't you like about your teacher? may elicit the child's feelings because it grants permission to state negative opinions.

Thus the phrasing of interview questions provides important cues that influence responses (Richardson, Dohrenwend, and Klein, 1965). Questions that can be answered with a simple yes or no are usually not very revealing, while questions that ask How? or What? are likely to receive elaborate answers. Questions that ask the child Why? regarding his own behavior are unlikely to elicit satisfactory or revealing responses, as most parents are well aware. More often than not, the assessor must infer the reasons a child behaves as he does from the data.

Richardson, Dohrenwend, and Klein (1965) present evidence that encouraging vocalizations by the interviewer, such as "uh huh" or "good," positively influence the length of children's responses to open-ended questions. However, approving remarks can bias the respondent's answers by implying approval of particular kinds of content. Silences during the interview sometimes encourage increased responsiveness, at other times raise anxiety or reduce responsiveness.

Interviews contribute to and elaborate on data from more standardized and formal mental status examinations. The interviewer can observe the child's physical appearance, behavior, orientation, memory, sensorium, mood and affect, intellectual functioning, perceptual processes, thought content, thought process, insight, and judgment (Maloney and Ward, 1979). Indeed, it is difficult to elicit meaningful information about a child's mood, affect, and insight without an interview, and these traits are highly relevant to the child's functioning in school and the types of interventions that will profit the child. A highly impulsive child with little demonstrated insight, for example, is unlikely to profit from verbal interventions like psychotherapy or discussions with his teacher.

Interviewing is useful for assessors who use a behavioristic model because they can observe target and terminal behaviors, their precipitants or antecedents, and consequences. (See Chapter Five for a discussion of a behavioral approach to observation.) The child, as well as older clients, may not be able to specify for the examiner what aspects of the classroom situation contribute to maintaining the target behaviors (Haynes, 1978). However, the interviewer can help the child to clarify the connections between reported or observed classroom behavior and the consequences. The interviewer can also discover possible positive reinforcers by asking, What do you enjoy doing in class? What would you do if you had the choice? What are you willing to work for?

Haynes (1978) warns against focusing in too early or too quickly on the problems mentioned in the referral because these may not be of central concern to the client or represent the most critical issues of the situation. The problems specified by a teacher or parent may differ from the problems experienced by the child. Most often, the child perceives others' reactions to his behaviors as the problem, and the target behaviors signal that something is wrong. What the target behaviors represent and how they are best remediated are the primary tasks of the assessor. If the decision is made to address the target behaviors by modifying the teacher's behavior or manipulating other classroom variables, the assessor can elicit the child's cooperation by appealing to his desires to get his teacher off his back, to be more successful, and to feel better and more capable. Initial remedial efforts are often best directed at the problems that concern the child rather than the behaviors mentioned in the referral.

Interviews of children may be unstructured or, depending on the nature of the referral issue, structured to fit the examiner's agenda. If the examiner is formulating hypotheses about the effect of family relations on the referral issue, he would probe this area. If the assessor is considering particular intervention procedures, he can explore the child's positive or negative predisposition to such interventions. However, children have varying degrees of spontaneity, particularly in their verbal expression, and the examiner must often be an astute follower and subtle leader, regardless of any particular agenda. Few children are accustomed to a prolonged, fairly serious conversation, and the examiner's attempts to involve the child can easily increase his anxiety. To reduce the child's anxiety, the assessor can conduct the interview in a piecemeal fashion, wedging conversation between less confrontive tasks.

Haynes (1978) discusses seven errors that interviewers commonly commit: insufficient reinforcement for the client, indiscriminate reinforcement, insufficient specification of behaviors and events, too large a proportion of closed to open-ended questions, comments that imply negative reactions, insufficient direction of the interview, and overestimation of the client's fragility in discussing certain topics.

The literature provides evidence of the validity, particularly the criterion validity, of interview data for adults, although conflicting evidence also exists. Haynes (1978) concludes that "the degree of validity is a function of situational, client, topic, and procedural variables" (p. 287). When using multiple sources of data, the assessor can check the interview data against other sources. If a child claims that his teacher picks on him, the assessor can substantiate this information by classroom observation. The examiner must also assess the reliability of the child as a source of information and observation.

Linehan (1977), defining an interview as "a method of obtaining verbal data about the client's behavior and interactions with the environment" (p. 32), points out several advantages of the interview as an assessment strategy. These include the potential for greater confidentiality than written tasks, the opportunity to assess a client who is not capable of responding by other means (for example, an illiterate), and the opportunities for the assessor to seek clarification of the client's responses. Linehan also discusses the effects of the client's memory, comprehension, and motivation on interview reliability and validity. Although adults are often motivated by the desire to be dutiful clients, especially if they initiated the contact, school children rarely feel this obligation and rarely initiate the contact. An essential task for the interviewer is to motivate the child to cooperate and participate.

In selecting questions to ask the child, the assessor must consider the conceptual demands of various questions. Sapir and Wilson (1978) provide some guidelines about the age at which children can be expected to answer questions about personal and temporal issues:

- How old are you? (four years, five months old)
- When is your birthday? (five years, seven months)
- Who lives in your house: brothers? sisters? (four years, six months)
- Are they bigger or smaller than you? (five years, six months)
- Are they older or younger than you? (six years, seven months)
- What is today? (five years, six months)
- What day comes before Wednesday? (seven years, nine months)
- What are the four seasons? (eight years, nine months)
- What time do you get up in the morning? (six years, eight months)
- How long did it take you to get here? (seven years, nine months)

If such estimates for a variety of interview questions can be confirmed by research, one could use such questions as an informal assessment measure to elaborate on, support, or contradict developmental data derived from other sources. The child's answers could also serve to indicate his level of functioning under a variety of conditions, such as structured and unstructured, relaxed and formal.

The validity of interviews with children is also complicated by children's language comprehension skills (Maccoby and Maccoby, 1954). Young children simply do not understand much of what is said to them, and if they do understand, they may have difficulty organizing a coherent response. Children also have a limited capacity for self-reflection and sometimes do not feel free to express their feelings about their experiences. The interviewer must also consider significant cultural differences and young children's natural egocentrism, which assumes that adults recognize all references in the child's conversation.

For the older child and adolescent, Meichenbaum (1977) recommends having the client close his eyes and imagine a scene in which the problem behavior occurs. The client is then asked to describe his thoughts, images, behaviors, and affects. For example, a teenager described in great detail examples of his encounters with his teacher. His description showed that he could acknowledge only his own anger, which he perceived as a response to his teacher's arbitrary anger; yet, his descriptions also revealed that he had clearly provoked his teacher. This interview data provided some of the most relevant and meaningful information of the entire assessment. Meichenbaum also suggests that the assessor solicit the client's ideas for improving his situation. This task is too difficult for some children, but others come up with good ideas, and most appreciate having been asked.

Burke and DeMers (1979) specifically discuss the interview as an assessment procedure for schoolchildren. They list three dimensions that characterize the format and structure of any interview: "(a) the degree to which the interviewer's questions are predetermined, (b) the type of response options allowed the interviewee, and (c) the breadth of content areas explored" (p. 53). The authors suggest seven appropriate content areas: the initial problem, clarification of the problem, the client's motivation, his developmental history, his self-control, his social relationships, and his social and cultural environment. Using these dimensions, the authors identify twenty-seven different types of interviews and suggest that such a typology enables researchers and assessors to discuss interviewing procedures with needed specificity.

Maccoby and Maccoby's (1954) hints for interviewing young children include: listening to how the child phrases questions for clues regarding how to phrase questions directed at the child and using nondirective phrasing that does not cue the child to a desirable response. The examiner should avoid establishing response sets that cause the child to perseverate on a particular type of response regardless of its appropriateness or accuracy. They also discuss building rapport and providing time for the child to explore the setting and satisfy his curiosity about the situation before beginning questioning.

Yarrow (1960) explains that interviews are most easily conducted with children older than six, but that some form of interview can be used with children as young as three. Most three-year-olds' language is comprehensible although children's developmental negativism often impedes verbal communication with an adult. Between the ages of four and five, children become increasingly interested in the use of language for the exchange of information. Yarrow suggests presenting dolls for children between three and five, using manipulative tasks, and involving the child in a game prior to questioning. He judges the effect of the interviewer's sex as possibly important but unresolved. The effect seems significant for children seven and older, and it acquires particular importance for adolescents.

Yarrow cites five types of nonverbal cues that the interviewer should note: physical posture, physiological-vasomotor (blushing, perspiring, muscle tension), formal characteristics of language (loquacity, fluency, tempo, speed), interactional behavior (dominance or passivity, resistance or compliance), and personality style (spontaneity, organization). Early studies of personality assessment emphasized the observation and measurement of such nonverbal behaviors as handshake grip, walking, and handwriting (Allport and Vernon, 1933; Eisenberg, 1937, and Wolff, 1941). Nonverbal behaviors are of particular interest in the assessment of young children because of children's limited language skills and wavering motivation to cooperate. Wolff (1941) observed the nonverbal, expressive behaviors of preschool children as they finger painted, brush painted, and did pencil drawings. During a blind analysis of photographs of these children, observers characterized the elements of the child's body position or posture by indifference, balance, and tension. Wolff notes that the consistency of expressive behavior varies with the individual, yet was generally high for his subjects.

Interviewing can elicit the subjective aspect of the child that is inaccessible to other approaches. While observation reveals only the present, the interview, like the questionnaire, allows the assessor to explore the child's past. The interview is often more useful than the questionnaire, however, because it allows the assessor to probe the client's responses. Within both school and clinical settings, the interview is a useful procedure not only for eliciting cooperation and behavioral samples, but also because sometimes the best way for an assessor to find out what he wants to know is to ask.

Role Playing and Simulation

The behavioral literature describes two assessment procedures that are relevant to the classroom and that need not be interpreted within the confines of a behavioristic model: role playing and simulation.

Role playing is neither a new technique nor one restricted to assessment purposes; it has long been used as a therapeutic intervention. McReynolds and DeVoge (1978) review the uses of role playing in personality assessment. The client is asked to imagine and act out a prescribed situation. The assessor evaluates this enactment by a formal coding, rating, or informal discussion; audiovisual recording allows the client to view, discuss, and assess his own performance. Role playing can be used to have the client reveal how he currently handles a given situation or to have him try out unfamiliar behaviors; the former is more often used in assessment, the latter in therapeutic interactions.

Moreno (1964), the originator of psychodrama, presents two role-playing measures for assessment, the Spontaneity Test and the Role Test. The Spontaneity Test involves "a psychodramatic interaction between the subject and the tester, in which the subject imagines himself in a prescribed situation in interaction with the tester and improvises accordingly" (McReynolds and DeVoge, 1978, p. 226). The Role Test assesses the individual's ability to assume a range of roles. Children can be asked to act out roles such as policeman, parent, teacher, and other familiar figures.

In using these procedures, assessors must consider what is actually measured: the way a person responds in a real situation or his ability to assume roles and demonstrate spontaneity, flexibility, range of affect, degree of self-consciousness, compliance, and the like. Similarly, assessors must decide which is more relevant to assessment, the particular content or the range of behaviors elicited. Is the way a person responds to a fabricated, improvised situation an accurate reflection of how he responds to real circumstances? McReynolds and

DeVoge (1978) present some evidence of the consistency of adults' behavior in improvised situations and the correspondence of such behavior with actual observed behavior. They view the main strength of role playing as its ability to reveal interpersonal style, an area of functioning difficult to assess by means other than direct observation. Staging a simulated experience, the assessor controls the timing of the situation he wishes to observe, rather than having to wait for a natural occurrence (Anderson, Ball, Murphy, and Associates, 1975).

The most standardized role-playing assessment techniques are those used in evaluating assertiveness, social skills, and expression of anger. Such approaches are particularly useful in the assessment of children referred for inappropriate aggressiveness or shyness. However, the available standardized measures pertain to adults' behavior.

Young children spontaneously role play, and the assessor's task is to catch them doing it and have some means of evaluating their performance. Curry and Arnaud (1974), studying spontaneous role playing of children aged eighteen months through nine years, have determined developmental stages for six dimensions of behavior: symbolic elaboration of the role, thematic content, integration of affect and intellect, enactment of the good or idealized self, distinction between reality and fantasy, and modes of interpersonal transactions. Symbolic elaboration, for example, appears to relate to the child's level of cognitive development and proceeds from "simple, concrete imitation of perceived actions" to " 'wild,' 'fantastic' elaborations of imaginary roles that represent combinations and transformations of cultural models" (p. 274). Their developmental model guides an assessor in deriving some impressions about the child's cognitive and social development. Curry and Arnaud (1974) have a helpful, developmentally based guideline for observation of children's play.

Some role-playing techniques place demands on the examiner to be an actor, a behavior quite discrepant with the traditional neutral stance. As McReynolds and DeVoge (1978) point out, the assessor must be an actor capable of involving the client such that the client reveals his characteristic behavior. Not all assessors feel able and comfortable in this capacity, but training in carrying out this approach broadens the professional's repertory of assessment skills. Perhaps one of the greatest difficulties for the examiner is to behave in a way sufficiently realistic to the client and to describe the situations in terms the client can understand.

Role-playing and simulation are appropriate for assessing such areas as interpersonal style and skill, which are not assessable by other means. However, the validity of inferences from such data is moot and requires further study. Stanton and Litwak (1955) compared adults' social competence as assessed by role playing with descriptions of the individual's behavior by someone who knew him well. Three aspects of interpersonal competence were assessed: autonomy, creativity, and empathy. The correlations they report for autonomy are extremely high.

Breland and Gaynor (1979) and Levine and McGuire (1968) discuss problems of reliability that arise because of the inescapable elements of subjective judgment. However, reliability can be improved by the use of multiple situations to sample behavior. Content validity is the strongest aspect of role-playing strategies, particularly in the assessment of mastery. Construct validity appears to be the most difficult to establish, possibly because role playing is unique in the dimensions of behavior it elicits.

Santostefano (1962a) considers situational assessment (that is, the simulation of situations) as the best means of assessing a client's coping behavior, or behavior that is "goal-directed, adaptive, and instrumental," (p. 84) in the gratification of needs or the reduction of threats. Santostefano (1962b) devised a simulation measure, the Miniature Situations Test, for the assessment of children's coping responses. The child is given two pairs of situations and asked to act out one pair, making his choice as quickly as possible. Santostefano (1965) reports that several of the situations significantly discriminate between normal public schoolchildren and brain damaged children, public schoolchildren and orphaned children, and orphaned and brain damaged children; the children studied were between six and thirteen years of age. The responses that significantly discriminate the public schoolchildren from the brain damaged are:

Brain damaged children selected:	*Public school children selected:*
Tearing paper	Repairing torn paper
Student timing examiner on sorting cards	Examiner timing student

Drawing design freehand	Tracing design
Blaming test for failure	Blaming self for failure
Examining interior of box with hand	Looking at concealed picture

Santostefano and Wilson (1968) used a similar method with two samples of institutionalized delinquents and identified behavioral choices that discriminated between "honor delinquents" and those requiring maximum security and restriction. More research of this kind is needed to establish the relationship between children's performance on simulations and their behavior in real situations. Such correlations would enable assessors to determine the generalizability of results obtained by role playing and simulation.

Just as arithmetic measures are criterion referenced to classroom instructional content, there is a need for measures that are criterion referenced to critical behaviors in the classroom, such as persistence in frustrating circumstances, response to aggressive provocation, manner of coping with lack of knowledge, and the like. Of course, not all verbal or written measures are artificial; the results of many such measures are generalizable to classroom behavior. But in situations where successful performance matters, such as in the armed services and in a variety of businesses, the development of simulation and situational assessment is progressing rapidly (Fitzpatrick and Morrison, 1971; Santostefano, 1962b).

Work-sample tests, a variation of simulation, are used when the client's finished work, not the behaviors preliminary to his production, is the object of evaluation (Fitzpatrick and Morrison, 1971). The work sample is an ideal approach to assessing an area such as handwriting. By asking the child to copy some printed material, the assessor obtains a work sample of his handwriting. The assessor can then introduce modifications, such as change of slant or slope of the writing surface, to assess their effects on the child's productions. Like other performance assessments, the work sample directly elicits the behavior to be assessed. However, in recommending interventions, the assessor must rely on inference, speculation, and judgment—just as he must in using other assessment strategies. For example, if a child's sample shows poor handwriting, the assessor must test hypotheses that this behavior represents neurological dysfunction, inadequate instruction, or a passive-aggressive personality.

These simulation and applied performance tests are variations of criterion-referenced assessment (Sanders and Sachse, 1977), in which the criterion behaviors are adaptive behaviors not assessable by paper-and-pencil measures. Thus our discussion, in Chapter Four, of the development, advantages, and disadvantages of criterion-referenced assessment apply here as well. For role-playing strategies, the task analysis and establishment of behavioral objectives can be carried out by means of the critical incident technique, developed by Flanagan (1954). McFall (1977) reviews the issues involved in the development of these critical behaviors.

Physiological Assessment

Physiological assessment is an area of increasing importance in clinical psychology, particularly with regard to behaviorally oriented treatment (Haynes, 1978). Physiological assessment requires specific training not yet a part of most professional education programs. Among the few studies relevant to the educational setting is Simpson and Nelson's (1974), which combines physiological assessment with an intervention program for hyperactive learning disabled children. The authors used a special apparatus to record respiration and devices to assess auditory and visual vigilance. The authors were able to help their subjects modify their control of their breathing and attention and, in turn, their hyperactive behavior.

Luria (1961) describes a physiological technique used to differentiate among problems of hearing, listening, and understanding. Constriction of the blood vessels has been found to be reactive to otic stimulation. Thus Luria and his colleagues first determined the blood vessel constriction pattern for an unimpaired child of normal intelligence that is associated with active listening; they used this as an index of attention and distractability when testing children suspected of having mental deficiencies. As a measure of comprehension, a child was told to press a button only when he heard a designated stimulus word. Once the child was trained to do this, the examiners included words from the same semantic family as the stimulus word and measured the blood vessel reaction to these words. The normal child did not react to words of different families, but did respond to words in the same family. The mentally defective child made generalizations based on sound rather than semantics. If the stimulus was *cat*, they reacted to *calf* but not to *kitten*.

Self-Monitoring

Self-monitoring involves having the client record the occurrence of his own behaviors. Although self-monitoring is used primarily with adults, it has been used successfully with children. Children have been asked to monitor their incidents of studying during class and talking out of turn (Broden, Hall, and Mitts, 1971), frequency of class participation (Gottman and McFall, 1972), academic productivity (Fox, 1966; Glynn, 1970), frequency of whining (Kunzelman, 1970), cleaning behavior (Layne and others, 1976), and out-of-seat and hand-waving behaviors during class (Maletzky, 1974). Haynes (1978) reviews these studies, which have been carried out with pupils as young as seven years of age.

Self-monitoring can supplement the assessor's observational capacities, while serving as an intervention that gives the pupil some responsibility for his behavior. The procedure risks a lack of accuracy, but adequate preparation of a motivated and capable child can reduce this disadvantage. However, self-monitoring can affect the incidence of behavior, although research results have been equivocal (Haynes, 1978; Nelson, 1977).

The behaviors to be recorded or tallied must be specifically described to the child and easy for the child to identify. The child should be told about the importance of accurate assessment, the purpose for doing so, and the procedures to be used. Haynes (1978) recommends procedures that facilitate self-recordings by children, such as line drawings of the behaviors to be checked off and wrist counters. The assessor may also solicit the cooperation of a responsible classmate to help the child monitor his recordings.

Continuous Performance Testing

Most assessment tasks are short, and assessment sessions often comprise a series of short tasks that sample the student's performance.

However, some behaviors that interfere with the child's classroom performance may not be elicited by these assessment tasks because they make minimal demands on the pupil's attention span. For example, many neurologically impaired children work best when they move quickly from one highly focused and structured task to the next. If such conditions are those of the assessment itself, the assessor may not see the child's dysfunctional aspects that the teacher notices during longer tasks (Kalverboer, 1975). Thus the assessor may find it helpful, particularly if he suspects an organic deficiency, to have the child work on at least one task that involves continuous or prolonged performance and sustained attention.

Rosvold and others (1956) devised a Continuous Performance Test that elicited significantly poor performance from brain damaged adults and children. The Continuous Performance Tests, and the continuous performance tasks described by Sykes, Douglas, and Morgenstern (1973), however, involve an apparatus not accessible to most psychologists or examiners. The importance of these investigations is that a child's response to demands on his sustained attention may indicate minimal brain dysfunction. Tests that require attentiveness for only brief periods do not successfully discriminate between these children and normal children. This finding has both diagnostic and remedial implications. If inattentiveness interferes with a child's functioning in class, the assessor should consider administering a measure of prolonged performance.

Play Techniques

We discussed the usefulness and validity of allowing the child to play freely with the assessment materials in Chapter Six. Here, we present play as an approach in and of itself, independent of materials involved in other assessment measures. Play can be used to establish rapport, to provide a means of expression for a nonverbal child, to supplement cognitive measures by observation of the child in a less structured setting, and to elicit content regarding the child's emotional and social life.

Play is a valued assessment approach because it comes naturally to the young child (Palmer, 1970). The difficulties lie in stimulating play that elicits material relevant to the referral issues and in eliciting play from children who do not feel like playing when the examiner wishes them to.

Palmer (1970) reviews the situational aspects that are likely to elicit play from children, including the size and nature of room and choice of play materials. The room should be large enough for free movement, but not too large, with minimal clutter, and adequately suited for use of the more regressive materials, such as sand and water. For free play, he recommends providing "the miniature life toys: housekeeping objects and family dolls, tiny soldiers, animals, cars, planes, and so on; materials which will permit regressive play in conjunction with the miniature life toys: sand, water, clay; larger toys for more realistic play: regular dolls and trucks; materials which permit aggressive play: guns, rubber knives, punching bag, 'BoBo the Clown'; junk toys, containing fragments such as pegs, light switches, string, tops, balls; and materials which permit communication and expression: a toy telephone, crayons, pencils and paper, chalk, paints, and finger paints" (p. 153). For older children, more structured, competitive games are suggested. A one-way viewing mirror, if available, enables the assessor to observe the child's play without an adult present or to observe parent-child play interaction.

Palmer also points out that the idiosyncratic nature of free play precludes the devisal of a formal scoring procedure. One can analyze the child's themes and sequences, but all such analyses have the limited reliability and validity characteristic of all unsystematic observation measures. Observation of free play may be quite useful in assessing a child's internal consistency, that is, in supporting, contradicting, or elaborating upon observations derived from other sources. Studies such as Johnston and others's (1977) are encouraging in presenting evidence that supports the generalizability of play behavior; these investigators report very high correlations between play behavior elicited under "laboratory" conditions and behavior in a natural setting.

Becker and Wolfgang (1977) describe a Symbolic Play Scale, derived from the writings of Piaget and Smilanski, that presents a kindergartener with a structured play situation. The stimulus toys include miniature people, animals, furniture, and wood forms; the child is instructed to "Make the toys tell a story." The child is scored, during a twenty-minute observation, on six levels: no action, sensorimotor, construction, symbolic, complex symbolic, and dramatic. These scores were compared with drawings, a conservation of number test, and reading readiness. The authors report that the level of the kindergarteners' play had significant correlations with their reading readiness. Jurkovic (1978) used these same play instructions with a sample of white, disadvantaged, preschool children and reports highly significant correlations between level of play and psycholinguistic level. This study thus lends support to the hypothesis that a child's cognitive level can be inferred from qualitative aspects of his play.

Switsky, Ludwig, and Haywood (1979) suggest an important distinction between exploration (investigation) and play: exploration is as an activity that precedes play. For example, one can play catch with a ball without exploring the ball itself, or one can explore the ball without incorporating it into play. In exploration, the ball is an object of interest in and of itself; in play, the ball is a means toward realizing a broader objective. Switsky, Ludwig, and Haywood report a converse relationship between exploration and play; that is, as exploration time decreases, play increases. Retarded and nonretarded children's exploratory behavior differ in that the retarded spend more time exploring the less complex stimuli, whereas the nonretarded are more attracted by greater complexity.

McReynolds, Acker, and Pietila (1961) observed eleven-year-olds exploring a box filled with small objects, a measure of curiosity. They report a positive association between ratings on curiosity and the teacher's rating of the child's adjustment, but no association between curiosity and achievement level. Behaviors rated as exemplifying curiosity included the number of manipulations of the objects and questions asked about them. Such an assessment of exploratory behavior or curiosity provides the assessor with an unobtrusive means of observing children's energy levels and identifying children who lack sufficient energy to concentrate on school work. The examiner can also stimulate exploratory behavior by asking questions like How many things can this (for example, a flashlight) be used for? How many things can you tell me about this? The child's responses may provide information about his energy level for involvement with tasks.

The Squiggle Game

Establishing rapport and eliciting responses from nonverbal and otherwise inhibited children always present a challenge, if not a frustration, to an assessor. If the child does not participate in classroom activities, and was referred for evaluation for this very reason, observation may not be a fruitful strategy. Play techniques, interviews, and rating data from the parents may be the only effective assessment measures. For such children, ice-breaking strategies like the Squiggle Game (Kaplan, 1975) may be helpful.

This nonstandardized procedure requires paper and pencils. "The interviewer says, 'I shut my eyes and go like this' and makes a scribble on one of the sheets of paper. The interviewer then says to the child, 'Now you turn this into something. Then it will be your turn to do the same thing and I will turn yours into something.' After the fourth or fifth exchange of squiggles, one theme or sometimes several themes usually emerge" (p. 421). Kaplan cautions against using this game with severely disturbed children because of its potential disorganizing effects. The procedure's primary contributions to assessment are that it generates a shared experience between the child and the examiner and provides a relatively nonthreatening means of communication for the reluctant responder.

The Preschool Interpersonal Problem Solving Test (PIPS)

Shure and Spivak's (1974) PIPS, designed for preschoolers, combines the advantages of a variety of assessment models that have direct implications for classroom instruction. The test's variables were derived from a series of research studies that identified specific behaviors which significantly differentiate well-adjusted from both impulsive and inhibited children. The primary cognitive behavior associated with social behavior that teachers rate as well adjusted is the ability to generate alternative solutions to problems; the ability to anticipate consequences and facility in means-end thinking are also reported to be relevant. The PIPS assesses the generation of alternatives; Platt and Spivak (n.d.) offer a Means-Ends Problem Solving Test (MEPS Procedure) for use with adults.

Administration of the PIPS involves presenting the child with stories and pictures. One set of stories concerns a problem between peers, the other set depicts incidents that could provoke anger in a child's mother. The examiner encourages the child to generate different solutions to each situation on the two major parts of the test. The test package includes normative information and scoring guides. The authors have also devised a training manual for use by parents and teachers. The instructional program provided teaches two cognitive skills—generation of multiple solutions and anticipation of consequences—associated with social adjustment. The program requires five daily sessions a week for some six weeks.

Inventories for the Assessment of Adaptive Behavior and Environment

Measures such as adaptive behavior scales based on questionnaires fall outside the scope of this chapter. However, we will discuss several examples of modified approaches to the assessment of adaptive behavior that do not use parental report but rely on more direct measurement.

Bradley and Caldwell's (1979) HOME Inventory was not specifically formulated as a measure of adaptive behavior. It does, however, directly assess environmental variables that place a preschool child at risk for developmental problems. This measure enables the examiner to systematically explore the child's home and family. The assessor counts the number of specified objects (books, magazines, toys) but also samples "aspects of the quantity and quality of social, emotional, and cognitive support available to three- to six-year-old children within their homes" (p. 236). The direct observation items were derived from the authors' research regarding variables that are associated with optimal development. Information not accessible to direct observation, such as out-of-home activities, are elicited by interview.

The newest edition of the HOME Inventory has fifty-five items (a previous edition had eighty). The sample population included both black and white families. Factor analysis revealed eight subscales: stimulation through toys, games, and reading materials; language stimulation; physical environment; pride, affection, and warmth; stimulation of academic behavior; modeling and encouraging of social maturity; variety of stimulation; and physical punishment. While preliminary studies reveal acceptable internal consistency—higher for the whole measure than for subscales—the stability of the Inventory appears questionable, and the authors therefore recommend multiple assessment of any one family. They report the total scale score to be a reliable predictor of Stanford-Binet IQ. The correlation between score and socioeconomic status is only low to moderate, which suggests that this measure adequately confirms the common professional observation that the qualitative home environment is independent of socioeconomic status.

With regard to the assessment of adaptive behavior, Halpern, Irvin, and Landman (1979) compare direct measurement and rating scale approaches for mildly retarded adolescents and young adults. The authors developed five approaches to the assessment of the variables of purchasing, banking, and job search skills: three oral true-false and multiple-choice tests of knowledge, a behavior rating scale filled out by the parent during an interview, and an applied performance test. Using the adolescents' demonstrated knowledge and actual performance as criteria, the authors conclude that the validity of a parent interview as a measure of the teenagers' adaptive behavior is questionable.

For the preschool population, Zeitlin (1978) offers the Coping Inventory, an adaptive behavior measure that employs observer ratings derived from direct observation of the child's behavior in a peer group. This inventory is now being used and researched in a number of preschool programs in New Jersey. The inventory was devised to assess preschool children who are placed in a special program because of maladaptive social behaviors for whom an individualized educational program (IEP) must be derived. The two primary variables assessed are coping with self and coping with environment, and each variable comprises three dimensions: productivity, activity and flexibility. The Coping Inventory, based on a criterion-referenced model, defines optimal coping behaviors, and the child is rated by this standard, not by a normative scale. The child is rated on each dimension and on his total performance on the inventory's forty-eight items. The ratings derived from the inventory are interpreted on a continuum of minimal competence, developing competence, or functional competence (mastery). The items of the scale can then be transferred directly to an IEP to indicate the most and least adaptive behaviors.

Preliminary studies show a high degree of interrater agreement and internal consistency. The inventory has been shown to discriminate successfully between handicapped and nonhandicapped children, and further validity has been demonstrated by an association between increased coping ratings and increased learning success (Zeitlin, n.d.). Although the Coping Inventory is a rating scale that is most likely to be used to elicit information from a teacher, we include it here because it combines direct observation and criterion referencing, as well as presenting a unique concept of adaptive behavior.

A Free-Response Description Approach

Pervin (1976), studying the interaction of persons and situations, adapted a free-response description approach to investigate the question, "In what ways, and why, do people remain stable (consistent) in their behavior and feelings, and in what ways do they vary according to which situational characteristics?" (p. 466). Pervin's strategy, applicable to adolescents and older pupils, provides a picture of the individual's functioning in circumstances not likely to be directly observable by the examiner. The client is asked to do five things: (1) "List the situations in his or her current life"; (2) "Describe (adjectives, traits, phrases) each situation"; (3) "Describe how he or she feels in each situation"; (4) "Describe his/her behavior in each situation"; and (5) "Indicate the applicability of each situation trait, feeling, and behavior to each situation" (p. 466). While the fifth task is of interest to a researcher, it may be an overly tedious endeavor for individual assessment. The other items provide the assessor with information about the context of the client's life, a means of understanding the client's world from the client's perspective, and a method for comparing a student's functioning in the school with other aspects of his life.

A Structured Family Interview

The structured family interview, described by Friedman (1969), is another approach to assessing the contextual aspects of a child's functioning. The family is assessed in order to define the effects of any family difficulty on the child's learning disorder. The assessor interviews the family to determine their quality of communication, the function of the parents as role models for achievement, parent-child conflicts, patterns of family relationships, and family attitudes toward achievement. The assessor's questions focus attention on the child's functioning in school. The following script shows seven questions that Friedman (1969; p. 164) regularly includes in the interview:

1. (To the parent)   What do you expect of your child in school?
2. (To the child)   What did mother (or father) say? or
                     What does mother expect of you in school?
3. (To the parent)   Is your child meeting that expectation?
4. (To the child)   What did mother say? or
                     Are you meeting that expectation?
5. (To the parent)   Are you disappointed that he is not meeting that expectation?
6. (To the child)   Is mother disappointed about your not meeting that expectation?
7. (To the parent)   How have you tried to help him with this problem?

Friedman recommends that the interviewer and family also discuss how homework and report cards are handled, as well as the family's educational history and values. He points out the advantages of the interviewer spending time with various combinations of family members and with individuals. Of particular interest is Friedman's recommendation that the session include an observation of a sample tutoring session between parent and child.

Chapter 8

❧❧❧❦❦❦

Legal Requirements
for Assessing
Handicapped Children

Robert E. Paul

Like all other areas of human ser-
vices, the practice of school psychology has been irrevocably altered
by recent state and federal legislation that regulates the behavior and
action of practitioners.* This legislation provides that parents need

* Robert E. Paul was, at the time of writing this chapter, supervisor of
the Legal Advocacy Unit of Child Development Programs of the Hall-Mercer

not defer to a professional's training, experience, and skill. Rather, parents who question a professional's assessment and recommendations for placement can object to those recommendations and force the professional to justify and prove the efficacy of those recommendations for that child to an officer at an impartial hearing. Or, if they desire action, the parents can initiate legal proceedings to assert the "right" of their child to a particular educational program, despite the psychologist's professional judgment about the appropriateness of that placement. Thus all school psychologists must supplement their knowledge of their discipline with a thorough understanding of the new federal and state legal requirements for practice.

This chapter analyzes and reviews the most important requirements for educational placement as defined by the most controversial and far-reaching of these legal developments that affect the practice of school psychology, Public Law 94–142.[1] This law was enacted by Congress as the Education of All Handicapped Children Act of 1975, and the final regulations were issued on August 29, 1977 by the Office of Education within the Department of Health, Education, and Welfare. In this chapter, we will refer to these regulations, rather than the law itself, although we will use Pub. L. 94–142 as a convenient shorthand reference for the regulations. The regulations are more specific and detailed than the law itself and are equally binding.

Pub. L. 94–142 orders drastic changes in the procedures a school system's evaluators and testers must use in the identification and assessment of children for special attention and services. The law also establishes many new procedures for the placement of children in special education classes and the education they receive once assigned to a special program. Individual states can ignore these requirements if they do not apply for federal funds under the act.[2] However, local school districts and private schools that receive public money to

Community Mental Health and Mental Retardation Center of Pennsylvania Hospital in Philadelphia, Pennsylvania. In that position, he participated in many due process hearings and resolved cases before they went to hearing under the Education of All Handicapped Children Act (Pub. L. 94–142). He also submitted comments on state and federal proposed regulations to implement this law and assisted other programs and agencies in meeting the law's requirements.

educate children with special needs must conform to these rules if their state chooses to apply for federal funds under the act. Once the state has applied for the money, the local district is bound by the state's application to follow these procedures, whether or not the local district applies for funds.

The purpose of the act seems relatively straightforward; the act is designed: "to assure that all handicapped children have available to them, within the time periods specified by section 612(2)(B) [that is, by September 1, 1978 all children between five and eighteen; by September 1, 1980 all children between three and twenty-one, if the state law does not forbid the provision of schooling for that length of time] a free appropriate public education which emphasizes special education and related services designed to meet their unique needs, to assure that the rights of handicapped children and their parents or guardians are protected, to assist states and localities to provide for the education of all handicapped children, and to assess and assume the effectiveness of efforts to educate handicapped children."[3] This seemingly simple statement is actually fraught with great difficulties for those who must implement it. The difficulty arises from the fundamental contradiction and difficulty that Pub. L. 94–142 poses for psychologists.

Traditionally children identified as possessing a handicapping condition were placed in a class with other children having the same disability, and their teacher structured the class to meet the special needs of the students. Pub. L. 94–142 rejects such disability tracking as the programming of choice whenever possible in favor of mainstreaming. That is, the statute requires that children with special needs be placed in regular classes, supplemented by special services whenever possible, and creates the presumption that regular class placement with normal children is the better procedure.[4] Only if the nature of a child's handicap is so severe that he cannot be educated in regular classes, supplemented by special aids and services, may he be placed in a full-time special education class and receive related services. Pub. L. 94–142 does not prevent special class placement, but it requires that substantial evaluation and due process procedures precede such placement. The school system must first convince the child's parents and a neutral hearing officer of the need for special placement. The laborious nature of this process, designed to protect

children and their families from the effects of inappropriate placement, delays placement even when it is desired by the child's parents.

Thus Pub. L. 94-142 creates a strong presumption against
special education placement which must be rebutted by a substantial
amount of evidence. This presumption, deliberate or not, overrules
professional expertise, positing mainstreaming as the ideal placement, even when the practitioner believes that a restrictive, or special
education, setting would be more beneficial to the child. Pub. L.
94-142 also raises the question of whether a parent's desire to place or
willingness to allow his child to be placed in a special education
classroom violates the child's rights. Surprisingly, the law answers in
the affirmative. Finally, Pub. L. 94-142 creates the need for more
psychologists, a point we discuss at the end of this chapter, yet it
constrains their freedom to apply their professional skills.

Pub. L. 94-142 has created a new interdisciplinary field of law
and education. The most important term in this field is *handicapped
child:* only those children so labeled may receive special education.
The act states three criteria that define the handicapped child. First,
the child must have one of the following physical or emotional
conditions: "mental retardation, hard of hearing, deaf, speech impaired, visually handicapped, seriously emotionally disturbed,
orthopedically impaired, other health impaired, deaf-blind, multi-
handicapped, having specific learning disability."[5] Second, the child
must be identified as needing special education rather than regular
education with supportive services. Third, the child must be identified as needing related services such as transportation, counseling,
and so forth. Thus the act does not recognize a child who is handicapped as a "handicapped child" if he has not been identified as
needing special education.[6] That is, if a handicapped child does not
need special education, he is not "handicapped"; and if he is not
"handicapped," he is not eligible for the related services described by
the act.

Special education and *related services* are two other terms that
have special meaning under Pub. L. 94-142. *Special education* is
specifically designed instruction at no cost to the parents, to meet the
unique needs of a handicapped child, including classroom instruction, instruction in physical education, home instruction, and instruction in hospitals and institutions.[7] *Related services* are those

services such as transportation and other developmental, corrective, and supportive services that assist a handicapped child to benefit from special education. Among them are speech pathology, audiology, psychological services, physical and occupational therapy, recreation, early identification and assessment of disabilities in children, counseling services, medical services for diagnosis or evaluation only, school health services, school social work, and parent counseling and training.[8] Note that the act funds medical services only for identification purposes, but psychological services for treatment as well as diagnostic purposes. However, the latter can be provided only for a child who meets the three criteria that the act specifies as defining a handicapped child. We will now review the legal procedures by which a child is identified as fulfilling these criteria. Very different procedures govern identification, referral, and evaluation initiated by the school district and referral initiated by the child's parent.

Identification Initiated by the School District

Pub. L. 94–142 legislates procedures for protecting schoolchildren's rights during evaluations conducted by the school.[9] In the past the identification of a child as mentally retarded often resulted in his permanent placement in programs for the mentally retarded or his total exclusion from public education. Two landmark federal court cases, *PARC* v. *Pennsylvania* 343 F. Supp. 279 (E.D. Pa. 1972) and *Mills* v. *Board of Education* 348 F. Supp. 866 (D.D.C. 1972), sought respectively to end the classification of children by district employees as mentally retarded or emotionally disturbed. Congress, in adopting Pub. L. 94–142 clearly sought to prevent misclassification of children and their exclusion from full participation in school.

The regulations issued by the Office of Education define minimum standards that must be met in placement evaluations. An evaluator or psychologist must use tests that are:

1. Provided and administered in the child's native language
2. Validated for the specific purpose for which they are employed
3. Administered by trained personnel
4. Tailored to assess specific areas of educational need

5. Administered to children with impaired sensory, manual, or speaking skills in such a manner that the results reflect the child's aptitudes or achievement levels or other factors purportedly measured rather than the impairment.[10]

These requirements seem reasonably straightforward and in line with progressive practice in the field. In addition, the regulations require that no single procedure be the sole criterion for the determination of a child's appropriate educational placement and that no one person perform the entire evaluation and recommendation procedure. Only a multidisciplinary team, including at least one teacher or other person knowledgeable in the area of the child's alleged disability, may make recommendations for placement of children.

The requirement that a team perform the evaluation represents a major change from traditional procedures in which placement was determined by a single counselor, psychologist, teacher, or principal or by a series of reviews within the supervisory chain. The various team members review proposed educational plans and attempt to reconcile the most appropriate plan with the least restrictive placement. Placement is decided by a majority vote, providing an additional protection for the child against misclassification.

The decision of the professional team that a child needs a special education placement may, however, be challenged by the child's parent. If the parent demands a regular class placement, that request must be granted unless the district is prepared to ignore the requirements of Pub. L. 94-142 or to engage in a complicated hearing process to defend its recommendation. The law also subjects the individual psychologist to a possible malpractice suit by a parent who disagrees with a placement recommendation. The usual basis of a malpractice suit is the failure of the professional to comply with the usual standard practices and conduct of that profession. Since Pub. L. 94-142 now sets the professional standard of conduct for psychologists, failure to meet its requirements could be construed as grounds for a malpractice suit.

The testing requirements, like the placement requirements, result from cases in the federal courts. Two cases of note are *Larry P.* v. *Riles* 343 F. Supp. 1306 (N.D. Cal. 1972), aff'd 502 F.2d 963 (1973) and

Diana Martinez v. *Soledad* (unreported). In the latter, a school district that used English-language tests to measure the intelligence of children who spoke only Spanish agreed to use Spanish-language tests for the evaluation of Spanish-speaking children.

In the *Larry P.* case, the plaintiffs complained that the California school districts' admissions procedures for classes for the mentally retarded were racially discriminatory. The evidence showed that the large number of black pupils admitted to classes for the mentally retarded was disproportionate to their numbers in the school district's population. The trial court found that this imbalance resulted from the requirement by the state's department of education that the IQ tests that had sold the most copies be used as the tests to measure intelligence. These scores were then the primary factor in determining admission to classes for the mentally retarded. Evidence produced during a later phase of the trial showed that the state selected the tests on the basis of their sales, ignoring its own experts and statements by the test developers that such tests did not adequately or accurately measure the intelligence of minority children. The court ruled the use of such tests for the evaluation of minority children improper and in violation of Pub. L. 94-142. This case, as well as *PARC* v. *Pennsylvania* and *Mills* v. *Board of Education* (both described earlier), have brought courts into the management of educational systems in special education in a manner similar to the courts' interventions in school integration. School districts and state departments of education complained; Congress enacted Pub. L. 94-142 to require schools to provide better services to handicapped children but to allow the districts options so that they could continue to manage their schools rather than allow the federal courts to do so.

Pub. L. 94-142 mandates that the psychologist, on receiving a referral from a teacher or other employee of the school district, begin the evaluation process by administering a battery of instruments and procedures, not just one test. The assessor must determine that each assessment technique he uses is appropriate for evaluating the individual child, so that the results will reflect the child's true abilities and strengths rather than improperly measure his weaknesses. Further, a psychologist may not undertake any evaluations of the child for possible placement in a special education program without first obtaining written consent from the parents. This consent must describe the activities to be used in the evaluation and must inform the parents they may revoke their consent at any time. If the parents refuse or revoke consent, the child cannot be evaluated unless the district requests a due process hearing and receives a favorable ruling. This procedure, which we describe later in this chapter, requires the school district and the parents to appear before an impartial hearing officer, present whatever evidence or witnesses either side deems appropriate, and make whatever arguments they wish to make. The hearing officer then decides to uphold or overrule the parents' decision not to consent.

Having received consent and administered a series of tests, the psychologist must then present his recommendation to a multidisciplinary team that includes at least one teacher.[12] The team must be composed of persons who know the child, persons who understand the evaluative data, and persons who know the placement options. The team then reviews the child's scores on aptitude, adaptive behavior, and achievement measures; his teachers' recommendations; his physical health; and his social and cultural background. The team must select the least restrictive placement among the available alternatives: regular placement, regular placement with supportive services, part-time regular placement, special placement, home instruction, and institutionalized placement.[13] A special education placement can be made only when the nature or severity of the handicap is such that education in regular classes is unsatisfactory.

The team then meets to make its recommendation for placement and to develop an *individualized educational program* (IEP).[14] This conference ideally includes the parents and any person whose presence the parents desire. Required is the attendance of the child's teacher, a representative of the district qualified to provide or arrange for special education, and the evaluator or someone familiar with the techniques of assessment used and the results of the evaluation. If the district cannot convince the parents to attend, its attempts to involve the parents must be documented in writing; records of telephone calls, correspondence, visits to the parents and the like must appear in the child's records.

At the conference, the participants develop an IEP, which must include:

1. A statement of the child's present level of educational performance
2. Annual goals for the child, including short-term instructional objectives
3. Specific services to be provided and the portion of the regular educational program in which the child will participate, if any
4. Starting date and length of time that services will be provided
5. The criteria which will be applied to measure achievement of educational goals and when the evaluation of the child's progress will be made

A sample IEP would specify that a child entering school for the first time will learn to count to twenty-five and learn the letters of the alphabet within three months of admission to a program. He will remain in the particular program for six months. After three months, the teacher will test the child's ability to count and recognize the letters of the alphabet and will note his performance in his records.

If the parents consent to the IEP, the child is placed. If the parent disagrees with the placement, he is entitled to employ the due process procedures established under Pub. L. 94–142.[15] Individual states may elect to employ a mediation proceeding as an intervening step prior to the more formal procedures of a due process hearing. Such a conference is conducted by a school district employee not involved in the original placement decision. If the placement conference fails to resolve the differences between the school district and the parents, the school district must then notify the parents of their right to a full due process hearing.[16] This notice must contain the following:

1. Notice of the parents' right to review the records of the determination of placement
2. A description of the action proposed or refused by the agency, an explanation of the reasons for its decision, a description of options reviewed and rejected, and the reasons for rejection
3. A description of each evaluation procedure, test, record, or report the district used
4. Other factors used in the determination

The notice must be written in plain language and communicated to the parents in their native language or mode of communication. The district must insure that the parents understand the content of the notice and must document the manner in which it complied with this obligation.

The notice must also inform the parents of their right to an "independent educational evaluation" at public expense if they disagree with the evaluation of the school district.[17] The district has the right to ask for a hearing to shift the financial burden for this evaluation to the parent; but if the district loses that hearing, the district is obligated to pay for the evaluation or to ensure the evaluation is provided at no expense to the family. The evaluation must be conducted by a qualified examiner not employed by the district. If the parents request a hearing, the district must also inform them of any available free or low-cost legal and other relevant services, such as those provided by chapters of the Association for Retarded Citizens or other advocacy groups in the community that assist parents in such hearings.

The hearing must be conducted before an impartial hearing officer not employed by the school district or other educational entity mandated to provide education to that child.[18] At the hearing, the parents can be represented by counsel and other persons with special expertise in the problems of handicapped children. Parents can present evidence, cross-examine the district's witnesses, and prevent material that they received fewer than five days previous to the hearing from being used in the determination. Parents can obtain a written or electronic record of the proceeding and receive written findings of fact and the decision of the officer. The decision rendered by the hearing officer must relate to educational placement, must comport with the concept of least restrictive alternative (that is, attempt to provide an alternative to full-time placement in classes only for handicapped children), and must be made and issued within forty-five days of the parents' request for the hearing. The parents can appeal the hearing officer's decision to their state's department of education; if dissatisfied with a decision at that level, they may appeal to the state or federal courts. If the parents appeal to the state, the state must issue its decision in the matter within thirty days.

While this process is taking place, the child may not be transferred to another placement without agreement between the parents and the school system.[19] If the placement that is the subject of the hearing is to be the child's first school experience, the child must be placed in public school pending the outcome of the hearing, provided that the parents consent. However, and this is a crucial loophole in the protections afforded parents and children, the comment to the section describing such provisionary placement states that "While the placement may not be changed, this does not preclude the agency [that is, the school system] from using its normal procedures for dealing with children who are endangering themselves or others."[20]

Despite this language, at least one federal court has clearly held that the special education requirements of Pub. L. 94–142 take precedence over ordinary school disciplinary proceedings and that a special education student may not be expelled for ten days or more without a prior IEP—see *Stuart* v. *Danbury School District* 443 F. Supp. 235 (D. Conn. 1978). Many states have issued regulations that seek to protect the handicapped child from school disciplinary proceedings that approximate the rule set out in *Stuart*.

Procedures Initiated by Parents

The requirements designed to prevent the mislabeling and inappropriate placement of children unfortunately impede parents who wish to obtain appropriate education for their child who has special needs. In this section, we discuss the procedures for a parent who seeks to have his child assigned to a class other than the one in which he was placed by the district.

The requirement that the child's placement cannot be changed, unless the school district and the parents agree otherwise, works against the parents. Since the parents want a change and the district may not, any delay only adds further to the frustration that the parents may already feel because their child is experiencing educational difficulties. The requirement that the school use various instruments and evaluators forces more delay. Further, the parents' desire to place their child in a special education program or in a private school at public expense is frustrated under the law if the school district proposes a less restrictive setting that seems adequate to the child's problems.[21] There are legal precedents that parents can rely on in appealing decisions against private school placements (see, for example, *Levy* v. *Department of Education*, 399A, 2d 159, Pa. Commonwealth, 1979). However, as plaintiffs, the parents must retain a lawyer, incur various expenses, and wait for the case to be heard. Obviously, the court may finally rule against the parents; indeed, that parents may desire a more restrictive setting than the school district desires is a situation that challenges the theory of Pub. L. 94-142. Rightly or wrongly, the drafters believed that parents would always champion in-home placement and public school programming.[22]

To initiate a change in placement, the parents can ask the district for an evaluation of their child. However, federal law does not specify a deadline by which the evaluation must be completed, although states may mandate deadlines. To avoid delay, a parent may obtain an independent evaluation at his own expense. Pub. L. 94-142 requires that the independent evaluator meet the professional standards defined by the school system.[23] In practice, this requirement has the effect that if the evaluator is not a certified school psychologist accredited by the state educational authorities, the district can ignore the evaluation unless it is approved by a local district psychologist. Thus parents wishing to retain an independent evaluator may encounter difficulties in finding a qualified evaluator. Many local community mental health centers, for example, are reluctant to commit their resources to perform one-time evaluations for school placement if the family is not planning to enter a therapeutic program; the centers provide evaluations only as a precursor to therapy.

If the parents succeed in retaining an evaluator who is a certified school psychologist, the evaluator's report must be reviewed by the school's placement team. If the team takes no action, the parents' only recourse is to initiate a legal suit, a step many parents are reluctant to take. In the final analysis, then, parents who seek a special education placement against the views of the school district can challenge the district's choice of the least restrictive placement only through extraordinary efforts in the courts. A district that insists on regular class placement and supportive services usually prevails against the parents in these cases.

The Effects of Pub. L. 94-142 on School Psychologists

The full effects of Pub. L. 94-142 on school psychologists' practice will be unclear for many years to come. Many of these effects were unforeseen by the drafters of the legislation; some are beneficial to the children involved, and others not. The children who benefit most are those who would be placed in classes for the mentally retarded were it not for the new requirements for such placement. The children who do not benefit are those who need more restriction and structure than they will receive in the least restrictive alternative setting. These children may not benefit from such placements but will be so placed, often over the parents' or psychologist's objections.

The law's effects on school psychologists are somewhat more difficult to discover or to predict. Even at this early stage, it is obvious that the law creates a need for more school psychologists, particularly those with experience in administering and interpreting the newer assessment instruments. School districts will hire more psychologists to conduct the complex assessments required by the law and to answer parents' requests that their children be reassessed. These psychologists will encounter increased opportunities and responsibilities in the area of special education, as administrators and facilitators of special education placements. Other psychologists will be employed as hearing officers and some will enter private practice as independent evaluators.

Although this increased involvement with the legal system creates many career opportunities, the involvement of the legal system in various professional fields reduces the power of those professionals—as psychiatrists have discovered—because they are required to rely on legal, rather than clinical or evaluative, techniques in reviewing cases. Pub. L. 94–142 limits school psychologists' role and importance in the placement process. No longer can they administer the tests they deem most appropriate, make recommendations, and expect those recommendations to be followed. Instead, the psychologist is merely one member of a multidisciplinary team. The psychologist must present his findings to the team members, most of whom have no professional training in assessment; yet they can override the psychologist's opinion or exert pressure that impinges on the conduct of the psychologist. The psychologist's freedom to administer tests and to expect that his interpretations will prevail in special education decisions has been eroded and, in fact, destroyed. The school psychologist is now, like many other professionals, subject to scrutiny and questioning by persons with authority to overrule his professional judgment.

Every school psychologist must become intimately familiar with the new legal requirements. Pub. L. 94–142 now defines the standards of professional conduct in the placement of children with special needs.

Notes

1. 20 U.S.C.A. 1401 et seq.
2. On state compliance, see 45 C.F.R. 121a.2 (Federal Register, August 23, 1977).
3. Education of All Handicapped Children Act, Section 601, 20 U.S.C. 1401.
4. On mainstreaming, see 45 C.F.R. 121a.550(b)(1) and (2).
5. 20 U.S.C.A. 1402. See also 45 C.F.R. 121a.5a and the S.L.D. Regulations (Federal Register, December 29, 1977).
6. 45 C.F.R. 121a.14 comment (1).
7. 45 C.F.R. 121a.14.
8. 45 C.F.R. 121a.13.
9. See Conference Report on Pub. L. 94–142, U.S. Code Congressional and Administrative News, 94th Congress, First Session, p. 1428.
10. 45 C.F.R. 121a.532.
11. On consent, see 45 C.F.R. 121a.500(a)–(c).
12. For regulations regarding the placement team, see 45 C.F.R. 121a.532(e), 553(a)(1)–(4).
13. 45 C.F.R. 121a.550(b), 550(b)(2), 551, and 551(b)(2) discuss placement and the least restrictive alternative.
14. On IEP procedures, see 45 C.F.R. 121a.340–349; specifically, 344(a)(1)(2) and (b)(1)(2) on persons in attendance; 345(d) on documenting attempts to notify parents; 346 on criteria for an IEP.
15. See 45 C.F.R. 121a.500.
16. 45 C.F.R. 121a.504–505 describe the notification process.
17. 45 C.F.R. 121a.503(a)(3)(i), (a)(3)(ii), 503(b), and 506(c) describe the preparation for an independent educational evaluation.
18. 45 C.F.R. 121a.507, 508, and 510 describe the hearing; 550–552 describe the guidelines for the hearing officer's decision; 511, 512(a), and 512(b) describe the appeals procedure.
19. 45 C.F.R. 121a.513(a) and (b) discuss the placement of the child pending the completion of the hearing and the appeal.
20. 45 C.F.R. 121a.513 comment.
21. See 45 C.F.R. 121a.550 and 552.
22. See 45 C.F.R. 121a.552 comment 2.
23. 45 C.F.R. 121a.503(e).

Chapter 9

᷈᷈᷈᷈᷈᷈

Communicating Assessment Results and Anticipating Future Trends

As we have seen, assessment is a complex cognitive process. In this chapter, we discuss the participation of the child, the parents, and the teacher in the final stage of the assessment process—educational planning—and the communication of the results of assessments to teachers. We conclude by noting current trends that may predict the future of psychological assessment of schoolchildren.

Participation in Planning

During the administration of measures, the child, the referral agent, and family members serve largely to provide the assessor with the information and data he needs. In communicating his findings and devising educational plans for the child, the assessor is mandated to involve the teacher and family as active participants. Such involvement can increase the relevance of the assessment and enhance the participants' motivation and commitment to the plan.

Ozer (1977, 1980) increases the participant roles of teacher, parent, and child to the level of collaborators, so that the assessment not only elicits observations and information, but includes the participation of all concerned in the planning. The assessor does not provide solutions for the referral agent, but explores the problem in collaboration with those involved with the child. The assessors' primary function is to structure this exploration.

Concern with the role of the child and others as active collaborators reflects the values that these individuals have a right to reasonable control over what happens to them and that assessment can be a growth-enhancing process, not merely the collection and reporting of information (Fischer, 1970). The assessor expresses these values throughout the assessment by informing those involved about what is taking place and by asking those involved about their feelings and opinions. The assessor may share the child's test results with him, discussing his patterns of performance on achievement measures, areas of mastery, areas in need of intervention, and patterns of behavior that appear to obstruct or enhance his functioning. This procedure, when used judiciously, communicates a profound impression of respect to the child and may provide the assessor with additional information about the child. Intermittent reports to the teacher during the course of the assessment are similarly helpful.

After all testing is completed, the assessor can prepare the pupil for the upcoming family session by sharing his impressions and recommendations. Such preparation communicates to the child that he is an individual whose integrity is perceived and respected and allows the assessor to observe the child's reactions to this information. Koesel (1976) reports significantly higher academic achievement and attitude among ninth- and tenth-grade suburban students who participated in their own diagnosis, compared to students who did not receive information or those who were not allowed to participate.

The assessor's sharing his information with the pupil not only conveys the message that the pupil is considered a serious participant, but also reduces the problems that can occur when the parents reinterpret the findings to the child. However, there are situations in which the pupil should not attend the initial planning session. For example, if the assessor's diagnosis is mental retardation, it may be preferable for the assessor to meet with the parents and teachers first. The child's presence at such a session might interfere with a free discussion that allows the parents to voice their affective reactions. A second meeting can be arranged, during which the assessor can summarize for the child the proposed courses of action.

The presence of other family members, such as siblings, is a decision that many pupils can make by themselves. The assessor, however, should be aware of the family constellation and use his judgment in interpreting a child's ambivalent response to having his siblings present. If the assessor anticipates that the assessment results will provide ammunition for sibling rivalry, siblings should not be invited.

Assessment Reports

Tallent (1976) offers a comprehensive guide to writing assessment reports. Here we discuss several issues specific to reports in the school setting. If such reports are to be useful, they must address the problems mentioned in the original referral. While the assessor may find other issues during the course of the assessment, his attention to the referral questions serves to guide the assessment process, organize the material reported, and determine the nature of the recommendations. Attention to the referral issues will preclude the assessor from deriving lists of irrelevant recommendations and will compel him to think about appropriate remediations.

Hudgins and Shultz (1978, pp. 57–58) offer four commandments for report writing:

1. "Thou shalt first enter the referral agent's frame of reference."
2. "Thou shalt personalize the evaluation."

3. "Thou shalt write about behavior."
4. "Thou shalt respond to the referral question."

The third rule is particularly important. The report should not be a list of test results, but a statement about the individual's integrated behavior as revealed by these results. If the assessor uses the referral issues to organize the report and discusses the data in relationship to these issues, his report is likely to be more meaningful and more comprehensible to his readers. One can report that a child demonstrates a deficiency in the ability to give verbal definitions of vocabulary words and above average ability to describe socially expected behavior, but such descriptions reveal little or nothing about what should be done to help the child.

Although the assessor may wish to describe the data upon which he is basing his inferences, these citations can be reported as examples that supplement the interpretation. Hudgins and Shultz summarize their recommendations by advising that "(1) data should come from many sources, (2) these data should be integrated into a differentiated, coherent, referral-specific narrative, and (3) the narrative should culminate in personally relevant decisions concerning the client's functioning, together with specific plans for improvement in his/her functioning" (p. 63).

Making specific recommendations can be the most difficult aspect of the assessment process, depending on the assessor's expertise in addressing specific classroom and educational issues and depending on the willingness of other school professionals to view the assessor as an appropriate consultant on such issues. For example, if a teacher sees the assessor solely as a source of information about a pupil's cognitive level and appropriate placement of the pupil, it may be futile for the assessor to recommend specific remedial activities for the classroom. Our discussion assumes, however, that the assessor is in an educational setting in which he is expected to relate his assessment findings to the educational program and suggest remedial strategies.

Catterall (1970) outlines four categories of interventions that the assessor should consider in devising remedial strategies. Environmental interventions "indirectly attempt to help the student by making adequate provisions . . . in the total curriculum/environ-

mental setting" (p. 6). Environmental interventions include placement decisions, program planning, and recommendations about
rules that should structure the child's curriculum and behavior. Second, the assessor may recommend installed interventions in which
an element of the child's environment—a technique, person, or
stimulus—is changed. Installed interventions include the provision
of a catalyst, new stimulation or destimulation, positive reinforcement, punishment, or the imposition of a moratorium.

Third, assigned interventions, techniques and exercises that
help the child change his personal or social behavior, may be recommended. Behavior exercises and techniques for role shifting and
attitude shifting are examples of assigned interventions. Transac-
tional interventions are those in which "the interventionist works
with the student in a direct, personal way" (p. 9); for example,
sensitization techniques, records-production dialogues, group dialogue, and personal dialogue.

In determining specific interventions, the assessor must analyze the diagnostic data for patterns of strengths, weaknesses, and
coping strategies. The assessor's professional experience, his knowledge of the available options, and his familiarity with the literature
contribute to his analysis. Blanco (1971) surveyed psychologists to
determine their most frequent recommendations for specific circumstances. Although these recommendations have not been objectively
evaluated and the criteria of their applicability are not specified, this
list can be useful to assessors.

The assessor must also ensure that any proposed educational
recommendations are within the province of his expertise and do not
impinge on other professionals' specialties. As a general rule, it is
inappropriate for a psychologist to specify the instructional materials
to be used, although highly appropriate for him to identify areas of
need and strategies that may enhance the pupil's functioning. For
example, a psychologist could recommend that audiovisual materials
be included in a pupil's program for subjects that require considerable independent reading, based on the disparity between the child's
cognitive skills and his reading ability. An educational specialist
would then specify what types of audiovisual materials to obtain and
how to incorporate these into the child's program.

To supplement available assessment approaches, assessors
need an objective method to collect work samples of pupils' perfor-

mances in response to a number of instructional strategies. Such a method would enable the assessor to determine which instructional objectives and pedagogical approaches are most effective in helping a particular student. Lidz (1977b) has proposed a model for such comparative analyses, but it has not yet been thoroughly tested. Jenkins and Larson (1979) propose an approach that tests alternative instructional strategies for mastery of word recognition. The authors compared the effects of five methods of error correction and a "no correction" control. The authors explain how their procedure can be applied diagnostically to determine which method shows superiority for individual students.

Assessors should also maintain a file of lists of interventions for frequent dysfunctions, such as letter reversals, hyperactivity, memory deficits and auditory perceptual dysfunctions. These recommendations can be attached to reports to supplement more individualized recommendations. Recommended sources of such specific instructional activities include:

Canfield, J. and Wells, H. C. *One Hundred Ways to Enhance Self-Concept in the Classroom.* Englewood Cliffs, N.J.: Prentice-Hall, 1976.

Cantwell, D. P. (Ed.). *The Hyperactive Child.* N.Y.: Spectrum Publications, 1975.

Della-Piana, G. *Reading Diagnosis and Prescription.* N.Y.: Holt, Rinehart and Winston, 1968.

Fernald, G. M. *Remedial Techniques in Basic School Subjects.* N.Y.: McGraw-Hill, 1943.

Hammill, D. D. and Bartel, N. R. *Teaching Children with Learning and Behavior Problems.* Boston: Allyn & Bacon, 1975.

Johnson, D. J. and Myklebust, H. R. *Learning Disabilities.* N.Y.: Grune & Stratton, 1967.

Karnes, M. B. *Helping Young Children Develop Language Skills: A Book of Activities.* Washington, D.C.: Council of Exceptional Children, 1968.

Lovitt, T. C. *Managing Inappropriate Behaviors in the Classroom.* ED 157255, EC 111266. Reston, Va.: Council of Exceptional Children, 1978.

Spache, E. B. *Reading Activities for Child Involvement.* Boston: Allyn & Bacon, 1973.

Strain, P. S., Cooke, T. P., and Apollini, T. *Teaching Exceptional Children*. N.Y.: Academic Press, 1976.
Swift, M. S. and Spivak, G. *Alternative Teaching Strategies*. Champaign, Ill.: Research Press, 1975.

The psychologist, as clinician and consultant, must serve his clients and professional colleagues as a helpful resource, but must avoid implying that he has answers to every question. Even the most knowing psychologist obviously does not have all the answers, and he knows that providing answers does not always provide a solution. Defining areas of need, asking questions that provoke problem solving in others, providing examples of possible interventions, and promoting clearer perception of direction and objectives—all are valuable consultation skills.

These skills are particularly important in communicating recommendations to teachers. Teachers often hope for solutions external to themselves, while psychologists and assessors often suggest that teachers modify their behavior (Lambert, 1976). Lambert reports that about half of the solutions that teachers propose as interventions for referred pupils involve modifications intrinsic to the classroom. Intrinsic modifications include changes in presentation of subject matter, learning atmosphere, and curriculum. Extrinsic modifications include the provision of individual attention (necessitating an aide), changes in the pupil's behavior or ability, and referral for professional therapy or attention. Lambert concludes that many teachers need help in developing more specific descriptions of problem behaviors in order to increase the elicitation of appropriate solutions. She also cautions assessment consultants of the need to become informed of the teacher's expectations and ability to perceive and describe behavior.

Tombari and Bergan (1978) demonstrate the significant effect of the consultant's verbal cues on teachers. The cues that reflect medical versus behavioral models differentially affect beginning teachers' conceptualizations of pupil adjustment problems, so that these conceptualizations tend to coincide with the model communicated by the consultant. Furthermore, teachers who are provided with behavioral cues express greater optimism about their ability to solve their pupil's problems in the classroom setting. Thus the consultant's skill in improving the teacher's ability to describe problem behaviors increases the likelihood that the teacher will perceive the solution to the problem as lying within the dimensions of the classroom situation.

The Future of Assessment

We turn now to a discussion of current trends in the assessment literature that indicate the probable future course for the assessment of the child in school. Of course, current trends in research do not alone determine future practice; events in the educational disciplines and legislation such as Pub. L. 94-142 will also shape future practice. (See Chapter Eight for a discussion of Pub. L. 94-142.)

Pluralistic Norms

In the use of assessment for the purpose of classification, the development of pluralistic norms is of particular consequence to psychological assessors. Mercer and Lewis' (1977) SOMPA (System of Multicultural Pluralistic Assessment) adds to the medical model a more relativistic approach to educational classification by comparing the child not only with national, but with cultural, norms. Determination of "at risk" status is also established on the basis of physical performance, health, and adaptive behavioral information. Two assumptions of this approach are of particular concern because they have potentially negative consequences for the children assessed. First, it appears that the authors' solution to the inadequacies of traditional normative assessment has been to extend the normative basis for classification rather than to consider nonnormative dynamic approaches like those of Budoff (1974) and Feuerstein (1979). (See Chapter Three for a discussion of dynamic approaches.) One could use both national and cultural norms to determine "at risk" status and the dynamic strategies to measure a child's capacity to profit from instruction.

The second questionable assumption is that the definition of "at risk" is culturally relative. Certainly, it is inexcusable to label a child "retarded" if he is deficient only in terms of national but not cultural norms. The child who is deficient in national norms is nevertheless at risk for failure and needs special programming. Similarly, while physical aggression is an effective strategy in rough neighborhoods, the child whose repertory of problem solving is limited to this strategy is handicapped in his ability to negotiate societal demands and possibilities. Thus, while it is important to determine that a child is not retarded in the context of his own cultural group, the discrepancy between the child's level of functioning and a national norm is a useful index of the child's chances of mastering one of the basic developmental tasks of childhood— academic achievement. Both the mastery of specific content and the experience of accomplishment itself are important for childrens' development. To ensure that children of all cultural backgrounds have these opportunities, assessors can use an "at risk" index that signals the need for intervention.

Cognitive Style

Goldstein and Blackman (1977) define cognitive style as "a hypothetical construct that is posited to explain the mediation between stimuli and responses. The term . . . refers to how individuals conceptually organize the environment" (p. 462). Differences among individuals in their cognitive style is hypothesized to account for previously unexplained variance in individual cognitive behavior. Goldstein and Blackman list seven dimensions of cognitive style:

1. Tolerance for unrealistic experiences
2. Conceptual differentiation: ability to differentiate concepts into subcategories
3. Constricted-flexible control: susceptibility to distraction
4. Leveling-sharpening: assimilation of new concepts in terms of previous concepts
5. Scanning: ability to check one's judgments
6. Contrast reactivity: sensitivity to stimulus differences
7. Field articulation: field dependence

Other cognitive dimensions include authoritarianism, dogmatism, cognitive complexity, and integrative complexity. Goldstein and Blackman also discuss means of measuring these dimensions. Kagan (1965) introduces the dimension of reflection-impulsivity.

Concepts like cognitive style suggest that individuals' traits characterize their interaction with their environment and that an understanding of such traits would allow one to predict an individual's response. In the past, the primary trait of interest was "intelligence"; yet this aptitude predicted only about half of the variance of a child's level of interaction with instructional demands, particularly for children whose performance on the intelligence measures was average or above average. Current efforts to define traits and aptitudes relevant to educational performance seek to overcome the limitations of earlier trait theories by specifying aptitudes that are more clearly associated with criteria of interest to researchers and practitioners, and which can be reliably measured. Much research is required to determine the critical response tendencies for specified situations, to discern their origin, and to devise methods to modify inadequate response tendencies. But cognitive style has considerably greater potential relevance for the assessment of schoolchildren than more traditional trait concepts such as introversion-extroversion. Burger and Blackman (1978, 1979) are researching this area, and Abikoff (1979) reviews the current status of cognitive training studies.

The cognitive dimension of reflective and impulsive styles has had a considerable influence on educational psychology. Kagan (1965) defines this dimension as "the child's consistent tendency to display slow or fast response times in problem situations with high response uncertainty. The results are persuasive in suggesting that a tendency for reflection increases with age, is stable over periods as long as twenty months, manifests pervasive generality across varied task situations, and is linked to some fundamental aspects of the child's personality organization" (p. 309). Impulsivity signifies performance that is quick but inaccurate; accurate, fast responses are not impulsive ones. Not all children are readily classifiable as reflective or impulsive; that is, this characteristic is not equally meaningful for everyone, although about 60 percent of preschool and elementary children can be described in these terms (Margolis and Brannigan, 1978). Furthermore, reflection or impulsivity do not characterize all aspects and modalities of any one child's functioning; for example, a child may be impulsive on auditory tasks but not on visual ones (Kennedy and Butter, 1978). Kagan (1965) reports associations between this cognitive dimension and interactions with the environment; for example, reflective children tend to avoid risky situations.

Reflection and impulsivity consist of two variables: speed and accuracy. Some tasks require both; in social interactions, however, impulsivity may indicate better adaptability than reflection. Of course, impulsive responses are undesirable in situations requiring accuracy, and thus are maladaptive in many circumstances of the school situation (Digate and others, 1978). So, children who were perceived as active, spontaneous, and even delightful at home encounter difficulties in classes that require the inhibition of responses, regulation, and accuracy. Digate and her associates review six procedures to reduce impulsive responses and increase reflective ones: required delay, direct instruction, self-verbalization, differentiation training, modeling, and learning about the consequences of responses.

Several other dimensions of cognitive style seem promising in discriminating between adequate and dysfunctional learners (Beck, 1977; Keogh and Donlon, 1972). Witkin, Goodenough, and Karp (1967) report stability in the cognitive style dimension of field dependence-independence from age eight through seventeen, as well as consistency across tasks on measures of this variable. Witkin and others (1977) discuss the educational implications of this dimension of cognitive style. Field dependent individuals, for example, are generally more alert to social stimuli and are better at mastering material with social content. Field dependent learners respond more favorably to extrinsic reinforcers, and field independent learners to intrinsic ones. In their cognitive processing, the field independent rely more on mediating concepts in problem solving, while the field dependent tend to rely more on externally available information and external structure. Teachers' pedagogical preferences correlate with their own tendencies toward field dependence, and the match between the teacher's style and the pupil's affects the pupil's perception of his teacher.

The investigation of cognitive style during an assessment provides information about how a student learns, an important supplement to the information provided by other assessment procedures. Stott's (1978) screening assessment of learning styles yields an informal determination of strategies that appear to interfere with a pupil's success in learning. More research is needed to relate cognitive styles to pupils' functioning in class, to devise measures of these styles, and to determine how they influence other dimensions of the learning situation. That attention to cognitive processes will continue to orient future research is suggested by Mischel's (1979) comment that "In the decade now ending, many of us have come to recognize increasingly that an adequate analysis of behavior cannot proceed without serious attention to the cognitive processes of both the actors and the observers, the subjects and scientists of our field" (p. 752).

Aptitude-Treatment Interactions

As we have discussed earlier, few psychologists hold to a strict environmental or organismic theory to account for behavior. The most meaningful resolution of these extremes is a position that recognizes that organic and environmental factors interact (Mischel, 1977, 1979). The interactionist approach to assessment is expressed by Cronbach (1957) in the concept of aptitude-treatment interactions (ATI). The Aptitude-Treatment approach suggests that neither behavior nor prescriptions for intervention can be successfully described or predicted by looking solely at either the organism or environment. Behavior can be known only in the context of a situation, and intervention has no effects without considering such contextured interactions. Although the literature on ATI is already vast, the full development of the approach will continue to be a topic of future research.

The assumptions of aptitude-treatment interaction inform diagnostic-prescriptive teaching (Ysseldyke, 1973). (Diagnostic-prescriptive approaches are discussed in Chapter Four.) Diagnostic-prescriptive approaches require that the assessment focus on the result of the interaction of individual characteristics with specific materials, instructional strategies, and situational variables. Researchers have not yet determined which variables interact in what way with other variables to produce predictable outcomes, and thus ATI is an assessment procedure that can be used in individual cases, but has no body of data that can be readily applied to any given instructional situation. Ysseldyke (1973) describes a number of methodological problems that have hindered research in this area; the diagnostic measures employed have been a notable weak point in the research (Lilly and Kelleher, 1973). D. E. Hunt (1975) criticizes ATI as a model for person-environment interactions because it relies on too narrow, purely statistical definitions. Delaney (1978), however, reports significant ATI effects in studying university students if the variables are highly specific, for example, verbal fluency rather than verbal ability. Bryant and others (1977) are applying an interactional approach to the study of learning disabilities.

While interactional research is of interest and relevance to all education (Scandura, 1977), the ability to match individuals with specific instructional approaches is most important in treating children who require special attention because they fail to respond to traditional instruction. ATI specifications could guide assessment and special education pedagogy if researchers can determine the instances in which this refined approach is applicable (for example, see Yen, 1978). However, the mastery of some materials seems best effected by strategies irrelevant to individual idiosyncracies. For example, if one conceptualizes reading as primarily auditory-visual perception and memory in the early stages and as primarily a language processing activity once decoding is mastered, then matching the learner's strengths with the instructional mode is irrelevant; instead, strengthening the learner's weaknesses and helping him develop compensatory strategies are recommended. For those learning tasks for which no one instructional mode is best, one could explore available approaches to determine which hinder and which promote the child's success. Thus, it is an error to consider ATI as a panacea for all instructional questions, and only further research will define when an ATI approach is relevant and how it can be applied.

Neuropsychology

Neuropsychological assessment is the closest realization of the medical model available to psychologists. The critical assumption is that behavioral data are a source of inferences about the functioning of the central nervous system and remedial treatment (Boll, 1977; Schwalb, Blau, and Blau, 1969). As medical technology improves, the psychologist's contribution to neuropsychology will probably be less in the diagnosis, localization, and specification of neurological dysfunction than in the elaboration of how such disorders are manifested in the behavior of the affected individual and strategies for remediation and rehabilitation. However, screening for neuropsychological dysfunction will remain a useful assessment activity, as the psychologist is the professional most likely to become aware of the more complex and subtle chronic dysfunctions that often do not become manifest until a child is faced with the demands of school. The distinction between hyperkinetic syndrome and anxiety reaction, for example, is of direct relevance to treatment, and the psychologist is often in the position of contributing to this diagnosis. Diagnoses of organic dysfunction, however, cannot be made based on a pupil's performance on the WISC-R or other measures that narrowly sample behavior.

The search to relate neuropsychological factors and behavior resembles the diagnostic-remedial model (see Chapter One) in that the researcher seeks to determine cognitive-perceptual capacities that are necessary prerequisites for basic achievement, to specify the ways in which dysfunctions interfere with mastery, and to derive methods for remediation of such dysfunctions (Braun and others, 1965). The validity of available assessment procedures to measure such functions is questionable, however, and the sensory, perceptual, and motor correlates that have been specified may not be those critical to learning tasks (Adelman, 1978; Blackman and Burger, 1972).

Attempts to realize a diagnostic-remedial model have shown that there is no clear, direct, or necessary connection between diagnosis and remediation. A child with organically based hyperactivity and a child with anxiety based overactivity may both respond to the same remedial methods in the classroom, although recommendations for noneducational interventions are dependent on the diagnosis. For example, the former child might benefit from medication, the latter from psychotherapy.

Neuropsychological research may also help to clarify present confusion about learning disabilities. While most professionals now assert that the learning disabled are not a homogeneous population, this concept seems to provoke professional anxiety rather than the response that heterogeneity is a natural consequence of the brain itself being so multifaceted and complex (Sabatino, 1968). Perceptual-motor handicaps were the first learning disability to be diagnosed and identified. Central processing language disorders, however, in many instances are diagnosed as emotional or volitional disturbances rather than as neurological impairments. In other words, researchers have identified the behavioral manifestations of perceptual-motor dysfunction and inconsistency in function, but have not yet done so for verbal processing mechanisms.

Neuropsychological assessment is just beginning to make a significant contribution. In the future, this approach may incorporate the study of cognitive styles and strategies, discussed earlier, and yield significant information about aptitudes in aptitude-treatment interactions.

Measurement of Cognitive Functioning

Federal and state legislation have already forced changes in the ways that intelligence is measured, and we are likely to see continuing changes in this area. Current alternatives to traditional cognitive assessment include pluralistic norms, dynamic procedures, and supplementary social, adaptive, and other noncognitive measures (Brooks, 1979; Fischer, 1969; Messick, 1979; Sundberg, Snowden, and Reynolds, 1978). Too, the prediction of grades or achievement test scores will probably not continue to be considered an adequate criterion for the validity of cognitive measures. Whether intelligence tests should strive to assess and define that abstraction called "intelligence" or whether they should merely predict intelligent behavior, however defined, continues to be a moot point; researchers are exploring both goals. The criticism of intelligence tests as poor predictors of "success in life" is obviously invalid, unless one naively believes that success in life depends primarily or solely on cognitive capacity. Clearly, there is more to life (and even intelligence) than cognition, and one cannot criticize measures designed to assess a limited variable for failing to incorporate a host of variables. Some researchers and test designers, recognizing that intelligence is too complex a variable to be measured by any one test, use *cognitive skills* or *academic aptitude* to label the abilities assessed by testing. The McCarthy Scales of Children's Abilities (McCarthy, 1972), for example, has a General Cognitive Index.

In the future, assessors will rely less on cognitive measures for classification; the determination of a numerical point on a cognitive scale will be replaced by analyses of error patterns, coping strategies, strengths and weaknesses, patterns of performance suggestive of etiology, and remedial strategies. Furthermore, if intelligence is the product of interactions between an organism and its environment, then certain environmental opportunities are required for organisms to realize their functional potential. Evidence that a group of individuals consistently scores lower on measures of intelligence need not imply genetic differences but environmental factors that inhibit cognitive development. Research is more appropriately directed at factors that limit environmental opportunities rather than at factors purported to document genetic inferiority.

Assessment continues to be a vital activity for the professional. Although many changes are necessary, such changes promise to increase the pertinence of assessment for the educational setting and the level of challenge and excitement for the assessor. It is hoped that this book's message is clear—assessment is a tool of, not an alternative to, consultation.

References

Abikoff, H. "Cognitive Training Interventions in Children: Review of a New Approach." *Journal of Learning Disabilities*, 1979, *12*(3), 65.

Adams, H. E., Doster, J. A., and Calhoun, K. S. "A Psychologically Based System of Response Classification." In A. R. Ciminero, K. S. Calhoun, and H. E. Adams (Eds.), *Handbook of Behaviorial Assessment*. New York: Wiley, 1977.

Adelman, H. S. "The Not So Specific Learning Disability Population." *Exceptional Children*, 1970–1971, *37*, 528–533.

Adelman, H. S. "Diagnostic Classification of Learning Problems." *American Journal of Orthopsychiatry*, 1978, *48*(4), 717–726.

Ahr, A. E. "The Psychological Referral: A Procedural Approach." *Psychology in the Schools*, 1965, *2*(2), 224–228.

Airasian, P. W., and Bart, W. M. "Validating A Priori Instructional

Hierarchies." *Journal of Educational Measurement*, 1975, *12*(3), 163–173.

Aliotti, N. C. "Covert Assessment in Psychoeducational Testing." *Psychology in the Schools*, 1977, *14*(4), 438–443.

Alker, H. A. "Is Personality Situationally Specific or Intrapsychically Consistent?" *Journal of Personality*, 1972, *40*(1), 1–16.

Allen, R. M., and Collins, M. G. "Suggestions for the Adaptive Administration of Intelligence Tests for Those with Cerebral Palsy." *Cerebral Palsy Review*, 1955, *16*, 1174.

Allport, G. W., and Vernon, P. E. *Studies in Expressive Movement*. New York: Macmillan, 1933.

Alper, T. G., and White, O. R. "The Behavior Description Referral Form: A Tool for the School Psychologist in the Elementary School." *Journal of School Psychology*, 1971, *9*(2), 177–181.

Anastasi, A. "Psychology, Psychologists, and Psychological Testing." *American Psychologist*, 1967, *22*, 297–305.

Ancevich, S. S., and Payne, R. W. "The Investigation and Treatment of a Reading Disability in a Child of Normal Intelligence." *Journal of Clinical Psychology*, 1961, *17*, 416–420.

Anderson, S. B., Ball, S., Murphy, R., and Associates. *Encyclopedia of Educational Evaluation: Concepts and Techniques for Evaluating Education and Training Programs*. San Francisco: Jossey-Bass, 1975.

Arrington, R. E. "Time Sampling in Studies of Social Behavior: A Critical Review of Techniques and Results with Research Suggestions." *Psychological Bulletin*, 1943, *40*(2), 81–124.

Arter, J. A., and Jenkins, J. R. "Examining the Benefits and Prevalence of Modality Considerations in Special Education." *Journal of Special Education*, 1977, *11*(3), 281–298.

Arthur, A. Z. "Diagnostic Testing and the New Alternatives." Psychological Bulletin, 1969, *72*(3), 183–192.

Babad, E. Y., and Budoff, M. "Sensitivity and Validity of Learning-Potential Measurement in Three Levels of Ability." *Journal of Educational Psychology*, 1974, *66*(3), 439–447.

Bachor, D. G. "Suggestions for Modifications in Testing Low-Achieving Adolescents." *Journal of Special Education*, 1979, *13*(4), 443–452.

Baker, E. L. "Beyond Objectives: Domain-Referenced Tests for Evaluation and Educational Improvement." *Educational Technology,* 1974, *14*(6), 10–16.

Baker, H. L. "Psychological Services: From the School Staff's Point of View." *Journal of School Psychology,* 1965, *3,* 36–42.

Baldwin, C. P. "Naturalistic Studies of Classroom Learning." *Review of Educational Research,* 1965, *35*(2), 107–113.

Barclay, A., and others. "Parental Evaluations of Clinical Services for Retarded Children." *American Journal of Mental Deficiency,* 1962, *67*(2), 232–237.

Barclay, J. R. "Descriptive, Theoretical, and Behavioral Characteristics of Subdoctoral School Psychologists." *American Psychologist,* 1971, *26,* 257–280.

Bardon, J. I., and Bennett, V. C. *School Psychology.* Englewood Cliffs, N.J.: Prentice-Hall, 1974.

Bardon, J. I., and others. "Psychosituational Classroom Intervention: Rationale and Description." *Journal of School Psychology,* 1976, *14*(2), 97–104.

Bateman, B. "Three Approaches to Diagnosis and Educational Planning for Children with Learning Disabilities. *Academic Therapy Quarterly,* 1967, *2*(4), 215–222.

Bealing, D. "Issues in Classroom Observation Research." *Research in Education,* 1973, *9,* 70–82.

Beck, A. D. "Learning Disabilities and Cognitive Style: The Coherence of Cognitive Style Constructs and Implications of Cognitive Styles for Children with Academic Difficulties. *Dissertation Abstracts International,* 1977, *37B,* 412B.

Becker, R. M., and Wolfgang, C. H. "An Exploration of the Relationship Between Symbolic Representation in Dramatic Play and Art and the Cognitive and Reading Readiness Levels of Kindergarten Children." *Psychology in the Schools,* 1977, *14*(3), 377–381.

Bem, D. J., and Allen, A. "On Predicting Some of the People Some of the Time: The Search for Cross-Situational Consistencies in Behavior." *Psychological Review,* 1974, *81,* 506–520.

Berger, N. S. "Beyond Testing: A Decision-Making System for Providing School Psychological Consultation." *Professional Psychology,* 1979, *10,* 273–277.

Berko, M. J. "Mental Evaluation of the Aphasic Child." *American Journal of Occupational Therapy,* 1951, *5,* 241–246.

Bersoff, D. N., "'Current Functioning' Myth: An Overlooked Fallacy in Psychological Assessment." *Journal of Consulting and Clinical Psychology,* 1971, *37,* 391–393.

Bersoff, D. N. "Silk Purses into Sow's Ears: The Decline of Psychological Testing and a Suggestion for Its Redemption. *American Psychologist,* 1973, *28*(10), 892–899.

Bersoff, D. N., and Grieger, R. M. "An Interview Model for the Psychosituational Assessment of Children's Behavior." *American Journal of Orthopsychiatry,* 1971, *41*(3), 483–493.

Biddle, B. J. "Methods and Concepts in Classroom Research." *Review of Educational Research,* 1967, *37*(3), 337–357.

Birch, H. B. "Introduction." In E. Haeussermann, *Developmental Potential of Preschool Children.* New York: Grune & Stratton, 1958.

Blackman, L. S., and Burger, A. L. "Psychological Factors Related to Early Reading Behavior of EMR and Nonretarded Children." *American Journal of Mental Deficiency,* 1972, 77(2), 212–229.

Blanco, R. F. "A Focus on Remediation in School Psychology." *Journal of School Psychology,* 1971, *9*(3), 261–277.

Blank, M. "The Wrong Response." In M. Blank (Ed.), *Teaching Learning in the Preschool.* Columbus, Ohio: Merrill, 1973.

Bloom, B. S. "Toward a Theory of Testing Which Includes Measurement-Evaluation-Assessment." In M. C. Wittrock and D. E. Wiley (Eds.), *The Evaluation of Instruction.* New York: Holt, Rinehart and Winston, 1967.

Bluestein, V. W. "An Analysis of Training Programs in School Psychology." *Journal of School Psychology,* 1967, *5*(4), 301–309.

Bluestein, V. W., and Milofsky, C. A. "Certification Patterns and Requirements for School Psychologists." *Journal of School Psychology,* 1970, *8*(4), 270–277.

Boeding, M. A. "A Multi-Process, Multi-Modality Approach to the Diagnosis of Learning Disabilities." *Dissertation Abstracts International,* 1976, *36A,* 5139–5140.

Boehm, A. E., and Weinberg, R. A. *The Classroom Observer: A Guide for Developing Observation Skills.* New York: Teachers College Press, 1977.

Boll, T. J. "A Rationale for Neuropsychological Evaluation." *Professional Psychology,* 1977, *8,* 64–71.

Bortner, M., and Birch, H. G. "Cognitive Capacity and Cognitive Competence." *American Journal of Mental Deficiency*, 1970, *74*, 167–178.

Bowers, K. S. "Situationalism in Psychology: An Analysis and a Critique." *Psychological Review*, 1973, *80*(5), 307–336.

Bowers, N. E. "Public Reaction and Psychological Testing in the Schools." *Journal of School Psychology*, 1971, *9*(2), 114–119.

Boyd, R. D., and DeVault, M. V. "The Observation and Recording of Behavior." *Review of Educational Research*, 1966, *36*(5), 529–551.

Bradley, R. H., and Caldwell, B. M. "Home Observation for Measurement of the Environment: A Revision of the Preschool Scale." *American Journal of Mental Deficiency*, 1979, *84*(3), 235–244.

Brandt, H. M., and Giebink, J. W. "Concreteness and Congruence in Psychologists' Reports to Teachers." *Psychology in the Schools*, 1968, *5*(1), 87–89.

Brandt, R. M. "An Historical Overview of Systematic Approaches to Observation in School Settings." In R. A. Weinberg and F. H. Wood (Eds.), *Observation of Pupils and Teachers in Mainstream and Special Education Settings: Alternative Strategies*. Minneapolis: University of Minnesota, 1975.

Braun, J. S., and others. "Cognitive-Perceptual-Motor Functions in Children—a Suggested Change in Approach to Psychological Assessment." *Journal of School Psychology*, 1965, *3*(3), 13–17.

Breger, L. "Psychological Testing: Treatment and Research Implications." *Journal of Consulting and Clinical Psychology*, 1968, *32*(2), 176–181.

Breland, H. M., and Gaynor, J. L. "A Comparison of Direct and Indirect Assessments of Writing Skill." *Journal of Educational Measurement*, 1979, *16*(2), 119–127.

Breyer, N. L., and Calchera, D. J. "A Behavioral Observation Schedule for Pupils and Teachers." *Psychology in the Schools*, 1971, *8*(4), 330–337.

Brison, D. W. "The School Psychologist's Use of Direct Observation." *Journal of School Psychology*, 1967, *5*(2), 109–115.

Broden, M., Hall, R. V., and Mitts, B. "The Effect of Self-Recording on the Classroom Behavior of Two Eighth-Grade Students." *Journal of Applied Behavior Analysis*, 1971, *4*, 191–199.

Brodsky, H. S. "The Assessment of Social Competence in Adolescents." *Dissertation Abstracts International,* 1975, *36B,* 4144–4145.

Brodt, A. M., and Walker, R. E. "Techniques of WISC Vocabulary Administration." *Journal of Clinical Psychology,* 1969, *25,* 180–181.

Brooks, R. "Psychoeducational Assessment: A Broader Perspective." *Professional Psychology,* 1979, *10*(5), 708–722.

Brophy, J. E., and others. "Classroom Observation Scales: Stability Across Time and Context and Relationships with Student Learning Gains." *Journal of Educational Psychology,* 1975, *67*(6), 873–881.

Brown, D. T., and Lindstrom, J. P. "The Training of School Psychologists in the United States: An Overview." *Psychology in the Schools,* 1978, *15*(1), 37–45.

Bryant, N. D., and others. "Summary of Activities for the Research Institute for the Study of Learning Disabilities." New York: Teachers College, Columbia University, 1977.

Budoff, M. "Learning Potential as a Supplementary Assessment Procedure." In J. Hellmuth (Ed.), *Learning Disorders. Vol. 3.* Seattle: Special Child Publications, 1968.

Budoff, M. "Measuring Learning Potential: An Alternative to the Traditional Intelligence Test." In G. R. Gredler (Ed.), *Ethical and Legal Factors in the Practice of School Psychology.* Harrisburg, Pa.: State Department of Education, 1974.

Burger, A. L., and Blackman, L. S. "Imagery and Verbal Mediation in Paired-Associate Learning of Educable Mentally Retarded Adolescents." *Journal of Mental Deficiency,* 1978, *22,* 125–130.

Burger, A. L., and Blackman, L. S. "Digit Span Estimation and the Effects of Explicit Strategy Training on Recall of EMR Individuals." *American Journal of Mental Deficiency,* 1979, *83*(6), 621–626.

Burke, J. P., and DeMers, S. T. "A Paradigm for Evaluating Assessment Interviewing Techniques." *Psychology in the Schools,* 1979, *16,* 51–60.

Buros, O. K. (Ed.). *The Seventh Mental Measurements Yearbook. Vol. 1.* Highland Park, N.J.: Gryphon Press, 1972.

Cairns, E., and Harbison, J. I. "Impulsivity: Self-Report and Performance Measure." *British Journal of Educational Psychology,* 1975, *45,* 327–329.

Camp, B. W. "Psychometric Tests and Learning in Severely Disabled Readers." *Journal of Learning Disabilities,* 1973, *6*(7), 512–517.

Carlson, J. S., and Wiedl, K. H. "Use of Testing-The-Limits Procedures in the Assessment of Intellectual Capabilities of Children with Learning Difficulties." *American Journal of Mental Deficiency,* 1978, *82*(6), 559–564.

Carroll, J. B. "Review of Illinois Test of Psycholinguistic Abilities." In O. K. Buros (Ed.). *The Seventh Mental Measurements Yearbook.* Highland Park, N.J.: Gryphon Press, 1972.

Carrubba, M. J. "The Effect of Two Timing Procedures, Level of Trait Anxiety, and Their Interaction on Performance on the Wechsler Intelligence Scale for Children-Revised." *Dissertation Abstracts International,* 1976, *37A,* 2070.

Cartwright, G. P., Cartwright, C. A., and Ysseldyke, J. E. "Two Decision Models: Identification and Diagnostic Teaching of Handicapped Children in the Regular Classroom. *Psychology in the Schools,* 1973, *10,* 4–11.

Cason, E. B. "Some Suggestions on the Interaction Between the School Psychologist and the Classroom Teacher." *Journal of Consulting Psychology,* 1945, *9,* 132–135.

Catterall, C. D. "A Taxonomy of Prescriptive Interventions." *Journal of School Psychology,* 1970, *8*(1), 5–12.

Chalfant, J. C., and Scheffelin, M. A. *Central Processing Dysfunctions in Children.* Bethesda, Md.: U.S. Department of Health, Education, and Welfare, 1969.

Chartoff, M. B., and Bardon, J. I. "Doctoral School Psychology Program Graduates in the United States: The First Seventeen Years." *Journal of School Psychology,* 1974, *12*(2), 102–113.

Clark, W. D. "Problem Clarification Consultation as a Response to Referral for Testing: A Means of Initiating Consultation Relationships." Paper delivered at meeting of the National Association of School Psychologists, Kansas City, Mo., 1975.

Cleveland, S. E. "Reflections on the Rise and Fall of Psychodiagnosis." *Professional Psychology,* 1976, *7*(3), 309–318.

Cohen, S. A. "Dyspedagogia as a Cause of Reading Retardation: Definition and Treatment." In B. Bateman (Ed.), *Learning Disorders, Vol. 4. Reading:* Seattle: Special Child Publications, 1971.

Connolly, A. J., Nachtman, W., and Pritchett, E. M. *Key Math Diagnostic Arithmetic Test.* Circle Pines, Minn.: American Guidance Service, 1971.

Cornell, E. L. "The Psychologist in the School System." *Journal of Consulting Psychology,* 1942, *6*(4), 185–192.

Coulter, W. A., and Morrow, H. W. (Eds.). *Adapative Behavior-Concepts and Measurements.* New York: Grune & Stratton, 1978.

Cox, R. C. "Evaluative Aspects of Criterion-Referenced Measures." In W. J. Popham (Ed.), *Criterion-Referenced Measurement: An Introduction.* Englewood Cliffs, N.J.: Educational Technology Publications, 1971.

Crambert, A. C. "Concepts and Issues in Criterion-Referenced Measurement." *Dissertation Abstracts International,* 1975, *36A,* 774.

Crocker, L., and Benson, J. "Achievement, Guessing, and Risk-Taking Behavior under Norm-Referenced and Criterion-Referenced Testing Conditions." *American Educational Research Journal,* 1976, *13*(3), 207–215.

Cronbach, L. J. "The Two Disciplines of Scientific Psychology." *American Psychologist,* 1957, 12, 671–684.

Cronbach, L. J. "Five Decades of Public Controversy over Mental Testing." *American Psychologist,* 1975, *30,* 1–14.

Cronbach, L. J., and Gleser, G. C. *Psychological Tests and Personnel Decisions.* Urbana: University of Illinois Press, 1957.

Curry, N. E., and Arnaud, S. H. "Cognitive Implications in Children's Spontaneous Role Play." *Theory into Practice,* 1974, *13*(4), 273–277.

Dansinger, S. S. "A Five Year Follow-Up Survey of Minnesota School Psychologists." *Journal of School Psychology,* 1968–1969, 7(3), 37–53.

Delaney, H. D. "Interaction of Individual Differences with Visual and Verbal Elaboration Instructions." *Journal of Educational Psychology,* 1978, *70*(3), 306–318.

Dempster, J.J.B. "Symposium on the Effects of Coaching and Practice in Intelligence Tests." *British Journal of Educational Psychology*, 1954, *24*, 1-4.

Deno, S. L. "Behavioral Approaches to Observations: Common Problems and Some Suggestions." In R. A. Weinberg and F. H. Wood (Eds.), *Observation of Pupils and Teachers in Mainstream and Special Education Settings: Alternative Strategies*. Minneapolis: University of Minnesota, 1975.

Deutsch, M., and Associates. *The Disadvantaged Child*. New York: Basic Books, 1967.

Dickinson, D. J. "Direct Assessment of Behavioral and Emotional Problems." *Psychology in the Schools*, 1978, *15*(4), 472-477.

Digate, G., and others. "Modification of Impulsivity: Implications for Improved Efficiency in Learning for Exceptional Children." *Journal of Special Education*, 1978, *12*(4), 459-467.

Dillon, R., and Carlson, J. S. "Testing Competence in Three Ethnic Groups." *Educational and Psychological Measurement*, 1978, *38*, 437-443.

"Do Specialists Help Teachers? Most Teachers Don't Think So." *Phi Delta Kappan;* 1969, *50*(7), 417.

Donlon, T. "Referencing Test Scores: Introductory Concepts." In W. Hively and M. C. Reynolds (Eds.), *Domain-Referenced Testing in Special Education*. Minneapolis: University of Minnesota, 1975.

Duchastel, P. C., and Merrill, P. F. "The Effects of Behavioral Objectives on Learning: A Review of Empirical Studies." *Review of Educational Research*, 1973, *43*(1), 53-69.

Duffey, J. B., and Fedner, M. L. "Educational Diagnosis with Instructional Use." *Exceptional Children*, 1978, *44*(4), 246-251.

Duncan, A. D. "Tracking Behavioral Growth: Day-To-Day Measures of Frequency over Domains of Performance." *Educational Technology*, 1974, *14*(6), 54-59.

Dunn, J. A. "Michigan's School Psychologists: A Profile Analysis of Personal and Professional Characteristics of School Psychologists in the State of Michigan." *Psychology in the Schools*, 1965, *2*(4), 340-344.

Dunn, L. M. "Special Education for the Mentally Retarded—Is Much of It Justifiable?" *Exceptional Children*, 1969, *35*, 5-22.

Eaves, R. C., and McLaughlin, P. "A Systems Approach for the Assessment of the Child and His Environment: Getting Back to Basics." *Journal of Special Education*, 1977, *11*(1), 99-111.

Ebel, R. L. "The Social Consequences of Educational Testing." In D. A. Payne and R. F. McMorris (Eds.), *Educational and Psychological Measurement*. Waltham, Mass.: Blaisdell, 1967.

Ebel, R. L. "Criterion-Referenced Measurements: Limitations." *School Review*, 1971, *79*, 282–298.

Ebel, R. L. "Evaluation and Educational Objectives." *Journal of Educational Measurement*, 1973, *10*(4), 273–279.

Ebel, R. L. "Educational Tests: Valid? Biased? Useful?" *Phi Delta Kappan*, October 1975, pp. 83–93.

Eisenberg, P. "A Further Study in Expressive Movement." *Character and Personality*, 1937, *5*(4), 296–301.

Ekehammar, B. "Interactionism in Personality from a Historical Perspective." *Psychological Bulletin*, 1974, *81*(12), 1026–1048.

Ellett, C. D., and Bersoff, D. N. "New Tricks for Old Dogs: A Modern Approach to Psychological Assessment." Paper presented at the annual meeting of the American Psychological Association, Montreal, Que., August 1973.

Ellett, C. D., and Bersoff, D. N. "An Integrated Approach to the Psychosituational Assessment of Behavior." *Professional Psychology*, 1976, *7*, 435–494.

Engel, M. "Time and the Reluctance to Diagnose." *Journal of School Psychology*, 1966, *4*(2), 1–8.

Ewing, N., and Brecht, R. "Diagnostic/Prescriptive Instruction: A Reconsideration of Some Issues." *Journal of Special Education*, 1977, *11*(3), 323–327.

Fairchild, T. N. "An Analysis of the Services Performed by a School Psychologist in an Urban Area: Implications for Training Programs." *Psychology in the Schools*, 1974, *11*, 275–281.

Fairchild, T. N. "School Psychological Services: An Empirical Comparison of Two Models." *Psychology in the Schools*, 1976, *13*(2), 156–162.

Federal Register. *Rules and regulations, Education of Handicapped Children. Pt. 2.* Implementation of part B of the Education of the Handicapped Act. Washington, D.C.: U.S. Government Printing Office, 1977.

Feuerstein, R. "Cognitive Assessment of the Socioculturally Deprived Child and Adolescent." In *Proceedings of the Conference on Men-

tal Tests and Cultural Adaptation. Istanbul, Turkey: 1971.

Feuerstein, R. *The Dynamic Assessment of Retarded Learners.* Baltimore: University Park Press, 1979.

Feuerstein, R., and Krasilowsky, D. "Interventional Strategies for the Significant Modification of Cognitive Functioning in the Disadvantaged Adolescent." *Journal of the American Academy of Child Psychiatry,* 1972, *11*(3), 572–581.

Fischer, C. T. "Intelligence Defined as Effectiveness of Approaches." *Journal of Consulting and Clinical Psychology,* 1969, *33*, 668–674.

Fischer, C. T. "The Testee as Co-Evaluator." *Journal of Counseling Psychology,* 1970, *17*(1), 70–76.

Fischer, C. T. "Exit I.Q.: Enter the Child." In G. J. Williams and S. Gordon (Eds.), *Clinical Child Psychology—Current Practices and Future Perspectives.* New York: Behavioral Publications, 1974.

Fitts, L. D. "The School Psychologist as Perceived by Superintendents of Education in Alabama." Unpublished doctoral dissertation, University of Pennsylvania, 1972.

Fitzpatrick, R., and Morrison, E. J. "Performance and Product Evaluation." In R. Thorndike (Ed.), *Educational Measurement.* Washington, D.C.: American Council on Education, 1971.

Flanagan, J. C. "The Critical Incident Technique." *Psychological Bulletin,* 1954, *51*(4), 327–358.

Flanders, N. "The Problems of Observer Training and Reliability." In E. J. Amidon and J. B. Hough (Eds.), *Interaction Analysis: Theory, Research and Application.* Reading, Mass.: Addison-Wesley, 1967.

Flax, M. L., and Anderson, D. E. "A Survey of School Psychologists in Colorado." *Psychology in the Schools,* 1966, *3*(1), 52–54.

Fleishman, E. A., and Hempel, W. E., Jr. "The Relation Between Abilities and Improvement with Practice in a Visual Discrimination Task." *Journal of Experimental Psychology,* 1955, *49*(5), 301–312.

Forness, S. R. "Implications of Recent Trends in Educational Labeling." *Journal of Learning Disabilities,* 1974, 7(7), 57–61.

Forness, S. R., and Esveldt, K. C. "Classroom Observation of Children with Learning and Behavior Problems." *Journal of Learning Disabilities,* 1975, *8*(6), 49–52.

Forness, S. R., Guthrie, D., and Hall, R. J. "Follow-Up of High-Risk

Children Identified in Kindergarten Through Direct Classroom Observation." *Psychology in the Schools,* 1976, *13*(1), 45–49.

Fox, L. "Effecting the Use of Efficient Study Habits." In R. Ulrich, T. Stachnik, and J. Mabry (Eds.), *Control of Human Behavior Journal.* Glenview, Ill.: Scott, Foresman, 1966.

Frick, T., and Semmel, M. I. "Observer Agreement and Reliabilities of Classroom Observational Measures." *Review of Educational Research,* 1978, *48*(1), 157–184.

Friedman, R. "A Structured Family Interview in the Assessment of School Learning Disorders." *Psychology in the Schools,* 1969, *6*(2), 162–171.

Frostig, M. "Testing as a Basis for Educational Therapy." *Journal of Special Education,* 1968, *2*(1), 15–33.

Garfield, S. L., and Kurtz, R. M. "Attitudes Toward Training in Diagnostic Testing: A Survey of Directors of Internship Training." *Journal of Consulting and Clinical Psychology,* 1973, *40,* 350–355.

Garvin, A. D. "The Applicability of Criterion-Referenced Measurement by Content Area and Level." In W. J. Popham (Ed.), *Criterion-Referenced Measurement—An Introduction.* Englewood Cliffs, N.J.: Educational Technology Publications, 1971.

Gellert, E. "Systematic Observation: A Method in Child Study." *Harvard Educational Review,* 1955, *25*(3), 179–195.

Gerweck, S., and Ysseldyke, J. E. "Limitations of Current Psychological Practices for the Intellectual Assessment of the Hearing Impaired: A Response to the Levine Study." *The Volta Review,* 1975, *77,* 243–248.

Gibson, E. J. "Learning to Read." *Bulletin of the Orton Society,* 1965, *15,* 32–47.

Giebink, J. W., and Ringness, T. A. "On the Relevance of Training in School Psychology." *Journal of School Psychology,* 1970, *8*(1), 43–47.

Gilmore, G. E., and Chandy, J. "Educators Describe the School Psychologist." *Psychology in Schools,* 1973a, *10*(3), 397–403.

Gilmore, G. E., and Chandy, J. "Teachers' Perceptions of School Psychological Services." *Journal of School Psychology,* 1973b, *11*(2), 139–147.

Glaser, R. "Instructional Technology and the Measurement of Learning Outcomes." *American Psychologist,* 1963, *18,* 519–521.

Glaser, R. "Evaluation of Instruction and Changing Educational Models." In M. C. Wittrock and D. C. Wiley (Eds.), *The Evaluation of Instruction*. New York: Holt, Rinehart and Winston, 1967.

Glaser, R. "A Criterion-Referenced Test." In W. J. Popham (Ed.). *Criterion-Referenced Measurement—an Introduction*. Engiewood Cliffs, N.J.: Educational Technology Publications, 1971.

Glaser, R. "Individuals and Learning: The New Aptitudes." *Educational Researcher*, 1972, *1*, 5–13.

Glaser, R., and Nitko, A. J. "Measurement in Learning and Instruction." In R. L. Thorndike (Ed.), *Educational Measurement*. Washington, D.C.: American Council on Education, 1971.

Glaser, R., and Resnick, L. B. "Instructional Psychology." *Annual Review of Psychology*, 1972, *23*, 207–276.

Glynn, E. L. "Classroom Applications of Self-Determined Reinforcement." *Journal of Applied Behavior Analysis*, 1970, *3*, 123–132.

Goldfried, M. R., and Kent, R. N. "Traditional Versus Behavioral Personality Assessments: A Comparison of Methodological and Theoretical Assumptions." *Psychological Bulletin*, 1972, *77*, 409–420.

Goldfried, M. R., and Sprafkin, J. N. *Behavioral Personality Assessment*. Morristown, N.J.: General Learning Press, 1974.

Goldstein, K. M., and Blackman, S. "Assessment of Cognitive Style." In P. McReynolds (Ed.), *Advances in Psychological Assessment IV*. San Francisco: Jossey-Bass, 1977.

Good, T. L., and Brophy, J. E. "Teacher-Child Dyadic Interactions: A New Method of Classroom Observation." *Journal of School Psychology*, 1970, *8*(2), 131–137.

Goodman, Y. M. "Using Children's Reading Miscues for New Teaching Strategies." *The Reading Teacher*, 1970, *23*(5), 555–564.

Gordon, E. W. "Introduction." In J. Hellmuth (Ed.), *Disadvantaged Child. Vol. 2*. New York: Brunner/Mazel, 1968.

Gordon, I. J., and Jester, R. E. "Techniques of Observing Teaching in Early Childhood and Outcomes of Particular Procedures." In R.M.W. Travers (Ed.), *Second Handbook of Research on Teaching*. Chicago: Rand McNally, 1973.

Gorth, W. P., and Hambleton, R. K. "Measurement Considerations for Criterion-Referenced Testing and Special Education." *Journal of Special Education*, 1972, *6*(4), 303–314.

Gottman, J. M., and McFall, R. M. "Self-Monitoring Effects in a Program for Potential High School Dropouts: A Time-Series Analysis." *Journal of Consulting and Clinical Psychology*, 1972, *39*, 275–281.

Graham, E. E., and Shapiro, E. "Use of the Performance Scale of the Wechsler Intelligence Scale for Children with the Deaf Child." *Journal of Consulting Psychology*, 1953, *17*(5), 396–398.

Gray, S. W. *The Psychologist in the Schools*. New York: Holt, Rinehart and Winston, 1963.

Greco, T. H., Jr. "Is There Really a Difference Between Criterion-Referenced and Norm-Referenced Measurements?" *Educational Technology*, 1974, *14*(2), 22–25.

Greenspoon, J., and Gersten, C. D. "A New Look at Psychological Testing: Psychological Testing from the Standpoint of a Behaviorist." *American Psychologist*, 1967, *22*, 848–853.

Greenstein, J., and Strain, P. S. "The Utility of the Key Math Diagnostic Arithmetic Test for Adolescent Learning Disabled Students." *Psychology in the Schools*, 1977, *14*(2), 275–282.

Greenwood, C. R., Walker, H. M., and Hops, H. "Issues in Social Interaction/Withdrawal Assessment." *Exceptional Children*, 1977, *43*(8), 490–499.

Grieger, R. M., and Abidin, R. R. "Psychosocial Assessment: A Model for the School Community Psychologist." *Psychology in the Schools*, 1972, *9*(2), 112–119.

Griffiths, A. N. "The WISC as a Diagnostic-Remedial Tool for Dyslexia." *Academic Therapy*, 1977, *12*(4), 401–409.

Gronlund, N. E. *Preparing Criterion-Referenced Tests for Classroom Instruction*. New York: Macmillan, 1973.

Gross, F. P., and Farling, W. H. "Analysis of Case Loads of School Psychologists." *Psychology in the Schools*, 1969, *6*(1), 98–101.

Grubb, R. D., Petty, S. Z., and Flynn, D. L. "A Strategy for the Delivery of Accountable School Psychological Services." *Psychology in the Schools*, 1976, *13*, 39–44.

Gump, P. V., Schoggen, P., and Redl, F. "The Behavior of the Same Child in Different Milieus." In R. G. Barker (Ed.), *The Stream of Behavior*. New York: Appleton-Century-Crofts, 1963.

Haeussermann, E. *Developmental Potential of Preschool Children*. New York: Grune & Stratton, 1958.

Hakim, C. S. "Task Analysis: One Alternative." *Academic Therapy*, 1974–1975, *10*(2), 201–209.

Hall, L. P., and La Driere, M. L. "Evaluation of WISC Similarities Responses According to Cognitive Style and Error Analysis: A Comparative Study." *Psychological Reports*, 1970, *26*, 175–180.

Hall, R. V., Hawkins, R. P., and Axelrod, S. "Measuring and Recording Student Behavior: A Behavior Analysis Approach. In R.A. Weinberg and F. H. Wood (Eds.), *Observation of Pupils and Teachers in Mainstream and Special Education Settings: Alternative Strategies.* Minneapolis: University of Minnesota, 1975.

Halpern, A. S., Irvin, L. K., and Landman, J. T. "Alternative Approaches to the Measurement of Adaptive Behavior." *American Journal of Mental Deficiency*, 1979, *84*(3), 304–310.

Halpern, F. "The Individual Psychological Examination." In M. G. Gottsegen and G. B. Gottsegen (Eds.), *Professional School Psychology. Vol. 1.* New York: Grune & Stratton, 1960.

Hambleton, R. K., and Gorth, W. P. *Criterion-Referenced Testing: Issues and Applications.* Technical Reports, No. 13. Amherst, Mass.: School of Education, University of Massachusetts, 1971.

Hambleton, R. K., and Novick, M. R. "Toward an Integration of Theory and Method for Criterion-Referenced Tests." *Journal of Educational Measurement*, 1973, *10*(3), 159–170.

Hambleton, R. K., and others. "Criterion-Referenced Testing and Measurement: A Review of Technical Issues and Developments." *Review of Educational Research*, 1978, *48*(1), 1–47.

Hammarback, F., and Koenig, C. H. "Precise Behavior Measurement in the RIC Tutorial Program for Handicapped Children." In W. Hively and M. C. Reynolds (Eds.), *Domain-Referenced Testing in Special Education.* Minneapolis: University of Minnesota, 1975.

Hammill, D. D. "Evaluating Children for Instructional Purposes." *Academic Therapy*, 1971, *6*(4), 341–353.

Hammill, D. D., and Bartel, N. R. *Teaching Children with Learning and Behavior Problems.* Boston: Allyn & Bacon, 1975.

Hammill, D. D., and Larsen, S. C. "The Effectiveness of Psycholinguistic Training." *Exceptional Children*, 1974, *41*, 5–14.

Hammill, D. D., and Larsen, S. C. "The Effectiveness of Psycholinguistic Training: A Reaffirmation of Position." *Exceptional Children*, 1978, *44*(6), 402–414.

Handler, L., Gerston, A., and Handler, B. "Suggestions for Improved Psychologist-Teacher Communication." *Psychology in the Schools*, 1965, *2*(1), 77–81.

Hanesian, H. "Classroom/Psychological Evaluation of the Handicapped Child." Mimeograph, n.d.

Hardy, J. B., and others. "Pitfalls in the Measurement of Intelligence: Are Standard Intelligence Tests Valid Instruments for Measuring the Intellectual Potential of Urban Children?" *Journal of Psychology*, 1976, *94*, 43–51.

Haring, N. G., and Bateman, B. *Teaching the Learning Disabled Child*. Englewood Cliffs, N.J.: Prentice-Hall, 1977.

Hartlage, L. C., and Hartlage, P. L. *The Application of Neuropsychological Principles in the Diagnosis of Learning Disabilities*. Augusta, Ga.: Medical College of Georgia, n.d.

Haynes, S. N. *Principles of Behavioral Assessment*. New York: Gardner Press, 1978.

Haywood, H. C., and Switsky, H. N. "Children's Verbal Abstracting: Effects of Enriched Input, Age and IQ." *American Journal of Mental Deficiency*, 1974, *78*(5), 556–565.

Heim, A. W., and Watts, K. P. "An Experiment in Practice, Coaching and Discussion of Errors in Mental Testing." *British Journal of Educational Psychology*, 1957, *27*, 199–210.

Herbert, J., and Attridge, C. "A Guide for Developers and Users of Observation Systems and Manuals." *American Educational Research Journal*, 1975, *12*(1), 1–20.

Herron, W. G., and Psaila, J. "Diagnosing Children's Problems." *Psychology in the Schools*, 1970, *7*(4), 397–403.

Heyns, R. W., and Lippitt, R. "Systematic Observational Techniques." In G. Lindzey (Ed.), *Handbook of Social Psychology. Vol. 1*. Reading, Mass.: Addison-Wesley, 1954.

Hively, W. "Introduction to Domain-Referenced Testing." *Educational Technology*, 1974a, *14*(6), 5–9.

Hively, W. "Some Comments on This Issue." *Educational Technology*, 1974b, *14*(6), 60–64.

Hively, W., and Reynolds, M. C. *Domain-Referenced Testing in Special Education*. Minneapolis: University of Minnesota Press, 1975.

Hobbs, N. *The Futures of Children: Recommendations of the Project on Classification of Exceptional Children.* San Francisco: Jossey-Bass, 1975.

Hofmeister, A. "Integrating Criterion-Referenced Testing and Instruction." In W. Hively and M. C. Reynolds, (Eds.), *Domain-Referenced Testing in Special Education.* Minneapolis: University of Minnesota Press, 1975.

Holden, R. H. "Improved Methods in Testing Cerebral Palsied Children." *American Journal of Mental Deficiency,* 1951, *56,* 349–353.

Hollenbeck, A. R. "Problems of Reliability in Observational Research." In G. P. Sackett (Ed.), *Observing Behavior. Vol. 2.* Baltimore: University Park Press, 1978.

Holm, R. A. "Techniques of Recording Observational Data." In G. P. Sackett (Ed.), *Observing Behavior. Vol. 2.* Baltimore: University Park Press, 1978.

Holt, R. R. "Diagnostic Testing: Present Status and Future Prospects." *Journal of Nervous and Mental Disease,* 1967, *144*(6), 444–465.

Honigfeld, G. "In Defense of Diagnosis." *Professional Psychology,* 1971, *2*(3), 289–291.

Hudgins, A. L., and Schultz, J. L. "On Observing: The Use of the Carkhuff Model in Writing Psychological Reports." *Journal of School Psychology,* 1978, *16*(1), 56–63.

Hunt, D. E. "Person-Environment Interaction: A Challenge Found Wanting Before It Was Tried." *Review of Educational Research,* 1975, *4*(2), 209–230.

Hunt, J. McV. "Psychological Assessment in Education and Social Class." In B. Z. Friedlander, G. M. Sterritt, and G. E. Kirk (Eds.), *Exceptional Child. Vol. 3.* New York: Brunner/Mazel, 1975.

Hunter, C. P. "Classroom Observation Instruments and Teacher Inservice Training by School Psychologists." *School Psychology Monograph,* 1977, *3*(2), 45–88.

Hutson, B. A. "Psychological Testing: Misdiagnosis and Half-Diagnosis." *Psychology in the Schools,* 1974, *11,* 388–391.

Hutson, B. A., and Niles, J. A. "Trial Teaching: The Missing Link." *Psychology in the Schools,* 1974, *11*(2), 188–191.

Hutt, M. L. "A Clinical Study of 'Consecutive' and 'Adaptive' Testing with the Revised Stanford-Binet." *Journal of Consulting Psychology,* 1947, *11,* 93–103.

Ivens, S. *An Investigation of Item Analyses, Reliability, and Validity in Relation to Criterion-Referenced Tests.* No. 71-7036. Ann Arbor, Mich.: University Microfilms, 1970.

Ivnik, R. J. "The Uncertain Status of Psychological Tests in Clinical Psychology." *Professional Psychology,* 1977, *8,* 206-213.

Jason, L. A., Ferone, L., and Anderegg, T. "Evaluating Ecological, Behavioral, and Process Consultation Interventions." *Journal of School Psychology,* 1979, *17*(2), 103-115.

Jedrysek, E., and others. *Psychoeducational Evaluation of the Preschool Child.* New York: Grune & Stratton, 1972.

Jenkins, J. R., and Larson, K. "Evaluating Error-Correction Procedures for Oral Reading." *Journal of Special Education,* 1979, *13*(2), 145-156.

Jensen, A. R. "Learning Abilities in Mexican-American and Anglo-American Children." *California Journal of Educational Research,* 1961, *12*(4), 147-159.

Jensen, A. R. "Learning Ability in Retarded, Average, and Gifted Children." *Merrill-Palmer Quarterly,* 1963, *9*(2), 123-140.

Jensen, A. R. "Verbal Mediation and Educational Potential." *Psychology in the Schools,* 1966, *3,* 99-109.

Jewell, B. T., and Wursten, H. "Observations of the Psychological Testing of Cerebral Palsied Children." *American Journal of Mental Deficiency,* 1952, *56,* 630-637.

Johnston, A., and others. "Validation of a Laboratory Play Measure of Child Aggression." *Child Development,* 1977, *48,* 324-327.

Jones, R. R., Reid, J. B., and Patterson, G. R. "Naturalistic Observation in Clinical Assessment." In P. McReynolds (Ed.), *Advances in Psychological Assessment, III.* San Francisco: Jossey-Bass, 1975.

Joselyn, G. "Ethical Considerations in the Use of Standardized Tests." In W. Hively and M. C. Reynolds (Eds.), *Domain-Referenced Testing in Special Education.* Minneapolis: University of Minnesota Press, 1975.

Jurkovic, G. J. "Relation of Psycholinguistic Development to Imaginative Play of Disadvantaged Preschool Children." *Psychology in the Schools,* 1978, *15*(4), 560-564.

Kagan, J. "Impulsive and Reflective Children: Significance of Conceptual Tempo." In J. D. Krumboltz (Ed.), *Learning and the Educational Process.* Chicago: Rand McNally, 1965.

Kahn, L. J., and Fine, M. J. "Teachers' Perceptions of the School

Psychologist as a Function of Teaching Experience, Amount of Contact, and Socioeconomic Status of the School." *Psychology in the Schools*, 1978, *15*(4), 577–582.

Kalverboer, A. F. *A Neurobehavioral Study in Pre-School Children.* Clinics in Developmental Medicine, No. 54. Philadelphia: Lippincott, 1975.

Kaplan, L. J. "Testing Nontestable Children." *Bulletin of the Menninger Clinic*, 1975, *39*(5), 420-435.

Kaplan, M. S., Chrin, M., and Clancy, B. "Priority Roles for School Psychologists as Seen by Superintendents." *Journal of School Psychology*, 1977, *15*(1), 75–79.

Kaplan, M. S., and Sprunger, B. "Psychological Evaluations and Teacher Perceptions of Students." *Journal of School Psychology*, 1967, *5*(4), 289–291.

Katz, E. "The 'Pointing Modification' of the Revised Stanford-Binet Intelligence Scales, Forms L and M, Years II Through VI: A Report of Research in Progress." *American Journal of Mental Deficiency*, 1958, *62*, 698–707.

Kauffman, J. M., and Hallahan, D. P. "The Medical Model and the Science of Special Education." *Exceptional Children*, 1974, *41*, 97–102.

Kaufman, M. R. "Psychiatry: Why a 'Medical' or 'Social' Model?" *Archives of General Psychiatry*, 1967, *17*, 347–360.

Keenan, L. "A Job Analysis of School Psychologists in the Public Schools of Massachusetts." *Psychology in the Schools*, 1964, *1*(2), 185–186.

Kennedy, C. B., and Butter, E. J. "Cognitive Style in Two Modalities: Vision and Audition." Journal of Educational Psychology, 1978, *70*(2), 193–199.

Keogh, B. K. "A Compensatory Model for Psychoeducational Evaluation of Children with Learning Disorders." *Journal of Learning Disabilities*, 1971, *10*(4), 544–548.

Keogh, B. K. "Psychological Evaluation of Exceptional Children: Old Hangups and New Directions." *Journal of School Psychology*, 1972, *10*(2), 141–145.

Keogh, B. K., and Donlon, G. McG. "Field Dependence, Impulsivity and Learning Disabilities." *Journal of Learning Disabilities*," 1972, *5*(6), 331–336.

Keogh, B. K., and Macmillan, D. L. "Effects of Motivational and Presentation Conditions of Digit Recall of Children of Differing Socioeconomic, Racial, and Intelligence Groups." *American Educational Research Journal*, 1971, *8*(1), 27–38.

Keogh, B. K., and others. "School Psychologists' Services in Special Education Programs." *Journal of School Psychology*, 1975, *13*(2), 142–147.

"Key Math: A Review." *Journal of Learning Disabilities*, 1978, *11*, 43–44.

Klopfer, W. G. "The Blind Leading the Blind—Psychotherapy Without Assessment." *Journal of Projective Techniques*, 1964, *28*, 387–392.

Koesel, J. G. "Student Participation in Learning, Diagnosis, and Its Effects on Academic Achievement and Attitudes Toward School." *Dissertation Abstracts International*, 1976, *37A*, 1406.

Kowatrakul, S. "Some Behaviors of Elementary Children Related to Classroom Activities and Subject Areas." *Journal of Educational Psychology*, 1959, *50*(3), 121–128.

Krathwohl, D. R., and Payne, D. A. "Defining and Assessing Educational Objectives." In R. L. Thorndike (Ed.), *Educational Measurement*. Washington, D.C.: American Council on Education, 1971.

Kratochwill, T. R. "The Movement of Psychological Extras into Ability Assessment." *Journal of Special Education*, 1977, *11*(3) 299–311.

Kratochwill, T. R., and Severson, R. A. "Process Assessment: An Examination of Reinforcer Effectiveness and Predictive Validity." *Journal of School Psychology*, 1977, *15*(4), 293–300.

Kunzelman, H. D. (Ed.). *Precision Teaching*. Seattle: Special Child Publications, 1970.

Lacey, H. M. "Pre-Conditions for the Psychological Evaluation of Young Cerebral Palsied Children." *Cerebral Palsy Review*, 1962, *57*, 92–99.

Lambert, N. M. "Children's Problems and Classroom Interventions from the Perspective of Classroom Teachers." *Professional Psychology*, 1976, *7*, 507–517.

Lambert, N. M., Wilcox, M. R., and Gleason, W. P. *The Educationally Retarded Child*. New York: Grune & Stratton, 1974.

Layne, C. C., and others. "Accuracy of Self-Monitoring on a Variable Ratio Schedule of Observer Verification." *Behavior Therapy*, 1976, 7, 481–488.

Ledford, B. R. "The Synthesis of a Technique of Comprehensive Analysis of Individual Learners." *Dissertation Abstracts International*, 1975, *35A*, 4923–4924.

Lerner, J. W. "Systems Analysis and Special Education." *Journal of Special Education*, 1973, 7(1), 15–26.

Levine, H. G., and McGuire, C. "Role-Playing as an Evaluative Technique." *Journal of Educational Measurement*, 1968, 5(1), 1–8.

Levy, M. R., and Fox, H. M. "Psychological Testing is Alive and Well." *Professional Psychology*, 1975, *37*, 43–49.

Lewandowski, D. G., and Saccuzzo, D. P. "The Decline of Psychological Testing." *Professional Psychology*, 1976, 7, 177–185.

Lidz, C. S. "Issues in the Assessment of Preschool Children." *Journal of School Psychology*, 1977a, *15*(2), 129–135.

Lidz, C. S. "Alternative Assessment Strategies for the School Psychologist." Unpublished doctoral dissertation, Rutgers University, Graduate School of Applied and Professional Psychology, 1977b.

Lidz, C. S. "Criterion-Referenced Assessment: The New Bandwagon?" *Exceptional Children*, 1979, *46*(2), 131–132.

Lilly, M. S. "Special Education: Tempest in a Teapot." *Exceptional Children*, 1970, *37*, 43–49.

Lilly, M. S., and Kelleher, J. "Modality Strengths and Aptitude-Treatment Interaction." *Journal of Special Education*, 1973, 7, 5–13.

Linehan, M. M. "Issues in Behavioral Interviewing." In J. D. Cone and R. P. Hawkins (Eds.), *Behavioral Assessment: New Directions in Clinical Psychology*. New York: Brunner/Mazel, 1977.

Lipinski, D., and Nelson, R. "Problems in the Use of Naturalistic Observation as a Means of Behavioral Assessment." *Behavior Therapy*, 1974, 5, 341–351.

Little, V. L., and Bailey, K. G. "Potential Intelligence or Intelligence Test Potential: A Question of Empirical Validity." *Journal of Consulting and Clinical Psychology*, 1972, *39*, 168.

Lovitt, T. C. "Assessment of Children with Learning Disabilities." *Exceptional Children*, 1967, *34*, 233–239.

Lucas, M. S., and Jones, R. L. "Attitudes of Teachers of Mentally Retarded Children Toward Psychological Reports and Services." *Journal of School Psychology,* 1970, *8*(2), 122-130.

Lund, K. A., Foster, G. E., and McCall-Perez, F. C. "The Effectiveness of Psycholinguistic Training, a Reevaluation." *Exceptional Children,* 1978, *44*(5), 310-319.

Luria, A. R. "An Objective Approach to the Study of the Abnormal Child." *American Journal of Orthopsychiatry,* 1961, *31,* 1-14.

Lutey, C. *Individual Intelligence Testing—a Manual and Sourcebook.* Greeley, Colo.: Carol L. Lutey Publishing, 1977.

Lynch, W. W. "Guidelines to the Use of Classroom Observation Instruments by School Psychologists." *School Psychology Monograph,* 1977, *3*(1), 1-22.

McCarthy, D. *McCarthy Scales of Child Development.* New York: Psychological Corporation, 1972.

McClelland, D. C. "Testing for Competence Rather than for 'Intelligence'." *American Psychologist,* 1973, *28,* 130-151.

Maccoby, E. E., and Maccoby, N. "The Interview: A Tool of Social Science." In G. Lindzey (Ed.), *Handbook of Social Psychology.* Reading, Mass.: Addison-Wesley, 1954.

McFall, R. M. "Analog Methods in Behavioral Assessment: Issues and Prospects." In J. D. Cone and R. P. Hawkins (Eds.), *Behavioral Assessment: New Directions in Clinical Psychology.* New York: Brunner/Mazel, 1977.

McGaw, B., Wardrop, J. L., and Bunda, M. A. "Classroom Observation Schemes: Where Are the Errors?" *American Educational Research Journal,* 1972, *9*(1), 13-27.

Mackay, G.W.S., and Vernon, P. E. "The Measurement of Learning Ability." *British Journal of Educational Psychology,* 1963, *33,* 177-186.

McKenzie, M., and Wendla, K. "Evaluating Learning." *Urban Review,* 1976, *9,* 59-72.

McKinney, J. D., and others. "Relationship Between Classroom Behavior and Academic Achievement." *Journal of Educational Psychology,* 1975, *67*(2), 198-203.

McMorris, R. F., and Ambrosino, R. J. "Self-Report Predictors: A Reminder." *Journal of Educational Measurement,* 1973, *10*(1), 13-17.

McReynolds, P. "An Introduction to Psychological Assessment." In P. McReynolds (Ed.), *Advances in Psychological Assessment. Vol. 1.* Palo Alto: Science and Behavioral Books, 1968.

McReynolds, P., Acker, M., and Pietila, C. "Relationship of Object Curiosity to Psychological Adjustment in Children." *Child Development,* 1961, *32,* 393–400.

McReynolds, P., and DeVoge, S. "Use of Improvisational Techniques in Assessment." In P. McReynolds (Ed.), *Advances in Psychological Assessment IV.* San Francisco: Jossey-Bass, 1978.

Magary, J. F. (Ed.). *School Psychological Services—in Theory and Practice: A Handbook.* Englewood Cliffs, N.J.: Prentice-Hall, 1967.

Maletsky, B. M. " 'Assisted' Covert Sensitization in the Treatment of Exhibitionism." *Journal of Consulting and Clinical Psychology,* 1974, *42,* 34–40.

Maloney, M. P., and Ward, H. P. *Psychological Assessment—a Conceptual Approach.* New York: Oxford University Press, 1979.

Mann, L. "Perceptual Training: Misdirections and Redirections." *American Journal of Orthopsychiatry,* 1970, *40*(1), 30–38.

Mann, L. "Psychometric Phrenology and the New Faculty Psychology: The Case Against Ability Assessment and Training." *Journal of Special Education, 1971, 5*(1), 3–14.

Mann, L. Review of *Frostig Developmental Test of Visual Perception.* In O. K. Buros (Ed.), *The Seventh Mental Measurements Yearbook.* Highland Park, N.J.: Gryphon Press, 1972.

Mann, L., and Phillips, W. A. "Fractional Practices in Special Education: A Critique." *Exceptional Children,* 1966–1967, *33,* 311–319.

Margack, C., and Kern, K. C. "Visual Impairment, Partial-Sight and the School Psychologist." *Journal of Learning Disabilities,* 1969, *2*(8), 407–414.

Margolis, H., and Brannigan, G. G. "Conceptual Impulsivity as a Consideration in Test Interpretation." *Psychology in the Schools,* 1976, *13*(4), 484–486.

Margolis, H., and Brannigan, G. G. "Conceptual Tempo as a Parameter for Predicting Reading Achievement." *Journal of Educational Research,* 1978, *71,* 342–345.

Marshall, H. H., and others. "Stability of Classroom Variables as Measures of a Broad Range Observational System." *Journal of Educational Research,* 1976–1977, *70,* 304–311.

Martin, R. P., Duffey, J. and Fischman, R. "A Time Analysis and Evaluation of an Experimental Internship Program in School Psychology." *Journal of School Psychology*, 1973, *11*(3), 263–268.

Masling, J., and Stern, G. "The Effect of an Observer in the Classroom." *Journal of Educational Psychology*, 1969, *60*, 351–355.

Medley, D. M. "Systematic Observation Schedules as Measuring Instruments." In R. A. Weinberg and F. H. Wood (Eds.), *Observation of Pupils and Teachers in Mainstream and Special Education Settings: Alternative Strategies*. Minneapolis: University of Minnesota Press, 1975.

Medley, D. M., and Mitzel, H. E. "Measuring Classroom Behavior by Systematic Observation." In N. L. Gage (Ed.), *Handbook of Research on Teaching*. Chicago: Rand McNally, 1963.

Medway, F. C. "Teachers' Knowledge of School Psychologists' Responsibilities." *Journal of School Psychology*, 1977, *15*, 301–307.

Meichenbaum, D. "Cognitive-Functional Approach to Cognitive Factors as Determinants of Learning Disabilities." In R. M. Knights and D. J. Bakker (Eds.), *The Neuropsychology of Learning Disorders*. Baltimore: University Park Press, 1976.

Meichenbaum, D. *Cognitive-Behavior Modification*. New York: Plenum Press, 1977.

Meier, J. H. "Innovations in Assessing the Disadvantaged Child's Potential." In J. Hellmuth (Ed.), *Disadvantaged Child. Vol. 1*. New York: Brunner/Mazel, 1967.

Mercer, J. R. *Labeling the Mentally Retarded*. Berkeley: University of California Press, 1973.

Mercer, J. R., and Lewis, J. *System of Multicultural Pluralistic Assessment*. New York: Psychological Corporation, 1977.

Mercer, J. R., and Ysseldyke, J. "Designing Diagnostic-Intervention Programs." In T. Oakland (Ed.), *Psychological and Educational Assessment of Minority Children*. New York: Brunner/Mazel, 1977.

Merwin, J. C. "Historical Review of Changing Concepts of Evaluation." In R. W. Tyler (Ed.), *Educational Evaluation: New Roles, New Means*. Chicago: University of Chicago Press, 1969.

Meskaukas, J. A. "Evaluation Models for Criterion-Referenced Testing: Views Regarding Mastery and Standard Setting." *Review of Educational Research*, 1976, *46*(1), 133–158.

Messick, S. "Potential Uses of Noncognitive Measurement in Education." *Journal of Educational Psychology*, 1979, *71*(3), 281–292.

Meux, M. O. "Studies of Learning in the School Setting." *Review of Educational Research*, 1967, *37*(5), 539–561.

Meyers, C. E., Sundstrom, P. E., and Yoshida, R. K. "The School Psychologist and Assessment in Special Education." *School Psychology Monograph*, 1974, *2*(1), 1–57.

Meyers, J. "A Consultation Model for School Psychological Services." *Journal of School Psychology*, 1973, *11*(1), 5–15.

Michael, D. C. "The Training of School Psychologists." *Psychology in the Schools*, 1965, *2*, 345–349.

Milham, J., Chilcutt, J., and Atkinson, B. L. "Comparability of Naturalistic and Controlled Observation Assessment of Adaptive Behavior." *American Journal of Mental Deficiency*, 1978, *83*(1), 52–59.

Miller, J. N. "Consumer Response to Theoretical Role Models in School Psychology." *Journal of School Psychology*, 1974, *12*(4), 310–317.

Millman, J. "Reporting Student Progress: A Case for a Criterion-Referenced Marking System." *Phi Delta Kappan*, December 1970, pp. 226–230.

Millman, J., and Popham, W. J. "The Issue of Item and Test Variance for Criterion-Referenced Tests: A Clarification." *Journal of Educational Measurement*, 1974, *11*(2), 137–138.

Mills, R. E. *The Learning Methods Test*. Fort Lauderdale, Fla.: The Mills School, 1970. (Distributed by Robert Mills, The Mills School, 1512 E. Broward Blvd., Ft. Lauderdale, Fla.)

Mischel, W. *Personality and Assessment*. New York: Wiley, 1968.

Mischel, W. "Direct Versus Indirect Personality Assessment." *Journal of Consulting and Clinical Psychology*, 1972, *38*(3), 319–324.

Mischel, W. "Toward a Cognitive Social Learning Reconceptualization of Personality." *Psychological Review*, 1973, *80*, 252–283.

Mischel, W. "On the Future of Personality Measurement." *American Psychologist*, 1977, *32*(4), 246–264.

Mischel, W. "On the Interface of Cognition and Personality: Beyond the Person-Situation Debate." *American Psychologist*, 1979, *34*(9), 740–754.

Moreno, J. L. *Psychodrama. Vol. 1*. (3rd Ed.). New York: Beacon, 1964. (Originally published in 1946).

Morris, J. D., and Arrant, D. "Behavior Ratings of Emotionally Disturbed Children by Teachers, Parents, and School Psychologists." *Psychology in the Schools*, 1978, *15*(3), 450–455.

Moughamian, H. "General Overview of Trends in Testing." *Review of Educational Research*, 1965, *35*(1), 5–16.

Mussman, M. C. "Teachers' Evaluations of Psychological Reports." *Journal of School Psychology*, 1964, *3*(1), 35–37.

Nelson, R. O. "Methodological Issues in Assessment via Self-Monitoring." In J. D. Cone and R. P. Hawkins (Eds.), *Behavioral Assessment—New Directions in Clinical Psychology*. New York: Brunner/Mazel, 1977.

Nelson, R. O., and Bowles, P. E., Jr. "The Best of Two Worlds—Observations with Norms." *Journal of School Psychology*, 1975, *13*(1), 3–9.

Neuhaus, M. "Modifications in the Administration of the WISC Performance Subtests for Children with Profound Hearing Losses." *Exceptional Children*, 1967, *33*, 573–574.

Newland, T. E. "Assumptions Underlying Psychological Testing." *Journal of School Psychology*, 1973, *11*(4), 316–322.

Nitko, A. J., and Hsu, T. "Using Domain-Referenced Tests for Student Placement, Diagnosis, and Attainment in a System of Adaptive, Individualized Instruction." *Educational Technology*, 1974, *14*(6), 48–54.

Northeast Regional Resource Center. *A Position Statement on Non-biased Assessment of Culturally Different Children*. Hightstown, N.J.: Northeast Regional Resource Center, 1976

Oakland, T. "Diagnostic Help 5¢: Examiner Is In." *Psychology in the Schools*, 1969, *6*(4), 359–367.

Oakland, T. "Assessment, Education, and Minority-Group Children." *Academic Therapy*, 1974–1975, *10*(2), 133–140.

Oakland, T. (Ed.). *Psychological and Educational Assessment of Minority Children*. New York: Brunner/Mazel, 1977.

O'Leary, K. D. "Behavioral Assessment: An Observational Slant." In R. A. Weinberg and F. H. Wood (Eds.), *Observation of Pupils and Teachers in Mainstream and Special Education Settings: Alternative Strategies*. Minneapolis: University of Minnesota, 1975.

Olson, G. H. "A Multivariate Examination of the Effects of Behavioral Objectives, Knowledge of Results, and the Assignment of Grades on the Facilitation of Classroom Learning." *Dissertation Abstracts International*, 1972, *32A*, 6214–6215.

O'Reilly, R. P. "Objective and Item-Banking: A Resource for Curriculum and Test Development." In W. Hively and M. C. Reynolds (Eds.), *Domain-Referenced Testing in Special Education*. Minneapolis: University of Minnesota, 1975.

Ortar, G. R. "Improving Test Validity of Coaching." *Educational Research*, 1959, *2*, 137–142.

Ozer, M. N. "The Neurological Evaluation of School-Age Children." *Journal of Learning Disabilities*, 1968a, *1*(1), 84–86.

Ozer, M. N. "The Neurological Evaluation of Children in Head Start." In J. Hellmuth (Ed.), *Disadvantaged Child. Vol. 2*. New York: Brunner/Mazel, 1968b.

Ozer, M. N. "Diagnostic Evaluation as an Information Processing System." *Journal of Learning Disabilities*, 1969, *2*(8), 39.

Ozer, M. N. "The Assessment of Children with Developmental Problems." *Exceptional Children*, 1977, *44*(1), 37–38.

Ozer, M. N. *Solving Learning and Behavior Problems of Children: A Planning System to Integrate Assessment and Treatment*. San Francisco: Jossey-Bass, 1980.

Ozer, M. N., and Dworkin, N. E. "The Assessment of Children with Learning Problems: An In-Service Teacher Training Program." *Journal of Learning Disabilities*, 1974, *7*(9), 15–20.

Ozer, M. N., and Richardson, H. B., Jr. "The Diagnostic Evaluation of Children with Learning Problems: A 'Process' Approach." *Journal of Learning Disabilities*, 1974, *7*(2), 30–34.

Ozer, M. N., and others. "Diagnostic Evaluation of Children with Learning Problems: An Interdisciplinary Clinic Model." *Clinical Proceedings, Childrens Hospital, Washington, D.C.*, 1970, *26*(6), 161–178.

Palmer, J. O. *The Psychological Assessment of Children*. New York: Wiley, 1970.

Pastor, D. L., and Swap, S. M. "An Ecological Study of Emotionally Disturbed Preschoolers in Special and Regular Classes." *Exceptional Children*, 1978, *44*, 213–215.

Payne, D. A. (Ed.). *The Assessment of Learning: Cognitive and Affective*. Lexington, Mass.: Heath, 1974.

Pervin, L. A. "A Free-Response Description Approach to the Analysis of Person-Situation Interaction." *Journal of Personality and Social Psychology*, 1976, *34*(3), 465–474.

Pikulski, J. J. "Criterion-Referenced Measures for Clinical Evaluations." *Reading World*, 1974a, *14*, 116–128.

Pikulski, J. J. "A Critical Review: Informal Reading Inventories." *The Reading Teacher*, 1974b, *28*, 141–150.

Piotrowski, R. J. "The Effect of Omitting a Limited Number of Subtests on the Full Scale Reliability of the WISC-R." *Psychology in the Schools*, 1976, *13*(3), 298–301.

Platt, J. J., and Spivak, G. *The MEPS Procedure—Brief Scoring Guide*. Philadelphia: Division of Research and Evaluation, Hahnemann Medical College and Hospital, n.d.

Pope, L., and Haklay, A. "A Follow-Up Study of Psychoeducational Evaluations Sent to Schools." *Journal of Learning Disabilities*, 1974, *7*(4), 56–61.

Popham, W. J. "Indices of Adequacy for Criterion-Referenced Items." In W. J. Popham (Ed.), *Criterion-Referenced Measurement—an Introduction*. Englewood Cliffs, N.J.: Educational Technology Publications, 1971.

Popham, W. J. "Teacher Evaluation and Domain-Referenced Measurement." *Educational Technology*, 1974, *14*(6), 35–38.

Popham, W. J., and Husek, T. R. "Implications of Criterion-Referenced Measurement." *Journal of Educational Measurement*, 1969, *6*(1), 1–9.

Post, J. M. "The Effects of Vocalization on the Ability of Third-Grade Students to Complete Selected Performance Subtests from the Wechsler Intelligence Scale for Children." *Dissertation Abstracts International*, 1970, *31A*, 1579.

Powell, W. R. "The Nature of Diagnosis." In B. Bateman (Ed.), *Learning Disorders. Vol. 4: Reading*. Seattle: Special Child Publications, 1971.

Proger, B. B. "Test Review No. 18—Woodcock Reading Mastery Tests." *Journal of Special Education*, 1975, *78*, 221–225.

Proger, B. B., and Mann, L. "Criterion-Referenced Measurement: The World of Gray Versus Black and White." *Journal of Learning Disabilities*, 1973, *6*(2), 18–30.

Quay, H. C. "The Facets of Educational Exceptionality: A Conceptual Framework for Assessment, Grouping, and Instruction." *Exceptional Children*, 1968, *35*(1), 25–31.

Randhawa, B. A., and Fu, L.L.W. "Assessment and Effect of Some Classroom Environment Variables." *Review of Educational Research*, 1973, *43*(3), 303–321.

Reed, H.B.C., Jr. "Biological Defects in Special Education—An Issue in Personnel Preparation." *Journal of Special Education*, 1979, *13*(1), 9–33.

Reid, J. B. "Reliability Assessment of Observation Data: A Possible Methodological Problem." *Child Development*, 1970, *41*,1143–1150.

Repp, A. C., and others. "A Comparison of Frequency, Interval, and Time-Sampling Methods of Data Collection." *Journal of Applied Behavior Analysis*, 1976, *9*(4), 501–508.

Reynolds, C. H., and Gentile, J. R. "Performance Under Traditional and Mastery Assessment Procedures in Relation to Students' Locus of Control: A Possible Attitude by Treatment Interaction." *Journal of Experimental Education*, 1975–1976, *44*, 55–60.

Reynolds, M. C. "Trends in Special Education: Implications for Measurement." In W. C. Hively and M. C. Reynolds (Eds.), *Domain-Referenced Testing in Special Education*. Minneapolis: University of Minnesota, 1975.

Richardson, H. B., Jr., and Ozer, M. N. "Structure of the Collaborative Service Program in the Schools." Washington, D.C.: Childrens Hospital, 1973. (Mimeograph.)

Richardson, S. A., Dohrenwend, B. S., and Klein, D. *Interviewing: Its Forms and Functions*. New York: Basic Books, 1965.

Ritter, D. R., and Sabatino, D. A. "The Effects of Method of Measurement upon Children's Performance on Visual Perceptual Tasks." *Journal of School Psychology*, 1974, *12*(4), 296–304.

Rivkind, H. C. "The Development of a Group Technique in Teaching Word Recognition to Determine Which of Four Methods is Most Effective with Individual Children." *Dissertation Abstracts*, 1959, *19*(2), 1620–1621.

Roberts, R. D. "Perceptions of Actual and Desired Role Functions of School Psychologists by Psychologists and Teachers." *Psychology in the Schools*, 1970, *7*(2), 175–178.

Roberts, R. D., and Solomons, G. "Perceptions of the Duties and Functions of the School Psychologist." *American Psychologist*, 1970, *25*(6), 544–549.

Rohwer, W. D., Jr., and others. "Population Differences and Learning Proficiency." *Journal of Educational Psychology*, 1971, *62*(1), 1–14.

Roper, R., and Hinde, R. A. "Social Behavior in a Play Group: Consistency and Complexity." *Child Development*, 1978, *49*, 570–579.

Rosenwald, G. C. "Psychodiagnostics and Its Discontents." *Psychiatry*, 1963, *26*, 222–240.

Rosner, J. "Testing for Teaching in an Adaptive Educational Environment." In W. C. Hively and M. C. Reynolds (Eds.), *Domain-Referenced Testing in Special Education*. Minneapolis: University of Minnesota, 1975.

Ross, A. O. *"Psychological Aspects of Learning Disabilities and Reading Disorders."* New York: McGraw-Hill, 1976.

Rosvold, H. E., and others. "A Continuous Performance Test of Brain Damage." *Journal of Consulting Psychology*, 1956, *20*(5), 343–350.

Roth, L. "Psychological Assessment: A Rebirth or Struggle for Life?" Trenton: Department of Institutions and Agencies, State of New Jersey, 1976. (Mimeograph.)

Rowley, G. L. "The Reliability of Observational Measures." *American Educational Research Journal*, 1976, *13*(1), 51–59.

Rowley, G. L. "The Relationship of Reliability in Classroom Research to the Amount of Observation: An Extension of the Spearman-Brown Formula." *Journal of Educational Measurement*, 1978, *15*(1), 165–180.

Rucker, C. N. "Report Writing in School Psychology—a Critical Investigation." *Journal of School Psychology*, 1967a, *5*(2), 101–108.

Rucker, C. N. "Technical Language in the School Psychologist's Report." *Psychology in the Schools*, 1967b, *4*(2), 146–150.

Rudnick, M., and Berkowitz, H. "Preparation of School Psychologists: For What?" *Psychology in the Schools*, 1968, *5*, 53–59.

Sabatino, D. A. "The Information Processing Behaviors Associated with Learning Disabilities." *Journal of Learning Disabilities*, 1968, *1*(8), 440–450.

Sabatino, D. A., and Miller, T. L. (Eds.), *Describing Learner Characteristics of Handicapped Children and Youth*. New York: Grune & Stratton, 1979.

Sackett, G. P. "Measurement in Observational Research." In G. P.

Sackett (Ed.). *Observing Behavior. Vol. 2* Baltimore: University Park Press, 1978.

Saigh, P. A., and Payne, D. A. "The Influence of Examiner Verbal Comments on WISC Performances of EMR Students." *Journal of School Psychology,* 1976, *14*(4), 342–345.

Salkind, N. J., and Wright, J. C. "The Development of Reflection-Impulsivity and Cognitive Efficiency: An Integrated Model." *Human Development,* 1977, *20,* 377–387.

Salvia, J., and Clark, J. "Use of Deficits to Identify the Learning Disabled." *Exceptional Children,* 1973, *39,* 305–308.

Salvia, J., and Ysseldyke, J. E. *Assessment in Special and Remedial Education.* Boston: Houghton Mifflin, 1978.

Sanders, J. R., and Sachse, T. P. "Applied Performance Testing in the Classroom." *Journal of Research and Development in Education,* 1977, *10*(3), 92–103.

Santostefano, S. "Performance Testing of Personality." *Merrill-Palmer Quarterly,* 1962a, *8,* 83–97.

Santostefano, S. "Miniature Situations as a Way of Interviewing Children." *Merrill-Palmer Quarterly,* 1962b, *8,* 261–269.

Santostefano, S. "Construct Validity of the Miniature Situation Test: I. The Performance of Public School Orphaned and Brain-Damaged Children." *Journal of Clinical Psychology,* 1965, *21,* 418–421.

Santostefano, S. "Cognitive Controls Versus Cognitive Styles: An Approach to Diagnosing and Treating Cognitive Disabilities in Children." *Seminars in Psychiatry,* 1969, *1*(3), 291–300.

Santostefano, S., and Wilson, G. "Construct Validity of the Miniature Situations Test: II. The Performance of Institutionalized Delinquents and Public School Adolescents." *Journal of Clinical Psychology,* 1968, *24,* 355–358.

Sapir, S., and Wilson, B. *A Professional Guide to Working with the Learning Disabled Child.* New York: Brunner/Mazel, 1978.

Sarason, I. G., Smith, R. E., and Diener, E. "Personality Research: Components of Variables Attributable to the Person and Situation." *Journal of Personality and Social Psychology,* 1975, *32,* 199–204.

Sattler, J. M. "Effects of Cues and Examiner Influence on Two Wechsler Subtests." *Journal of Consulting and Clinical Psychology,* 1969, *33*(6), 716–721.

Sattler, J. M. *Assessment of Children's Intelligence.* Philadelphia: Saunders, 1974.

Sattler, J. M., and Anderson, N. E. "The Peabody Picture Vocabulary Test, Stanford-Binet, and the Modified Stanford-Binet with Normal and Cerebral Palsied Preschool Children." *Journal of Special Education,* 1973, 7(2), 119-123.

Scandura, J. M. "Structural Approach to Instructional Problems." *American Psychologist,* 1977, 32(1), 33-53.

Schmidt, W. I., and Thompson, M. L. "Guidelines for Psychological Testing." *Psychology in the Schools,* 1969, 6, 192-197.

Schowengerdt, R. V., Fine, M. J., and Poggio, J. P. "An Examination of Some Bases of Teacher Satisfaction with School Psychological Services." *Psychology in the Schools,* 1976, 13, 269-275.

Schucman, H. "Evaluating the Educability of the Severely Mentally Retarded Child." *Psychological Monographs,* 1960, 14, (501, entire issue).

Schwalb, E., Blau, H., and Blau, H. "Child with Brain Dysfunction." *Journal of Learning Disabilities,* 1969, 2(4), 182-188.

Schwebel, A. I., and Bernstein, A. J. "The Effects of Impulsivity on the Performance of Lower-Class Children on Four WISC Subtests. *American Journal of Orthopsychiatry,* 1970, 40(4), 629-636.

Severson, R. A. "Environmental and Emotionally Based Influences upon the Learning Process." Paper presented at annual meeting of the American Psychological Association, Washington, D.C., September 1976.

Sewell, T. E. "Intelligence and Learning Tasks as Predictors of Scholastic Achievement in Black and White First-Grade Children." *Journal of School Psychology,* 1979, 17(4), 325-332.

Sewell, T. E., and Severson, R. A. "Learning Ability and Intelligence as Cognitive Predictors of Achievement in First-Grade Black Children." *Journal of Educational Psychology,* 1974, 66(6), 948-955.

Shapiro, M. B. "An Experimental Approach to Diagnostic Psychological Testing." *Journal of Mental Science,* 1951, 9, 748-764.

Shimoni, N. "A Case Study Approach to Delivering and Evaluating Services by a School Psychologist." *Journal of School Psychology,* 1978, 16(3), 257-264.

Shively, J. J., and Smith, A. E. "Understanding the Psychological Report." *Psychology in the Schools,* 1969, *6*(3), 272–273.

Shoemaker, D. M. "Criterion-Referenced Measurement Revisited." *Educational Technology,* 1971, *11,* 61–62.

Shore, M. F. "The Utilization of the Patient-Examiner Relationship in Intelligence Testing of Children." *Journal of Projective Techniques,* 1962, *26,* 239–243.

Shure, M. B., and Spivak, G. *The PIPS Test Manual—a Cognitive Measure of Interpersonal Problem-Solving Ability.* Philadelphia: Hahnemann Community Mental Health/Mental Retardation Center, Department of Mental Health Sciences, Hahnemann Medical College and Hospital, 1974.

Siegel, E. "Task Analysis and Effective Teaching." *Journal of Learning Disabilities,* 1972, *5*(10), 519–532.

Sigel, I. E. "How Intelligence Tests Limit Understanding of Intelligence." *Merrill-Palmer Quarterly,* 1963, *9*(1), 39–56.

Simon, A., and Boyer, E. G. (Eds.). *Mirrors for Behavior: An Anthology of Classroom Observation Instruments.* Philadelphia: Research for Better Schools, 1967.

Simon, G. B. "Comments on 'Implications of Criterion-Referenced Measurement'." *Journal of Educational Measurement,* 1969, *6*(4), 259–260.

Simpson, D. D., and Nelson, A. E. "Attention Training Through Breathing Control to Modify Hyperactivity." *Journal of Learning Disabilities,* 1974, *7,* 274–286.

Simrall, D. "Intelligence and the Ability to Learn." *Journal of Psychology,* 1947, *23,* 27–43.

Sitko, M. C., Fink, A. H., and Gillespie, P. H. "Utilizing Systematic Observation for Decision Making in School Psychology." *School Psychology Monograph,* 1977, *3*(1), 23–44.

Sloves, R. E., Docherty, E. M., Jr., and Schneider, K. C. "A Scientific Problem-Solving Model of Psychological Assessment." *Professional Psychology,* 1979, *10,* 28–34.

Small, L. "The Uncommon Importance of Psychodiagnosis." *Professional Psychology,* 1972, *3*(2), 111–119.

Smead, V. S. "Ability Training and Task Analysis in Diagnostic/Prescriptive Teaching." *Journal of Special Education,* 1977, *11*(1), 113–125.

Smith, D. C., and Martin, R. A. "Use of Learning Cues with the Bender Visual Motor Gestalt Test in Screening Children for Neurological Impairment." *Journal of Consulting Psychology,* 1967, *31,* 205–209.

Sommers, R. K., Erdige, S., and Peterson, M. K. "How Valid are Children's Language Tests?" *Journal of Special Education,* 1978, *12*(4), 393–407.

Stake, R. E. "Language, rationality and assessment." In W. H. Beatty (Ed.), *Improving Educational Assessment and an Inventory of Measures of Affective Behavior.* Washington, D.C.: Association for Supervision and Curriculum Development, National Education Association, 1969.

Stallings, J. *Training Manual for Classroom Observation.* Menlo Park, Calif.: Stanford Research Institute, 1972.

Stanton, H. R., and Litwak, E. "Toward Development of a Short Form Test of Interpersonal Competence." *Sociological Review,* 1955, *20,* 668–674.

Sternlicht, M., Deutsch, M., and Alperin, N. "Psychological Evaluations and Teacher Assessments of Institutionalized Retardates." *Psychology in the Schools,* 1970, *7*(2), 161–166.

Stetz, F. P. "Providing Relevant Test Data for Decision Making Purposes." *Elementary School Journal,* 1978, *78,* 221–225.

Stoneman, Z., and Gibson, S. "Situational Influences on Assessment Performance." *Exceptional Children,* 1978, *45,* 166–169.

Stott, D. H. *The Hard-to-Teach Child—a Diagnostic-Remedial Approach.* Baltimore: University Park Press, 1978.

Styles, W. A. "Teachers' Perceptions of the School Psychologist's Role." *Journal of School Psychology,* 1965, *3*(4), 23–27.

Sundberg, N. D., Snowden, L. R., and Reynolds, W. M. "Toward Assessment of Personal Competence and Incompetence in Life Situations." *Annual Review of Psychology,* 1978, *29,* 179–221.

Sweet, R. C., and Ringness, T. A. "Variations in the Intelligence Test Performance of Referred Boys of Differing Racial and Socio-economic Backgrounds as a Function of Feedback or Monetary Reinforcement." *Journal of School Psychology,* 1971, *9*(4), 399–409.

Switsky, H. N., Ludwig, L., and Haywood, H. C. "Exploration and Play in Retarded and Nonretarded Preschool Children: Effects of Object Complexity and Age." *American Journal of Mental Deficiency*, 1979, *83*(6), 637–644.

Sykes, D. H., Douglas, V. I., and Morgenstern, G. "Sustained Attention in Hyperactive Children." *Journal of Child Psychology and Psychiatry*, 1973, *14*, 213–220.

Szmuk, M.I.C., Docherty, E. M., and Ringness, T. A. "Behavioral Objectives for Psychological Consultation in the School as Evaluated by Teachers and School Psychologists." *Psychology in the Schools*, 1979, *16*, 143–148.

Tallent, N. *Psychological Report Writing*. Englewood Cliffs, N.J.: Prentice-Hall, 1976.

Tarver, S. G., and Dawson, M. M. "Modality Preference and the Teaching of Reading." *Journal of Learning Disabilities*, 1978, *11*(1), 17–29.

Theye, F. W. "Violation of Standard Procedure on Wechsler Scales." *Journal of Clinical Psychology*, 1970, *26*, 70–71.

Thomas, A., and Chess, S. *Temperament and Development*. New York: Brunner/Mazel, 1977.

Tidwell, R., and Wetter, J. "Parental Evaluations of Psycho-Educational Reports: A Case Study." *Psychology in the Schools*, 1978, *15*(2), 209–215.

Tolor, A. "Diagnosing the State of the Diagnostic Function: An Analysis of the Literature." *Journal of Clinical Psychology*, 1973, *29*, 338–342.

Tombari, M. L., and Bergan, J. R. "Consultant Cues and Teacher Verbalizations, Judgments, and Expectations Concerning Children's Adjustment Problems." *Journal of School Psychology*, 1978, *16*(3), 212–219.

Towle, M., and Ginsberg, A. "An Educator's Mystery: Where Do Performance Problems Come From?" *Journal of Learning Disabilities*, 1975, *8*(8), 486–489.

Trione, W. W. "One Hundred Eighty Cases: A Follow-Up by a Rural School Psychologist." *California Journal of Educational Research*, 1958, *9*(2), 86–90.

Tryon, W. W. "The Test-Trait Fallacy." *American Psychologist*, 1979, *34*(5), 402–410.

Tucker, J. "Operationalizing the Diagnostic-Intervention Process." In T. Oakland (Ed.), *Psychological and Educational Assessment of Minority Children*. New York: Brunner/Mazel, 1977.

Tyler, R. W. "The Purposes of Assessment." In W. H. Beatty (Ed.), *Improving Educational Assessment and an Inventory of Measures of Affective Behavior*. Washington, D.C.: Association for Supervision and Curriculum Development, National Education Association, 1969.

Valett, R. E. "Developmental Task Analysis and Psychoeducational Programming." *Journal of School Psychology*, 1972, *10*(2), 127–133.

Vance, H. B. "Information Assessment Techniques with LD Children." *Academic Therapy*, 1977, *12*(3), 291–303.

Venezky, R. L. *Testing in Reading: Assessment and Instructional Decision Making*. Urbana, Ill.: National Council of Teachers of English, 1974.

Vernon, P. E. "Symposium on the Effects of Coaching and Practice in Intelligence Tests." *British Journal of Educational Psychology*, 1954, *24*, 5–8.

Volle, F. O. "A Proposal for 'Testing the Limits' with Mental Defectives for Purposes of Subtest Analysis of the WISC Verbal Scales." *Journal of Clinical Psychology*, 1957, *13*(1), 64–67.

Wade, T. C., and others. "The Status of Psychological Testing in Clinical Psychology; Relationship Between Test Use and Professional Activities and Orientations." *Journal of Personality Assessment*, 1978, *42*(1), 3–9.

Wahler, R. G., House, A. E., and Stambaugh, E. E., II. *Ecological Assessment of Child Problem Behavior*. Elmsford, N.Y.: Pergamon Press, 1976.

Walker, N. W. "An Investigation into the Modification of Impulsive Responding to Four WISC Subtests." *Dissertation Abstracts International*, 1976, *36A*, 4369.

Wamba, D. E., and Marzolf, S. S. "Use of Eye Movements as a Response Indicator in Testing the Physically Handicapped." *Journal of Clinical Psychology*, 1955, *11*, 405–411.

Ward, J. "On the Concept of Criterion-Referenced Measurement." *British Journal of Educational Psychology*, 1970, *40*, 314–323.

Waters, L. G. "School Psychologists as Perceived by School Personnel: Support for a Consultant Model." *Journal of School Psychology*, 1973, *11*(1), 40–45.

Waugh, R. "On Reporting the Findings of a Diagnostic Center." *Journal of Learning Disabilities*, 1970, *3*(12), 30–35.

Wedell, S. "Diagnosing Learning Difficulties: A Sequential Strategy." *Journal of Learning Disabilities*, 1970, *3*(6), 15–21.

Weick, K. E. "Systematic Observation Methods." In G. Lindzey and E. Aronson (Eds.), *The Handbook of Social Psychology. Vol. 2 (2nd ed.)*. Reading, Mass.: Addison-Wesley, 1968.

Weiner, H. "The Illusion of Simplicity: The Medical Model Revisited." *American Journal of Psychiatry*, 1978, *135*, 27–33.

Weiner, I. B. "Does Psychodiagnosis Have a Future?" *Journal of Personality*, 1972, *36*, 534–546.

Wesman, A. G. "Intelligent Testing." *American Psychologist*, 1968, *23*(4), 267–274.

Westbury, I. "The Reliability of Measures of Classroom Behavior." *Ontario Journal of Educational Research*, 1967–1968, *10*(2), 125–138.

White, M. A., and Harris, M. W. *The School Psychologist*. New York: Harper & Row, 1961.

White, R. T. "Research into Learning Hierarchies." *Review of Educational Research*, 1973, *43*(3), 361–375.

Wiederholt, J. L., Hammill, D. D., and Brown, V. *The Resource Teacher: A Guide to Effective Practices*. Boston: Allyn & Bacon, 1978.

Wiseman, S. "Symposium on the Effects of Coaching and Practice in Intelligence Tests." *British Journal of Educational Psychology*, 1954, *24*, 5–8.

Wiseman, S., and Wrigley, J. "The Comparative Effects of Coaching and Practice on the Results of Verbal Intelligence Tests." *British Journal of Psychology*, 1953, *44*, 83–94.

Withall, J. "Research Tools: Observing and Recording Behavior." *Review of Educational Research*, 1960, *30*(5), 496–512.

Witkin, H. A., Goodenough, D. R., and Karp, S. A. "Stability of Cognitive Style from Childhood to Young Adulthood." *Journal of Personality and Social Psychology*, 1967, *7*(3), 291–300.

Witkin, H. A., and others. "Educational Implications of Cognitive Styles." *Review of Educational Research*, 1977, *47*(1), 1–64.

Wittrock, M. C. "The Evaluation of Instruction: Cause and Effect in Naturalistic Data." In M. C. Wittrock and D. E. Wiley (Eds.), *The*

Evaluation of Instruction. New York: Holt, Rinehart and Winston, 1967.

Wohl, J. "Traditional and Contemporary Views of Psychological Testing." In D. A. Payne and R. F. McMorris (Eds.), *Educational and Psychological Measurement.* Waltham, Mass.: Blaisdell, 1967.

Wolff, W. "Projective Methods for Personality Analysis of Expressive Behavior in Preschool Children." *Character and Personality,* 1941, *10,* 309–330.

Womer, F. B. "Tests: Misconceptions, Misuse and Overuse." In D. A. Payne and R. F. McMorris (Eds.), *Educational and Psychological Measurement.* Waltham, Mass.: Blaisdell, 1967.

Woodcock, R. W. *Woodcock Reading Mastery Tests.* Circle Pines, Minn.: American Guidance Service, 1973.

Woodrow, H. "The Effect of Practice on Groups of Different Initial Ability." *Journal of Educational Psychology,* 1938, *29,* 268–278.

Woodrow, H. "Factors in Improvement with Practice." *Journal of Psychology,* 1939, *7,* 55–70.

Woodrow, H. "The Ability to Learn." *Psychological Review,* 1946, *53,* 147–157.

Woodson, M. I. C. E. "The Issue of Item and Test Variance for Criterion-Referenced Tests: A Reply." *Journal of Educational Measurement,* 1974, *11*(2), 139–140.

Wright, H. F. *Recording and Analyzing Child Behavior.* New York: Harper & Row, 1967.

Wrightstone, J. W. "Observational Techniques." In C. W. Harris and M. R. Liba (Eds.), *Encyclopedia of Educational Research.* (3rd ed.) New York: Macmillan, 1960.

Yamamoto, K., Jones, J. P., and Ross, M. B. "A Note on the Processing of Classroom Observation Records." *American Educational Research Journal,* 1972, *9*(1), 29–44.

Yarrow, L. J. "Interviewing Children." In P. Mussen (Ed.), *Handbook of Research Methods in Child Development.* New York: Wiley, 1960.

Yates, A. "Symposium on the Effects of Coaching and Practice in Intelligence Tests." *British Journal of Educational Psychology,* 1953, *23,* 147–162.

Yen, W. M. "Measuring Individual Differences with an Information-

Processing Model." *Journal of Educational Psychology*, 1978, *70*(1), 72–86.

Ysseldyke, J. E. "Diagnostic-Prescriptive Teaching: The Search for Aptitude-Treatment Interactions." In L. Mann and D. Sabatino (Eds.), *The First Review of Special Education. Vol. 1.* Philadelphia: Journal of Special Education Press, 1973.

Ysseldyke, J. E. "Who's Calling the Plays in School Psychology?" *Psychology in the Schools*, 1978, *15*, 373–378.

Ysseldyke, J. E. "Issues in Psychoeducational Assessment." In G. D. Phye and D. J. Reschly (Eds.), *School Psychology: Perspectives and Issues.* New York: Academic Press, 1979.

Zach, L. "Current Thought on Intelligence Tests." *American Psychologist*, 1966, *3*(2), 116–123.

Zeitlin, S. *Coping Inventory—a Measure of Adaptive Behavior.* Cliffside Park, N.J.: Innovative Educational Materials, 1978.

Zeitlin, S. "Assessing Coping Behavior." Northdale, N.J.: PIE Validation Project, Northern Valley Regional High School District, n.d.

Index

&&&&&&&

A

Abidin, R. R., 88
Abikoff, H., 169
Acker, M., 140
Adaptive behavior scales, 142–144
Adelman, H. S., 76, 173
Ahr, A. F., 23
Airasian, P. W., 65–66
Aliotti, N. C., 99, 108
Alker, H. A., 13
Allen, A., 14
Allen, R. M., 117
Allport, G. W., 131
Alper, T. G., 23
Alperin, N., 4
Ambrosino, R. J., 124

Ammons Full Range Picture Vocabulary Test, 117
Anastasi, A., 5
Anderegg, T., 14
Anderson, N. E., 116
Anderson, S. B., 57, 76, 77, 133
Apollini, T., 166
Aptitude-Treatment Interactions (ATI), 171–172
Arnaud, S. H., 133
Arrant, D., 3
Arrington, R. E., 80, 82, 85
Arter, J. A., 10, 11, 41
Assessment, psychological: alternatives to standardized, 123–145; approaches to, 1–15; behaviorist model of, 12–14; communicating

results of, 160–167; consultation and, 20; criteria for, 21–22; defined, 1, 20–21; diagnostic remedial model of, 9–12; dissatisfaction with, 2–5; domains of, 26–30; dynamic, 33–45; ecological model of, 14; functions in, 67–69; future in, 167–175; of handicapped children, 146–159; for knowledge, 55–74; of learning potential, 33–54; medical model of, 5–9; methods in, 5–15; modifications in, 98–122; neurological evaluation model of, 43–45; observation for, 75–97; optimal model of, 16–32; and planning sessions, 161–162; process of, 19–26; and recommendations, 163–164; steps in, 22–26; task analysis model of, 12; terminology of, 17–19; trial teaching and, 45

Assessors: caseloads of, 3; dissatisfactions of, 3–5; effects of law on, 157–159; intervention by, 33, 38; malpractice liability of, 151; multidisciplinary team of, 151, 153; preparation of, 4–5; as resources, 165–166

Attridge, C., 84

B

Babad, E. Y., 36, 37
Baker, H. L., 2, 3
Ball, S., 57, 76, 77, 133
Barclay, A., 2
Bardon, J. I., 4–5, 18
Bart, W. M., 65–66
Bartel, N. R., 46, 56, 165
Bateman, B., 8, 9, 12
Bealing, D., 77, 80
Beck, A. D., 170
Becker, R. M., 139
Behavioral objectives, 57–58, 60, 61, 62, 66–67
Behaviorist model, 12–13
Bem, D. J., 14
Bender Gestalt test, 111–112

Bennett, V. C., 18
Benson, J., 59
Bergan, J. R., 166
Berger, N. S., 16
Berkeley Paired-Associate Learning Test, 45
Berko, M. J., 117–118
Berkowitz, H., 4
Bernstein, A. J., 108
Bersoff, D. N., 13, 76, 88, 90, 107, 110–111
Biddle, B. J., 84
Birch, H. B., 116
Blackman, L. S., 169, 173
Blackman, S., 168
Blanco, R. F., 164
Blank, M., 101, 108
Bloom, B. S., 17
Boeding, M. A., 28
Boehm, A. E., 76, 77, 84, 86
Boehm Test of Basic Concepts, 73–74
Boll, T. J., 172
Bowers, K. S., 13
Bowers, N. E., 5
Bowles, P. E., Jr., 87
Boyd, R. D., 82, 86
Boyer, E. G., 90
Bradley, R. H., 142
Brandt, H. M., 2
Brandt, R. M., 79
Brannigan, G. G., 108, 169
Braun, J. S., 173
Brecht, R., 46
Breland, H. M., 134
Breyer, N. L., 85
Brison, D. W., 76, 87
Broden, M., 137
Brodsky, H. S., 124
Brooks, R., 174
Brown, D. T., 4
Brown, V., 46
Bryant, N. D., 172
Budoff, M., 34, 35–38, 39, 167
Bunda, M. A., 79, 80
Burger, A. L., 169, 173
Burke, J. P., 130
Butter, E. J., 169

C

Calchera, D. J., 85
Caldwell, B. M., 142
Canfield, J., 165
Cantwell, D. P., 165
Carroll, J. B., 12
Carrubba, M. J., 106
Cartwright, C. A., 46
Cartwright, G. P., 46
Cason, E. B., 2
Catterall, C. D., 163–164
Chalfant, J. C., 100
Chandy, J., 2–3
Chartoff, M. B., 4–5
Chess, S., 7
Chrin, M., 2
Clancy, B., 2
Clark, J., 11
Clark, W. D., 20
Cognitive functioning, 174–175
Cognitive style, 168–171
Cohen, S. A., 6
Collaborative Service System, 43–45
Collins, M. G., 117
Columbia Mental Maturity Scale, 117
Columbia Test of Mental Maturity, 115
Connolly, A. J., 70
Continuous Performance Test, 138
Cooke, T. P., 166
Coping Inventory, 143–144
Correlated disability, 9
Cox, R. C., 60, 61, 62
Criterion-referenced tests: applications and limitations of, 67–70; and behavioral objectives, 57–58, 60, 61, 62, 66–67; case study for, 73–74; characteristics of, 57–58; critique of, 70–73; defined, 55; evaluation of, 62–63; and hierarchy, 65–66; and item analysis, 59–61; for knowledge, 55–74; and mastery, 63–65; reliability of, 61; validity of, 61–62
Crocker, L., 59
Cronbach, L. J., 5, 19, 171
Curry, N. E., 133

D

Dansinger, S. S., 3
Dawson, M. M., 41
Decision making, 20–21, 30, 32
Deficit, concept of, 11
Delaney, H. D., 172
Della-Piana, G., 165
DeMers, S. T., 130
Deno, S. L., 79
Deutsch, M., 4, 10
DeVault, M. V., 82, 86
DeVoge, S., 132–133
Diagnosis, 8, 19, 67, 68–69
Diagnostic remedial model, 9–11, 173
Diagnostic-Prescriptive teaching, 45–47, 52–54, 171
Diana Martinez v. *Soledad*, 152
Dickinson, D. J., 88
Digate, G., 170
Docherty, E. M., Jr., 2, 3, 16
Dohrenwend, B. S., 124, 126
Donlon, G. McG., 170
Douglas, V. I., 138
Duchastel, P. C., 67
Dworkin, N. E., 43
Dynamic assessment, 33–45

E

Ebel, R. L., 65, 66–67, 70
Education of All Handicapped Children Act of 1975, 147–159
Eisenberg, P., 131
Ekehammar, B., 13
Ellett, C. D., 88, 107, 110–111
Engel, M., 3
Erdige, S., 12
Error analysis, 99–104, 108
Esveldt, K. C., 84
Etiology, and diagnosis, 8
Evaluation, concept of, 17–18
Ewing, N., 46

F

Fairchild, T. N., 4
Farling, W. H., 3
Fernald, G. M., 165
Ferone, L., 14
Feuerstein, R., 34, 38–39, 167
Fink, A. H., 84
Fischer, C. T., 161, 174
Fitts, L. D., 2
Fitzpatrick, R., 135
Flanagan, J. C., 136
Flanders, N., 86
Fleishman, E. A., 35
Flynn, D. L., 3, 23
Formative assessment, 67, 68
Forness, S. R., 84
Foster, G. E., 11
Fox, H. M., 4
Fox, L., 137
Free-response description, 144
French Picture Vocabulary Test, 115
Frick, T., 78, 79, 86
Friedman, R., 144–145
Frostig, M., 10, 12
Fu, L.L.W., 84
Functioning domain, 28–30

G

Gaynor, J. L., 134
Gellert, E., 75, 80, 81, 82, 85
Gentile, J. R., 64
Gerweck, S., 113, 114
Gibson, S., 13
Giebink, J. W., 2, 4
Gillespie, P. H., 84
Gilmore, G. E., 2–3
Ginsberg, A., 101
Glaser, R., 17, 28–29, 55
Gleason, W. P., 45
Gleser, G. C., 19
Glynn, E. L., 137
Goldstein, K. M., 168
Goodenough, D. R., 170
Goodman, Y. M., 101
Gordon, I. J., 76
Gorth, W. P., 60, 61
Gottman, J. M., 137

Graham, E. E., 114
Gray, S. W., 18, 20
Greenstein, J., 73, 103
Greenwood, C. R., 79, 81
Grieger, R. M., 13, 17, 88
Griffiths, A. N., 104
Gronlund, N. E., 63, 64, 65, 67
Gross, F. P., 3
Grubb, R. D., 3, 23
Gump, P. V., 13
Guthrie, D., 84

H

Haeussermann, E., 41, 115
Haklay, A., 4
Hall, L. P., 104
Hall, R. J., 84
Hall, R. V., 137
Hallahan, D. P., 7
Halpern, A. S., 143
Halpern F., 6
Hambleton, R. K., 60, 61, 64, 71
Hammill, D. D., 10, 11, 46, 56, 165
Handicapped children: assessing,
   146–159; defined, 149; discipline
   of, 156; modifications for, 112–
   118; placement standards for,
   150–151; rights of, 150; school
   identification of, 150–156; special
   class placement of, 148–149
Hanesian, H., 87
Hardy, J. B., 108
Harris, M. W., 18
Haynes, S. N., 79, 80, 81, 83, 85, 127,
   128, 136, 137
Haywood, H. C., 140
Hempel, W. E., Jr., 35
Herbert, J., 84
Herron, W. G., 8
Heyns, R. W., 81, 83
Hinde, R. A., 13
Hiskey-Nebraska Test of Learning
   Aptitude, 112
Hively, W., 57, 62, 67
Holden, R. H., 117
Hollenbeck, A. R., 79, 81
Holt, R. R., 4
HOME Inventory, 142–143

Honigfeld, G., 7
Hops, H., 79, 81
House, A. W., 90
Hudgins, A. L., 162–163
Hunt, D. E., 171
Hunter, C. P., 87
Husek, T. R., 61
Hutson, B. A., 19, 45
Hutt, M. L., 109

I

Illinois Test of Psycholinguistic
  Abilities (ITPA), 10, 12, 115, 120
Individualized educational program
  (IEP), 153–154
Interviews: advantages of, 128–129;
  assessment function of, 124–132;
  dimensions of, 130–131; initial
  phase of, 124–126; nonverbal cues
  in, 131; questioning in, 126–127,
  129; and target behaviors, 127–
  128, 130; validity of, 128, 129–130
Irvin, L. K., 143
Ivens, S., 60, 61, 62

J

Jason, L. A., 14
Jedrysek, E., 40, 41–43, 47–49
Jenkins, J. R., 10, 11, 41, 165
Jensen, A. R., 34–35, 36–37
Jester, R. E., 76
Jewell, B. T., 116–117
Johnson, D. J., 165
Johnston, A., 139
Jones, J. P., 82
Jones, R. L., 3
Jones, R. R., 77, 81, 82, 85, 86
Joselyn, G., 66
Jurkovic, G. J., 140

K

Kagan, J., 168, 169
Kalverboer, A. F., 138
Kaplan, L. J., 141
Kaplan, M. S., 2, 4
Karnes, M. B., 165

Karp, S. A., 170
Katz, E., 117
Kauffman, J. M., 7
Kaufman, M. R., 7
Kelleher, J., 11, 171
Kennedy, C. B., 169
Keogh, B. K., 106, 170
Kern, K. C., 115
Key Math Diagnostic Arithmetic
  Test, 70, 72–73, 103
Klein, D., 124, 126
Koesel, J. G., 161
Kohs Block Designs Test, 35–36,
  37, 38
Kowatrakul, S., 86
Krasilowsky, D., 38
Krathwohl, D. R., 62, 65, 66, 67
Kratochwill, T. R., 34, 39, 44
Kunzelmann, H. D., 137

L

La Driere, M. L., 104
Lacey, H. M., 116
Lambert, N. M., 45, 166
Landman, J. T., 143
Larry P. v. *Riles*, 151, 152
Larsen, S. C., 10, 11
Larson, K., 165
Layne, C. C., 137
Learning disabilities, 173–174
Learning Methods Test, 40–41,
  50–51
Learning potential: assessment of,
  33–54; case studies in, 47–54;
  classification of, 34–39; and diag-
  nostic-prescriptive teaching, 45–
  47; 52–54; and programming,
  40–45
Learning Potential Assessment De-
  vice, 38–39
Learning Potential Assessment Strat-
  egy, 35–38
Ledford, B. R., 28
Legal requirements: for assessment,
  146–159; for mediation, notification, and hearings, 154–155; for
  parental procedures, 156–157; and
  psychologists, 157–159; purpose

Legal requirements (cont'd.)
of, 148; for school procedures,
150–156
Leiter International Performance
Scale, 117
Levine, H. G., 134
Levy, M. R., 4
Levy v. *Department of Education,*
156
Lewandowski, D. G., 4
Lewis, J., 167
Lidz, C. S., 85, 165
Lilly, M. S., 11, 171
Lindstrom, J. P., 4
Linehan, M. M., 128–129
Lipinski, D., 81
Lippitt, R., 81, 83
Litwak, E., 134
Lovitt, T. C., 87, 165
Lucas, M. S., 3
Ludwig, L., 140
Lund, K. A., 11
Luria, A. R., 136
Lutey, C., 113, 115, 118
Lynch, W. W., 78, 81, 84

M

McCall-Perez, F. C., 11
McCarthy, D., 174
McCarthy Scales of Children's Abili-
ties, 119, 120–121, 174
McClelland, D. C., 5
Maccoby, E. E., 129, 130
Maccoby, N., 129, 130
McFall, R. M., 136, 137
McGaw, B., 79, 80
McGuire, C., 134
Mackay, G.W.S., 35
McKenzie, M., 56
McKinney, J. D., 85
Macmillan, D. L., 106
McMorris, R. F., 124
McReynolds, P., 5, 132–133, 140
Magary, J. F., 18
Maletsky, B. M., 137
Maloney, M. P., 18, 20, 127
Mann, L., 10–11, 12, 69
Margack, C., 115

Margolis, H., 108, 169
Marshall, H. H., 79, 83
Martin, R. A., 111–112
Marzolf, S. S., 117
Masling, J., 82
Mastery, 63–65
Means-Ends Problem Solving Test,
141
Measurement, concept of, 18
Medical model, 5–9
Medley, D. M., 79, 85, 90
Medway, F. C., 3
Meichenbaum, D., 130
Meier, J. H., 15
Mercer, J. R., 16, 70, 167
Merrill, P. F., 67
Merwin, J. C., 17
Meskaukas, J. A., 57
Messick, S., 174
Meyers, C. E., 6
Miller, T. L., 26
Mills, R. E., 40–41, 50–51
Mills v. *Board of Education,* 150
Miniature Situations Test, 134
Mischel, W., 13, 171
Mitts, B., 137
Mitzel, H. E., 79, 85
Modifications: in assessment, 98–
122; of Bender Gestalt, 111–112;
for blind child, 114–115; case
studies of, 120–122; by contin-
gency reinforcement, 106; for
hearing impaired, 113–114; for
impulsivity, 108; for motor hand-
icaps, 115–118; need for, 99; for
preschoolers, 118–120; of projec-
tive tests, 110–111; in scoring,
106–107; for special groups, 112–
120; of Stanford-Binet, 109–110,
116, 117, 119; by testing limits,
106; of time, 106, 114; by verbalizations, 107; of WISC, 104–
108, 113–114, 116–117
Moreno, J. L., 132
Morgenstern, G., 138
Morris, J. D., 3
Morrison, E. J., 135
Moughamian, H., 3
Murphy, R. T., 57, 76, 77, 133

Mussman, M. C., 3
Myklebust, H. R., 165

N

Nachtman, W., 70
Nelson, A. E., 136
Nelson, R. O., 81, 87, 137
Neuhaus, M., 113
Neuropsychology, trends in, 172–174
Niles, J. A., 45
Nitko, A. J., 55
Norm-referenced tests, 58–59
Novick, M. R., 61

O

Oakland, T., 6
Observation: advantages of, 84–86; of behavior, 75–97; case studies of, 91–97; category systems for, 78–79, 84; defined, 77; event sampling in, 78, 84; generalizability in, 80, 84, 86; interobserver agreement in, 76, 80, 86–87; and observer's presence, 81–83; procedures for, 77–79; for psychosituational assessment, 87–90; rationale for, 76; reliability of, 79–80; selecting measure for, 83–84; sign system for, 78, 79; stability in, 79–80, 83; as technique, 75–77; time sampling in, 78, 84; and validity, 80–81
O'Leary, K. D., 82
Ortar, G. R., 35
Ozer, M. N., 43–45, 161

P

Palmer, J. O., 138, 139
PARC v. *Pennsylvania*, 150, 152
Parents, 146–147, 151, 152–153, 154–155, 156–157, 161–162
Pastor, D. L., 14
Patterson, G. R., 77, 81, 82, 85, 86
Paul, R. E., 146–159
Payne, D. A., 60, 61, 62, 65, 66, 67, 69, 84, 106

Peabody Picture Vocabulary Test, 48, 115
Pervin, L. A., 144
Peterson, M. K., 12
Petty, S. Z., 3, 23
Phillips, W. A., 10–11
Physiological assessment, 136–137
Pietila, C., 140
Pikulski, J. J., 46–47, 58
Piotrowski, R. J., 112
Platt, J. J., 141
Play techniques, 138–140
Pluralistic norms, 167–168
Pope, L., 4
Popham, W. J., 60, 61
Post, J. M., 107
Powell, W. R., 19
Preschool Interpersonal Problem Solving Test (PIPS), 141–142
Pretesting, 67–68
Pritchett, E. M., 70
Probing, 105
Problem solving, 20–21
Process Learning Assessment, 39
Proger, B. B., 69
Projective tests, 110–111
Psaila, J., 8
Psychoeducational Evaluation of the Preschool Child, 40, 41–43, 47–49
Psychosituational assessment, 87–90
Public Law 94–142, 147–159

Q

Quay, H. C., 28

R

Randhawa, B. A., 84
Raven Coloured Progressive Matrices, 37, 38
Raven's Progressive Matrices, 36, 37, 38, 117
Redl, F., 13
Reid, J. B., 77, 81, 82, 85, 86
Related services, 149–150
Reliability, 61, 79–80, 134
Reporting test results, 160–167

Repp, A. C., 78
Reynolds, C. H., 64
Reynolds, M. C., 62, 69
Reynolds, W. M., 16, 20, 174
Richardson, H. B., Jr., 44
Richardson, S. A., 124, 126
Ringness, T. A., 2, 3, 4, 106
Ritter, D. R., 12
Rivkind, H. C., 40
Roberts, R. D., 3
Rohwer, W. D., Jr., 39
Role playing, 132-134
Role Test, 132
Roper, R., 13
Rorschach test, 110
Rosner, J., 61
Ross, M. B., 82
Rosvold, H. E., 138
Rowley, G. L., 30
Rucker, C. N., 3
Rudnick, M., 4

S

Sabatino, D. A., 12, 26, 173
Saccuzzo, D. P., 4
Sachse, T. P., 136
Saigh, P. A., 106
Salvia, J., 11, 45, 46
Sanders, J. R., 136
Santostefano, S., 134, 135
Sapir, S., 129
Sattler, J. M., 99, 106, 107, 110, 113, 114, 116
Scandura, J. M., 172
Scheffelin, M. A., 100
Schneider, K. C., 16
Schoggen, P., 13
Schultz, J. L., 162-163
Schwalb, E., 172
Schwebel, A. I., 108
Self-monitoring, 137
Semmel, M. I., 78, 79, 86
Series Learning Potential Test, 37
Severson, R. A., 37, 39
Sewell, T. E., 37, 39
Shapiro, E., 114
Shapiro, M. B., 25
Shoemaker, D. M., 60

Shore, M. F., 104-105, 106
Shure, M. B., 141
Sigel, I. E., 101, 110
Simon, A., 90
Simpson, D. D., 136
Simrall, D., 35
Simulation, 134-136
Sitko, M. C., 84
Situation domain, 26, 28
Sloves, R. E., 16
Smith, D. C., 111-112
Snowden, L. R., 16, 20, 174
Solomons, G., 3
Sommers, R. K., 12
Spache, E. B., 165
Special education, concept of, 149
Spivak, G., 141, 166
Spontaneity Test, 132
Sprunger, B., 4
Squiggle Game, 141
Stake, R. E., 17
Stambaugh, E. E., II, 90
Stanford-Binet Intelligence Scale, 36, 109-110, 116, 117, 119, 143
Stanton, H. R., 134
Stern, G., 82
Sternlicht, M., 4
Stoneman, Z., 13
Stott, D. H., 170
Strain, P. S., 73, 103, 166
Structured family interview, 144-145
Stuart v. *Danbury School District*, 156
Summative assessment, 67, 69
Sundberg, N. D., 16, 20, 174
Sundstrom, P. E., 6
Swap, S. M., 14
Sweet, R. C., 106
Swift, M. S., 166
Switsky, H. N., 140
Sykes, D. H., 138
Symbolic Play Scale, 139
System of Multicultural Pluralistic Assessment (SOMPA), 167
Szmuk, M.I.C., 2, 3

T

Tallent, N., 162
Tarver, S. G., 41

Task analysis, 57, 99–104, 108
Teachers, 2–3, 161–162, 166–167
Testing, concept of, 18–19
Thematic Apperception Test, 110
Thomas, A., 7
Tidwell, R., 2
Tombari, M. L., 166
Towle, M., 101
Trione, W. W., 4

V

Vallett, R. E., 100–101
Validity, 61–62, 80–81, 128, 129–130, 134
Vance, H. B., 56
Venezky, R. L., 17
Vernon, P. E., 35, 131

W

Wahler, R. G., 90
Walker, H. M., 79, 81
Walker, N. W., 108
Wamba, D. E., 117
Ward, H. P., 18, 20, 127
Ward, J., 66
Wardrop, J. L., 79, 80
Waters, L. G., 2
Waugh, R., 3
Wechsler Intelligence Scales for Children (WISC), 36, 38, 39, 41, 104–108, 113–114, 116–117
Wechsler Intelligence Scales for Children—Revised (WISC—R), 107, 112, 114, 173
Weick, K. E., 80, 82, 85, 87, 90
Weinberg, R. A., 76, 77, 84, 86
Weiner, H., 7

Weiner, I. B., 14
Wells, H. C., 165
Wendla, K., 56
Westbury, I., 80
Wetter, J., 2
White, M. A., 18
White, O. R., 23
White, R. T., 65
Wiederholt, J. L., 46
Wilcox, M. R., 45
Wilson, B., 129
Wilson, G., 135
Withall, J., 75
Witkin, H. A., 170
Wittrock, M. C., 17
Wohl, J., 18, 20
Wolff, W., 131
Wolfgang, C. H., 139
Woodcock, R. W., 70–72
Woodcock Reading Mastery Test, 70–72
Woodrow, H., 35
Work-sample tests, 135–136
Wright, H. F., 80, 82
Wrightstone, J. W., 80
Wursten, H., 116–117

Y

Yamamoto, K., 82
Yarrow, L. J., 131
Yen, W. M., 172
Yoshida, R. K., 6
Ysseldyke, J. E., 16, 19, 21, 32, 45, 46, 70, 113, 114, 171

Z

Zeitlin, S., 143, 144